Andrew Arnold Lambing

The Sacramentals of the Holy Catholic Church

Andrew Arnold Lambing

The Sacramentals of the Holy Catholic Church

ISBN/EAN: 9783743392526

Manufactured in Europe, USA, Canada, Australia, Japa

Cover: Foto ©Lupo / pixelio.de

Manufactured and distributed by brebook publishing software (www.brebook.com)

Andrew Arnold Lambing

The Sacramentals of the Holy Catholic Church

THE SACRAMENTALS

OF

THE HOLY CATHOLIC CHURCH.

BY

Rev. A. A. LAMBING, LL.D.,

Author of "A History of the Catholic Church in the Dioceses of Pittsburg and Alleghany," "The Sunday-School Teacher's Manual," "Masses for the Dead," "Mixed Marriages," etc., etc.

NEW YORK, CINCINNATI, CHICAGO:
BENZIGER BROTHERS,
PRINTERS TO THE | PUBLISHERS OF
HOLY APOSTOLIC SEE | BENZIGER'S MAGAZINE

Nihil Obstat.
D. J. McMahon, D.D.,
Censor Librorum.

Imprimatur.
✠ Michael Augustine,
Archbishop of New York.

New York, September 1, 1892.

Copyright, 1892, by Benziger Brothers.

TO THE

Right Rev. RICHARD PHELAN, D.D.,

Bishop of Pittsburg.

Right Rev. Dear Bishop:

In pausing to review the period of more than thirty-three years during which time I have enjoyed the benefit of your direction as your penitent; the light of your example as your brother priest; and the advantage and encouragement of your paternal rule as a priest of your diocese, I beg the privilege, on this day, on which I complete my fiftieth year, of offering you this little volume as a memorial of the friendship which has so long existed between us, but of which it is a very inadequate expression.

I am, my dear Bishop,

Your devoted son in Christ,

A. A. LAMBING.

Feast of St. Ignatius, Bishop and Martyr,
February 1, 1892.

PREFACE.

NEARLY all the essays contained in this volume originally appeared in the *Ave Maria* or in the *American Ecclesiastical Review*, but they are here brought together, after a careful revision and rewriting, with a view of placing before Catholics a book that will give in a small compass a sufficiently full explanation of the principal devotions and sacred objects which they are accustomed to see or make use of in the practice of their religion. Unfortunately there is not in our language a work of this kind; and hence it is hoped this one will be acceptable to both the clergy and people. Father Barry published a small work on the Sacramentals about thirty-five years ago; but besides being long out of print and rare, it does not treat of many sacramentals a knowledge of which would be useful to Catholics, while it does treat of certain others not very useful, such as the Golden Rose and the Archbishop's Pallium. In a few other books of devotion or instruction short treatises are given on some of the sacramentals, but they are necessarily so brief as not to satisfy an inquiring mind, and the authorities from which the information is taken are not, as a rule, given.

The better we understand our religion the more intelligently and fruitfully we can practise it; yet it is a fact, of which we have no reason to be proud, that Catholics generally know far too little about their religion.

Account for it as we may, the fact cannot be denied that even educated and well-read Catholics very often know far less of the doctrines and practices of the Church than they do of almost any other branch of knowledge; and the information they possess is commonly of a general and indefinite character, and not of that precise nature which the clearly-defined teaching of the Church would enable them to acquire, and which is rendered necessary on account of the circumstances in which most of them are placed. The consequence is that many of them find little attraction in the devotions they practise or assist at and perform them rather as a task than as an intelligent act of loving worship; and they are neither prepared to explain the many beautiful practices of our holy religion to those who seek information nor to defend them against even the threadbare objections which they constantly hear.

But besides being useful to the Catholic laity this work will also be of service to the teachers and the more advanced pupils and students of our schools, academies, and colleges. It is also believed that it will be equally acceptable to the reverend clergy, both for their own reading and in the preparation of instructions on the subjects treated in its pages.[1]

The reader will observe that, as a rule, only the highest authorities are quoted; and the references are generally given, which will enable those who wish to study any of the questions more fully to go directly to reliable sources of information.

So numerous are the doubts addressed to the Roman Congregations and their replies, especially with regard to sacred rites and indulgences, that it is difficult to keep pace with their issue; but care has been taken to

---

[1] Concilii Baltimorensis II., Acta et Decreta, N. 350

consult the latest works on these subjects, and it is believed that few, if any, decrees bearing on the matters treated in this work have escaped notice.

Owing to the fact that these essays were written at different times and in the spare moments at command in an active ministry, the subjects will be found to be treated in different ways, references will be differently given, the style will not always be the same, etc.; but this, while detracting nothing from the value of the work, may prove of advantage, by giving the reader a greater variety of style and arrangement.

Some difficulty was also experienced in arranging the various subjects, so as to bring those together which appeared to be most closely related ; but the order adopted is perhaps as good as any other that could have been followed. The essays on the Missal and Ritual are rather foundations for others than treating of sacramentals themselves, but they will afford useful and interesting information on subjects of importance. The closing essay is given for the information it contains on a point that must be of interest to every American Catholic ; and it may perhaps be opportune in this the fourth centenary year of the discovery of our country.

The reader will meet with certain repetitions, which it was difficult or impossible to avoid, especially in such essays as those on Holy Water and the *Asperges ;* the Paschal Candle, Blessed Candles, and the *Agnus Dei ;* and a few others.

It may, however, be a matter of surprise to some readers that reference should have been made in a number of places to pagan customs somewhat similar to certain others found among Christians. This was done for two reasons : to state a fact that must have considerable weight against infidels ; and to prove that there must have been either a direct revelation made by God to man in the beginning or else that He implanted feelings in the heart of man requiring such forms of outward expression; as, for example, the offering of sacrifice, which is found in some form among all peoples, but which is not stated in the Sacred Scriptures to have been enjoined till long after the Deluge. However abominable many of the pagan rites may have been and are, those who practised them are as much to be pitied as blamed; for these are but the outward expression of that unquenchable longing of every rational creature to hold communion with the unseen world—with his first beginning and his last end.

The indulgences granted by the Holy See to the pious use of some of the sacramentals are given, thereby enabling the reader to see at a glance what spiritual benefits he is able to derive from their proper employment.

In sending this little volume out into the world the author does not regret the amount of labor and research its preparation entailed, but finds ample compensation in the hope that it may be instrumental in some small measure in promoting the interests of Holy Mother Church, by the diffusion of useful and solid information, thus imparting a clearer idea of some of her many beautiful devotions and practices.

WILKINSBURG, PA.,
FEAST OF ST. IGNATIUS MARTYR, FEBRUARY 1, 1892.

CONTENTS.

	PAGE
Dedication,	3
Preface,	5

I.
What are Sacramentals? 13

II.
The Treasures of the Missal, ... 17

III.
The Treasures of the Ritual, ... 31

IV.
The Treasures of the Breviary, ... 43

V.
The Sign of the Cross, ... 54

VI.
The Stations or Way of the Cross, . . . 71

VII.
The Holy Oils, ... 86

VIII.
Holy Water, ... 105

IX.
The Asperges, or Sprinkling of Holy Water before Mass, ... 117

X.
The Forty Hours' Adoration and the Benediction of the Most Blessed Sacrament, ... 124

XI.
The Rosary of the Blessed Virgin Mary, . . 135

XII.
The Scapular of Our Lady of Mount Carmel, or Brown Scapular, ... 152

XIII.
The Angelus, ... 165

XIV.
The Miraculous Medal, ... 176

XV.
The Little Office of the Blessed Virgin Mary, . . 185

XVI.
The Litanies, ... 193

XVII.
The Paschal Candle, ... 205

XVIII.
The Agnus Dei, ... 212

XIX.
Blessed Candles, ... 227

XX.
Blessed Ashes, ... 239

XXI.
Blessed Palms, ... 245

XXII.
The Nuptial Mass and Blessing, ... 253

XXIII.
The Churching of Women, ... 266

XXIV.
The Blessing and Thanksgiving at Meals, . . . 272

XXV.
Sacred Vestments, ... 279

XXVI.
Church Bells, ... 294

XXVII.
The Last Blessing, or Blessing "in Articulo Mortis," . 300

XXVIII.
The Burial Service, ... 311

XXIX.
Mary Conceived without Sin. the Patroness of the United States, ... 320

THE SACRAMENTALS

OF

THE HOLY CATHOLIC CHURCH.

I.—WHAT ARE SACRAMENTALS?

BEFORE treating of the sacramentals it will be necessary for us to inquire into their precise nature and the manner in which they produce their supernatural effects. In the beginning of our era and for several centuries the word *sacrament* had a wider and more indefinite signification than it has at present, being used by many of the early Christian writers to designate anything holy or a mystery; but in process of time it was restricted, as at present, to the seven sacraments, or principal sources of grace, instituted by our divine Saviour. The other pious objects or prayers came to be called *sacramentals*. This change, however, was gradually made, so that no precise time can be fixed for it.

For this reason it will be of advantage to begin by inquiring into the difference between a sacrament and a sacramental. There are two principal points of difference. In the first place, the sacraments were instituted by Christ, for all time, and their number was fixed, so that it can never be increased or diminished; while the sacramentals were instituted, for the most part, by the Church, and she can increase or diminish their number as circumstances may demand or the spiritual welfare of her children render expedient. In the second place, the sacraments have in themselves the power of giving grace to those who receive them with the requisite dispositions; while the sacramentals only excite such pious dispositions in those who make use of them as will prepare them for the more easy and effectual reception of grace. But of this later.

Theologians are not agreed with regard to the number of heads under which the sacramentals should be arranged; but the opinion of Sabetti will be sufficiently explicit for our purpose.[1]

Prayer must be placed first among the sacramentals, especially the Lord's Prayer and the public prayers of the Church. Second are such as refer to the *touch*, as the use of holy water, sacred unctions that are not connected with the administration of the sacraments, as those in the blessing of a church bell, etc. Third, *eating*, by which is meant the partaking of the holy bread which was formerly blessed in the Mass and distributed to those who did not communicate, of which mention will be found in the essay on the Sign of the Cross; also the eating of fruits blessed by the Church, especially new fruits, for which there is a special benediction given in the ritual. Fourth, *confessing*, which includes the public confessions sometimes made in the early Church, but more particularly the confession made by the priest and his ministers at the beginning of the Mass, and at times in the recitation of the Divine Office; and any act by which a person acknowledges himself a sinner: as striking the breast, receiving the ashes on Ash-Wednesday, etc. Fifth, *giving*, as the giving of alms and the performing of any spiritual or corporal work of mercy, especially such as are enjoined by the ecclesiasti-

---

[1] "Theologia Moralis." Aloisio Sabetti, S.J., NN. 651, 652.

cal authorities in times of a public calamity or during Lent. Sixth, *blessing*, which is the most comprehensive of all the heads, and includes every blessing given by proper ecclesiastical authority, whether it be that of the Pope, a bishop, or a priest, whether it be found in the ritual or not.

On the effects of the sacramentals and the manner in which they are produced the "Catholic Dictionary" (p. 732) has this: "If the sacramentals are used with pious dispositions they excite increased fear and love of God and detestation of sin, and so, not in themselves, but because of these movements of the heart toward God, remit venial sins. They have a special efficacy, because the Church has blessed them with prayer, and also when, for example, a person takes holy water, accompanying the outward act with the desire that God may cleanse his heart, the prayer of the whole Christian people is joined to his own." The opinion that sacramentals remit venial sins by a power given them by God over and above the good dispositions with which they are used is held by some theologians, but rejected by others as destitute of a warrant in Scripture or tradition. The weight of theological opinion is against it at the present time.

According to the more general opinion, which is held by Sabetti, the sacramentals produce two principal effects in those who make use of them according to the mind of the Church. First, the remission of venial sins, not, however, directly and by virtue of their own power, as the sacraments do, but indirectly, by the pious movements of the heart to contrition, which are rendered more frequent and easy by the use of the sacramentals. Secondly, the sacramentals are powerful means of overcoming the temptations of the spirit of evil and putting him to flight, and this not merely by way of impetration, but by way of command. This is, as will be seen in the following essays, besought of Almighty God in the prayers and exorcisms recited in the blessing of many of the sacramentals. The faith of the people in this power is illustrated in their use of them, especially in having the dying hold a crucifix or blessed candle in their hands, in having holy water or blessed objects in their sleeping apartments, etc. It is no less seen in the confidence they have in the use of certain sacramentals when threatened with danger from the elements; for, by the permission of God, the evil spirit has certain power over the atmosphere, and is, for that reason, called in Scripture the prince of the air.[1] The power to still the disturbances of the elements is also called down upon not a few of the sacramentals in the form of prayer by which they are blessed. With this explanation, which, though short, will be sufficient, let us proceed to a consideration of some of the principal sacramentals, with a view not only of increasing our knowledge of them but also of stimulating us to their more frequent and pious use.

[1] Ephesians, ii. 2

II.—THE TREASURES OF THE MISSAL.

By the transgression of our first parents man came into the power of the evil spirit to a lamentable extent, and the visible creation was burdened with the malediction of its Creator, as God said to Adam: "Cursed is the earth in thy work."[1] For this reason the spirit of evil is called in various places of the Scriptures the Prince of this world.[2] The earth itself bears evidence of the fall; for we cannot imagine a God of infinite goodness creating such a world as that which we now inhabit. So truly is it natural for man to entertain this view that even the pagan philosophers and the sages of all times and countries have regarded the earth as more or less a place of punishment, or at least of trial, for the human race. Their ideas may have been variously expressed, but they will invariably be found to have been based on the same fundamental belief. Deeply impressed with this truth, the children of God have at all times invoked the divine blessing upon such creatures as they had occasion to use, evidences of which are to be met with in numberless passages of the sacred writings and in sacred biography.

Apart from the use which man is necessitated to make of various creatures for the sustenance and conveniences of life, he is also required to use them in the worship of God, and this in a threefold manner: as victims to be sacrificed; as vessels, vestments, etc., in the service of religion; and as instruments or channels for the con

---

[1] Council of Trent, session v. canon i.; Genesis, iii. 17.
[2] St. John, xii. 31; Ephesians, vi. 12.

veying of supernatural assistance to the souls of men, as in the sacraments and sacramentals. The infinite dignity of Almighty God and the relation man bears to Him require that this should be done at all times and under all circumstances with becoming decorum; in other words, with certain liturgical observances. In patriarchal times the liturgy was very simple, and appears to have been regulated by the patriarch's own ideas of what was becoming, because at that early day he, or one appointed by him, was the sacrificing priest of the tribe or family of which he was the head. And this custom continued among the Gentiles even after the institution of the Mosaic Law, as may be learned from the case of holy Job, from whom God accepted sacrifices for himself, his family, and his friends. But when the Jews were set apart as the chosen people of God a special ritual was prepared for them by a revelation from heaven, in which the ceremonial law was laid down even to the most minute details, and its strict observance enjoined under the severest penalties.

With the abrogation of the Mosaic Law a new liturgy was called into existence to suit the changes brought about in divine worship by the institution of the sacrifice of the Mass and the sacraments. Our divine Redeemer unchangeably fixed all that relates to their essence, but it was fitting that He should leave to His Church the regulation of the minor details of their administration, both because it became His dignity to do so and because these depend in a measure on the circumstances of time, place, and people. The authority necessary for arranging these particulars is contained in the power of binding and loosing given in its plenitude to the teaching body of the Church. To the same authority was entrusted the power of instituting such sacramentals as might, from time to time, be found conducive to the welfare of the children of God.

All that relates to the offering of the adorable sacrifice of the Mass is found in the liturgical work known as the Roman Missal, or Mass Book, as it is commonly called. This, as well as the other liturgical books of the Church, is, of course, in the Latin language; and notwithstanding that prayer-books may readily be had in which some parts of the Missal are rendered into the vernacular, and even entire translations of the Missal are made, still this and the other liturgical books are more or less mysterious to the greater number of Catholics. And, what is worse, their lack of information too often renders them incapable of appreciating the value of sacred rites, and leaves them without the desire of increasing their knowledge. A short explanation of the Missal, and later one of the other liturgical books, must for these reasons be at once interesting, instructive, and useful. Interesting, because these works treat of matters in which all Catholics are concerned, and would be still more concerned if they knew more about them; instructive, because it will open up new and extensive fields of knowledge relating to our holy religion; and useful, because it will place within the reach of everyone many graces, the existence of which was partially or wholly unknown before—graces which will strengthen, console, and encourage them in the time of temptation, trial, and bereavement, and prepare them better for their final passage to eternity.

It is not my intention to treat in this place of the treasure we possess in the Holy Sacrifice of the Mass, since it is regarded by all as the clean oblation foretold by the prophet Malachy, which was to be offered up from the rising to the setting of the sun. It is the purpose to treat rather of the contents and arrangement of the Missal.

Time was necessarily required to bring the Missal to its present state of perfection; for, though from the beginning all the essential parts were in use in the Church, the Missal had not reached the form in which it now appears until after the lapse of centuries. Nor were the several parts at first arranged in the same manner as they are at present. A portion was found in one book and another portion in another, which different books were known as the *Antiphonary*, the *Lectionary*, the *Book of the Gospels*, and the *Sacramentary*. A vestige of this remains to our day in the Church, as may be seen in the more solemn functions when a bishop officiates. Besides, certain prelates arranged the Missals for their respective dioceses, more or less according to their own ideas. The necessity of adopting uniformity of ritual where there was uniformity of belief became more and more apparent as time went on and the faith became diffused; and the better to secure this the necessity became also apparent of restricting the power to make alterations to the highest authority in the Church. But it was not till the sixteenth century that the Missal was reduced to its present form, and all further changes forbidden under the severest penalties.

The Council of Trent [3] recommended this action, and it was taken by Pope St. Pius V., who thoroughly revised the Missal, and published it in its corrected form, making that the standard to which all subsequent editions should strictly conform, and forbidding, at the same time, under the severest penalties, the use of any other Missal or of any other prayers or ceremonies in the Holy Sacrifice except those found in the Missal which he

[3] Session xxv.

had approved. No person, however exalted his dignity, was exempted from the observance of this command; but churches or religious orders having different customs dating back at least two hundred years were excepted out of respect for the antiquity of their liturgy. The bull issued by the Holy Father enjoining the use of the revised Missal and prohibiting all others is dated July 16, 1570. But the disorder was not fully remedied, and Pope Clement VIII., under date of July 7, 1604, issued another bull on the same subject, increasing the penalties. He was followed, September 2, 1634, by Urban VIII., in a bull of the same tenor. These three bulls are placed at the beginning of every Missal, as well as certain decrees of the Sacred Congregation of Rites bearing on the same subject.

Thus it was that the Missal came to assume its present form. The first step, however, had been taken somewhat earlier by "Burchard, master of ceremonies under Innocent VIII., who set out at length both the words and the ceremonies of the Mass in his Roman pontifical, printed at Rome in 1485, and again in his *Sacerdotale*, printed a few years later. . . . After this the ceremonies were joined to the Ordinary of the Mass in some printed Missals, and were finally arranged under their present titles by Pius V."[4]

A matter which those not of the One Fold find it difficult to understand, and for which, unfortunately, the vast majority of Catholics are not able to give a satisfactory reason, is the use of the Latin language in the liturgy of the Church. While a spirit of submission to the Church and of confidence in the wisdom of her decrees follows necessarily from a lively faith, there are too many Catholics who rest satisfied with these, for-

[4] "Catholic Dictionary," p. 724.

getting the advice of the Apostle, that they should be able to give a reason for the faith that is in them. It may be questioned, however, whether it is the result of faith, and not rather of indifference, that so many Catholics feel a reluctance to study books of instruction. Faith is not founded on ignorance, nor is it nourished by ignorance; nor does the Church, as some of our enemies would fain have us believe, fear the light. On the contrary, she invites and desires the careful study of both friend and foe.

Latin is the language of the Church's liturgy for several very good reasons. In the first place, it was the language of the Roman Empire, and was generally understood, if not spoken, throughout the civilized world at the date of the establishment of the Christian religion; and as St. Peter fixed the centre of the Christian commonwealth in the city of the Cæsars, it was not only natural but also necessary for the Church to adopt the Latin tongue as that of her liturgy. Again, the Church is one, and oneness of language serves to illustrate and to preserve oneness of faith. Besides, living languages are constantly changing; new terms are being introduced, and those in use vary their meanings. As instances of this may be cited certain English words that have not only changed their signification, but have taken a diametrically opposite one; as, for example, *let*, *prevent*, etc. But it is of the very first importance that the well-defined doctrines of religion should be expressed in language that always conveys the same ideas. The advantage of a medium of communication between the members of the Church throughout the world, whether assembled in general council, addressing their common Father, or corresponding with one another, is too apparent to require comment. Other reasons might also be adduced, but these are sufficient.

Examining the parts of which the Missal is composed we find that, after the insertion of the Papal bulls already referred to, the first place is devoted to the arrangement of all that relates to the calendar of the movable and immovable feasts. It may be said briefly that this arrangement of the Masses for saints and seasons depends on the feasts of Christmas and Easter. The former fixes all from the first Sunday of Advent to the octave of Epiphany; and the latter all from Septuagesima to Trinity Sunday; and the two together regulate the number of Sundays that must intervene between Epiphany and Septuagesima and between Trinity Sunday and the first Sunday of Advent, in order to give fifty-two in the year. If Easter is late, there will be more of the former; if early, there will be more of the latter. The calendar of the feasts of saints is also placed here. Next come the rubrics, which are laws or rules for the guidance of the priests in the celebration of the Adorable Sacrifice.

It may be well to note that in the Missal, as also in the Ritual and in the Breviary, besides the general rubrics which are found in the beginning and at the opening of the several parts or divisions, there are other ones interposed throughout these works for the guidance of the minister in the performance of his sacred functions. If the reader is careful to bear this in mind as we proceed it will obviate the necessity of frequent repetitions.

The word rubric is derived from the Latin term *rubor* (red), and its application in this place is taken from the manner in which red was used in writing the Roman laws and decisions, the titles, maxims, and principal decisions being written in red. In early ages the rubrics of the Mass were not found in the Missal at all, much less in the place and order they now occupy, but were contained in other works known as Directories, Rituals, Ceremonials, and Ordos. They were finally incorporated into the Missal by Burchard, elsewhere referred to. The revision of the Missal by Pope St. Pius V. fixed them in the place they must ever occupy.

After the rubrics come a preparation for and a thanksgiving after Mass, which are not, however, strictly obligatory on the celebrant. Then begins what may be termed the Missal proper, or that part of the book which contains the Masses of the feasts and saints. It opens with the Mass for the first Sunday of Advent, which contains, as all the other Masses do, those portions only of the Mass which are peculiar to the several days or feasts to which they are assigned, omitting those parts which are found in what is called the Ordinary of the Mass, which will be considered presently. The Masses for each Sunday and for some of the feasts which cluster immediately around Christmas, as well as for all the days of Lent, make up this division, which closes with Holy Saturday. Then comes the Ordinary of the Mass, which comprises all that part, except the secret prayers, from the gospel to the post-communion exclusive. It is composed of the prefaces, eleven in number, which are given first in solemn chant, then in ferial or simple chant, and finally without music, with rubrics directing the celebrant during which seasons or on which feasts each is to be said.

Next there is the Canon of the Mass, so called from the Greek word *kanon*, which means a rule; because this part of the Mass, as it were, follows a rule, and admits of no changes, except of a few words on some of the more solemn feasts. To illustrate the firmness with which the Church resists all encroachments on the Canon, it may be stated that when the Holy Father, at the request of a very large number of the hierarchy of the Christian world, declared St. Joseph patron of the Universal Church, he at the same time refused the request of a large number of prelates to have the name of the chaste spouse of the holy Mother of God inserted in the Canon after the consecration, where the names of about a dozen other saints are found.

At the close of the Canon the feast of Easter begins the Masses, and it is followed by the Masses for all the Sundays till the last before Advent, with some other Masses in their proper places, as those within the octaves of Easter and Pentecost, and a few more. This closes what are called the Masses of seasons; the rest of the Missal is taken up almost entirely with the Masses of saints, of mysteries in the life and passion of Our Lord and of His holy Mother, votive Masses, and Masses for the dead. The feasts of saints are of six grades doubles of the first class; doubles of the second class greater doubles; lesser doubles; semi-doubles; and simples. The portion devoted to the Masses of saints is divided into two parts: the proper of saints and the common of saints. The former embraces all that is proper to each individual saint—as the collect; or, the collect, secret prayer, and post-communion; or, with these, the epistle and gospel; or, in some instances, the entire Mass, with the exception of the Canon. The latter contains Masses for each class of saints—as martyrs, confessors, virgins, etc.—of which there are two or more for each class, and separate Masses for martyrs during paschal time.

The next section of the Missal is taken up with the votive Masses; and these are followed by a number of prayers, one or more of which may be introduced into certain Masses at the option of the celebrant or the request of the person for whose intention the Holy Sacrifice is offered. Then come four different Masses for the dead: that for All-Souls' Day, which is also said for a deceased Pope or Bishop; that for the day of a person's death or interment, which has also a prayer for the third, seventh, and thirtieth day after death; that for the anniversary; and, lastly, that for any day upon which a Mass for the dead is permitted by the rubrics. To these Masses are appended twelve prayers for different individuals or classes of the faithful departed, one or more of which can be introduced into the Mass according to certain rules, at the discretion of the celebrant, or according to the intention of the person requesting the celebration of the Mass. But the number of prayers should always be an odd one. An odd number, being indivisible, has a mystic signification. One represents unity in the several forms in which it appears in religious teaching, as the unity of God, the unity of the Church, the unity of the hierarchy, etc.; three represents the three Persons of the Adorable Trinity, Christ praying thrice in the Garden of Gethsemani, His rising from the dead on the third day, the angels thrice repeating *Sanctus;* five represents the five wounds of Our Saviour; and seven, the seven gifts of the Holy Ghost, the seven sacraments, and the seven petitions of the Lord's Prayer. These apply equally to the number of prayers used in the blessings of the Ritual.[1]

Certain formulæ for blessing water, articles of food,

[1] De Herdt, vol i. no. 82; O'Brien, p. 213.

and a few other things, occupy the next place in the Missal; but inasmuch as they pertain rather to the Ritual they will be passed over for the present. After these we have the six votive Masses permitted by Pope Leo XIII. to be celebrated on the several days of the week upon which no saints' feasts occur or only feasts of minor rite. The rest of the Missal is taken up with Masses of saints that have been canonized, for the most part, since the time of St. Pius V., and others that are peculiar to certain religious orders or localities.

Such, in brief, is the Missal. It is believed that what has been said, though apparently very commonplace, will not be either useless or uninteresting. There are few priests who have not reason to regret the limited knowledge of many of their people; and hence simple and plain instructions must ever be regarded as the most useful, though they will never be the most attractive or popular.

But the purpose of this article is twofold: First, to give a general idea of the construction of the Missal; and, secondly, to call attention to the votive Masses and to the prayers that are permitted to be inserted in other Masses on some of the feasts of minor rite. But here the question naturally arises: What is a votive Mass, and why so named? The word is derived from the Latin *votum*, and, as found in the liturgy of the Church, means a Mass which does not correspond with the office of the day or feast, as found in the Breviary, and which is so named because it is celebrated by the free choice—or *votum*—of the priests. The following are the votive Masses found in the Missal: That of the Most Holy Trinity, with a special collect when it is offered as a Mass of thanksgiving; of the Angels; of the holy Apostles Peter and Paul; of the Holy Ghost;

of the Most Holy Sacrament; of the Cross; of the Passion of Our Lord Jesus Christ; of the Blessed Virgin Mary, which varies for the different seasons of the year; for the election of a Supreme Pontiff; for the election or consecration of a Bishop; for the destruction of schism; for every necessity; for the remission of sins; for the grace of a good death; against pagans; in time of war; for peace; as a protection against mortality in time of pestilence; for the sick, with a special prayer when it is said for those who are believed to be near their last hour; for those on a journey; and, finally, the Nuptial Mass, which is treated at length in another part of this work.

Besides the above votive Masses there are six others permitted, as was stated above, by the Holy See: namely, of the Angels; of the Apostles; of St. Joseph; of the Most Blessed Sacrament; of the Passion; and of the Immaculate Conception of the Blessed Virgin Mary; some of which differ a little from those of the same title given above. In addition to these, however, any Mass of a saint may be said as a votive Mass, for a sufficient reason, upon the observance of certain rules, which differ little from those governing other votive Masses.

Still another mine of spiritual wealth of the Missal are the prayers, of which mention has already been made, one of which must, and more than one of which may, be inserted in the Mass on some Sundays and other days at the option of the celebrant, or in compliance with the request of the person for whose intention the Holy Sacrifice is being offered. These prayers are thirty-five in number, each of which includes, of course, the collect, the secret prayer, and the post-communion. The following are some of them—and the devout reader cannot but admire the loving care with which the Church provides in them for our every necessity : To ask the intercession of the saints ; another of the same kind ; for every grade of persons in the Church ; for the Pope ; for prelates and congregations committed to their pastoral care ; against the persecutors of the Church ; for every necessity ; for every tribulation ; in time of famine ; in time of an earthquake ; for rain ; for fair weather ; against pests among animals ; for the celebrant himself ; for the gift of tears ; for the remission of sins ; for those who are afflicted with temptations and trials ; to repel evil thoughts ; for the gift of patience ; for the gift of charity ; for friends ; for enemies ; for the welfare of the living ; and for the living and the dead. To these must also be added the prayers found in the Mass of any saint or mystery, which may be taken upon certain conditions, that apply to but few of them.

From all this it must be apparent to the thoughtful reader that not only have we an inestimable treasure in the Mass itself, but also that the value of this treasure is greatly enhanced by the special Mass which he can have celebrated, and which, besides its value as the greatest act of worship that man can offer to God, has a worth of its own from its being adapted to the particular intention for which its celebration is requested—there being special Masses for so many different intentions, as we have just seen, besides one for every necessity. And, granting that for a sufficient reason this special Mass is not permitted to be said, the addition of one of the prayers just named, when it is allowed, enhances the value of the petition immensely, as being made to God through His divine Son and in the name of the Church. Hear St. Liguori on this point. After citing the opinion of a theologian, with which he concurs, that the prayer of a lay person when offered up in church at the time when Mass is being celebrated is on that account the more readily and more certainly heard, he adds: "How much more the prayer of the priest himself?" And speaking of the Divine Office, which, though more efficacious than any other form of prayer, is yet far less so than the Mass, he says: "Many private prayers do not equal in value only one prayer of the Divine Office, as being offered to God in the name of the whole Church."[1]

In the Old Law there were many sacrifices, suited to the manifold wants of the people of God; the sacrifice of the New Law has not only taken the place of all those in the sense of being the supreme act of worship of God, but also as being the supreme act of petition for man.

Serious reflection on the inestimable treasure we possess in the adorable sacrifice of the Mass, as briefly set forth in this essay, will convince the reader of the advantage he may derive from asking for the graces, both general and particular, which he stands in need of, by means of this holy sacrifice. The graces, as St. Liguori remarks, which are not obtained in the Mass are with difficulty obtained at any other time. Here it is not man who prays, but the God Man, who petitions His eternal Father for His people through the ministry of His priests.

[1] "Sacerdos Sanctificatus," pp. 36, 128.

III.—THE TREASURES OF THE RITUAL.

The formation of the Ritual was the same as that of the Missal; its contents were not in the beginning found in their present form, nor even in one book. The early Rituals—for such they really were—went by a variety of names, according to the nature of their contents and the sacred functions in which they were used, and embraced a more or less complete collection of the rules for the rites and ceremonies to be observed in the administration of the sacraments, funeral services, blessings, etc. At length, however, the name *Ritual* came to be regarded as the most appropriate term, and as such superseded all others in the Western or Latin Church.

But to whom, it may be asked, do we owe the Ritual in its present form? A *Sacerdotale*—another name for Ritual—was edited by Castellanus and printed at Rome in 1537. Previously different dioceses were free to follow their own Rituals, but in 1614 an edition with the title *Rituale* was drawn up under Pope Paul V., who, in the bull *Apostolicæ Sedi* exhorted all prelates, secular and regular, to conform to it exactly.[1] But the fact that all persons of whatever rank are only *exhorted in the Lord—hortamur in Domino* are the words of the bull —to use this one to the exclusion of all others, would indicate that the use of the Ritual is not of so strict obligation as that of the Missal. But this is a point which, though warmly discussed among the rubricists,

[1] "Catholic Dictionary," p. 721.

and not yet definitely settled, would not be of interest to the general reader.

But who was it that reduced the Ritual to its present form? It may be remarked in passing, that the Ritual, like the Missal, was revised in accordance with the recommendation of the Council of Trent, for the sake of securing uniformity, as far as possible, in the administration of the sacraments and the performance of the other sacred functions of religion. The Ritual was finally reduced to its present form by a commission of Cardinals appointed for that purpose by Pope Paul V., who were assisted by many other eminent divines; but, as we learn from the bull of the Pope, prefixed to the Ritual, and dated June 17, 1614, it was mainly the work of Julius Antonius, Cardinal Priest of St. Severinus— a man, as the same bull declares, of remarkable piety, zeal, and learning. From the time it came from his hands it has undergone little change, although it was revised by Pope Benedict XIV., who prefixed to his revision a bull—*Quoniam autem*—dated March 25, 1752. Several additions, for the most part in the form of appendices, have since been made to it, consisting of various blessings, etc.

Before discussing the blessings of the Ritual, it will be advisable to give the reader an idea of its divisions and contents.

After certain decrees of Sovereign Pontiffs with which the Ritual opens, there is a short chapter devoted to general remarks on the administration of the sacraments. The sacrament of Baptism is then taken up, with all the prayers and ceremonies for its administration to infants and adults by a priest or a bishop. Then follows the manner of administering the sacrament of Penance, with the form of absolution from censures in case a person has incurred any. A chapter follows on the manner of giving Holy Communion outside of Mass, and to the sick, with remarks on Easter Communion. After this comes Extreme Unction, with the Seven Penitential Psalms and the Litany of the Saints, which those in attendance in the sick room are directed to recite during the administration of the last sacraments. To these is added a chapter on the visitation of the sick, with prayers and selections from the gospels, to be read on such occasions, as far as time and circumstances permit or render advisable; also the method of assisting the dying, giving the last blessing, and recommending the departing soul to God. Then follows all that relates to the funeral obsequies, which the reader will find treated at length in the essay on that subject.

The sacrament of Matrimony, with churching, or the blessing of a woman after child-birth, closes that part of the Ritual which relates to the administration of the sacraments. And here it may not be out of place to remark parenthetically that for the convenience of priests on the mission, who have to go on frequent and often distant sick-calls, those portions of the Ritual necessary for such occasions are printed separately in a smaller book, that may be easily carried in the pocket. These books are sometimes, though improperly, called Rituals. The remainder of the Ritual is devoted principally to the blessings of various objects, from the majestic cathedral or extensive cemetery to the diminutive medal. But before treating of these it will be advisable to complete the survey of the contents and divisions of the remainder of the Ritual. The numerous blessings will then be discussed in detail.

A number of blessings, some of which are reserved to a bishop, or a priest having special faculties from him, come next; and these are followed by the ceremonies, prayers, psalms, hymns, etc., for the processions of Candlemas Day, Palm Sunday, the Greater Litany, which takes place on the feast of St. Mark, April 25, and Corpus Christi; the procession praying for rain, for fair weather, for the dispelling of tempests; in time of want or famine, in time of mortality or pestilence; prayers to be added to the Litany of the Saints in time of war; for whatever necessity, with prayers to be added when it is made in thanksgiving for favors received; and, finally, a procession for the translation—or solemn removal from one place to another—of sacred relics. Then comes in order an exorcism—which is quite long, and consists of prayers, psalms, and selections from the gospels for expelling the spirit of evil from those who are possessed or obsessed by him. Next are given the various formulas for making registries of marriages, baptisms, confirmations, etc., in the several books required to be kept in the archives of every church. With these the Ritual proper closes; but there are two appendices and a supplement which aggregate three-fourths its own size.

The first of these opens with a short form for blessing baptismal water for the use of missionaries who give stations in places to which they cannot conveniently carry water from the font in the church. This is followed by the ceremony by which a priest, with the necessary faculties—very rarely granted by the Holy See—administers Confirmation where there is as yet no bishop; instructions for a priest who is permitted to celebrate Mass twice the same day; and the Litanies of the Saints, of the Blessed Virgin, and of the Holy Name of Jesus. Then begin the blessings for various articles, some of which may be performed by any priest, others by a priest having special faculties, some by a bishop only, others by the members of certain religious orders or congregations, while not a few are peculiar to certain dioceses. But of these more anon.

The second appendix comprises an additional number of blessings. The Ritual closes with a brief supplement, which does not, properly speaking, form a part of it, but is given for the convenience of priests in this country, and will, therefore, be passed over without comment.

Such is the Roman Ritual, according to the latest revision. We shall now take up the principal blessings, and to these the reader's attention is earnestly invited, as they constitute a rich treasure for those who will draw from it in a spirit of lively faith.

The blessing of various objects by the Church proves three things: First, the fall of man, and the passing of the world into the power of him who is called "the prince of this world"; secondly, the solicitude of the Church that whatever is used by her children should be "sanctified by the word of God and prayer"; and, thirdly, it proves the faith of Catholics in times past; because many, if not all, of these blessings would never have been instituted had they not been asked for by the piety of the faithful. It may be further remarked that the prayers recited in the several blessings as a rule indicate or express both the desire that the article blessed may be conducive to the spiritual and temporal welfare of those for whom it is intended, and also the special grace for which the blessing petitions. The number of blessings in the Ritual is much greater than the majority of Catholics imagine, being at least one hundred and twenty-five. These are so many sacramentals or vehicles of grace, which the Church makes use of to impart not only spiritual but also temporal blessings to her children.

The general rules for the blessing of articles are: that the priest who performs the sacred function should be vested in surplice and violet stole, commonly, though another color is sometimes required; that he should stand, with head uncovered, attended by an acolyte carrying the holy-water pot with the sprinkler; and that he should begin with the versicle—in Latin, of course: "Our help is in the name of the Lord;" to which the acolyte responds: "Who made heaven and earth." *V.* "O Lord! hear my prayer." *R.* "And let my cry come to Thee." *V.* "The Lord be with you." *R.* "And with thy spirit." Then follow the prayer or prayers; for in many cases there are three or even more, but seldom two, for the Church prefers odd numbers, as was said above with regard to the collects of the Mass. Sometimes also an additional number of versicles and responses is found; or again, one or more psalms or hymns form part of the blessing; or, in certain cases, there is an exorcism. At the conclusion of the blessing the object is usually sprinkled with holy water, and in the more solemn blessings—as those of ashes, candles, palms, etc., to which the reader is referred—incense is also used.

So great is the variety of blessings found in the Ritual that it is not easy to classify them; but some attempt will be made to group those together that seem most nearly related to one another. And first, of blessings of persons. There is a blessing for those who make a pilgrimage to the holy places of Palestine and another for them on their return; a form of absolving and blessing persons and fields by a special indult from the Holy See. But these are special, and are rarely given in our day, at least in this country. Those that follow are in more general use. Of these is the blessing of St. Blase, which is commonly given on the feast of that saint (Feb. 3d) to children as a preventative against diseases of the throat. Next comes the blessing of sick adults, which is followed by that for pregnant women, for the grace of a happy delivery—a blessing that should be more frequently asked, when the natural difficulties of parturition are borne in mind, the transmission of original sin, and the unscrupulous methods resorted to by too many physicians, and permitted by irreligious or indifferently instructed mothers, which practices, called by their right names, are nothing more nor less, in most instances, than the wilful murder of the defenceless. Why should not mothers have recourse to the Creator to save His creatures from the peril in which they are temporarily placed rather than use improper means to destroy, most probably, their frail lives, and doom them to an eternal separation from God ?

Then there is a blessing for infants, that they may live to grow up in innocence and holiness, uncontaminated by sin ; another for a child, that it may obtain the mercy of God, and increase, like the divine Child, in wisdom, age, and grace with God and men, and attain to a ripe old age ; and still another for children, assembled in the church for that purpose, in which the virtues suitable for their age and state of life are besought of God. After these comes a blessing for sick children who have come to the use of reason, that they may be restored to health, to the Church, and to their parents. Finally, there is a blessing for boys and girls on the feast of the Union of the Holy Infancy, asking especially for spiritual strength and the grace to guard against temptation.

Next are found the various blessings of religious articles, several of which the reader will find treated in separate essays in this work. Among these may be mentioned the blessing of a new cross; the blessing of a statue of Our Lord, His blessed Mother, and the saints, in the countless styles in which they are designed; the blessing of a church-organ; of a processional banner; of the metal for a new bell; and of a girdle in honor of the Blessed Virgin, for health of body, purity of soul, and the divine protection. Then there is another blessing for a crucifix or a picture of the crucifixion; the simple blessing of a bell, which is not intended to be used for a church; and, lastly, the blessing for crosses, crucifixes, rosaries, chaplets, statues, etc., and imparting to them what are called the Papal indulgences.

Another class of objects to which the blessings of the Church are imparted are the several kinds of buildings. And first, there is the blessing of houses on Holy Saturday, in the performance of which the priest, clothed in surplice and white stole, and attended, as usual, by an acolyte, passes from house to house, begging that as the blood of the paschal lamb, which was a figure of the true Lamb of God, protected the Israelites in their houses in Egypt from the destroying angel, so God would deign to send His angels to guard the inmates of these houses from all harm. Besides this, there is another blessing for dwellings, which may be given at any time by a priest; another for a house; another for a place, which may also be applied to a house; and a blessing for a bed-chamber. Would it not be well for Christians, who spend so much of their time in their houses, particularly in their bed-chambers, where perhaps they were born, and where they expect to die, to have these fortified with the blessings of religion? It is the pious custom of many persons, and it should be that of all; and it is with a view of increasing their knowledge, and thus stimulating their piety and their confidence in the divine protection, so liberally imparted by the Church, the dispenser of the graces of the Redemption, that this essay is written. Still another blessing for houses is given, which is assigned to the feast of the Epiphany, in which reference is made to the mysteries which that solemnity commemorates.

The Church, the patron of education and all useful knowledge, has also a blessing for a new school, in which the spiritual and temporal favors desirable for the pupils are besought of Almighty God. Lastly there is the blessing of the first stone of any edifice, no matter for what purpose it is intended, begging of God that what is undertaken for His honor and glory may be brought to a successful termination.

Blessings of articles of food shall next be considered. There is, as has been said, a number of blessings in the Missal for eatables and a few other things; but they are reproduced in the Ritual, and properly come up for treatment in this place. Of living things, there is a blessing for the paschal lamb, beseeching God that He would deign to bless it through the resurrection of Our Lord Jesus Christ, for the welfare of those who wish to partake of it. Also a blessing for fowls, with a reference to the action of Noe in sacrificing of the animals and fowls saved in the ark from the ravages of the deluge, and to Moses, at the command of God drawing the line between clean and unclean creatures in the Old Dispensation. This benediction asks that those who partake of these creatures may be replenished with the divine benediction, and may merit to be nourished unto eternal life. Among the blessings for other articles of food may be mentioned a blessing for fruits and vines; for eggs; two for bread; for new fruits; for any eatable; for simple oil; and for wine, on the feast of St. John the Evangelist. This blessing, where it is given, usually takes place at the end of Mass, while the celebrant is still vested, with the exception of the maniple, which he lays aside. It is imparted in honor of the apostle St. John, who is said to have drunk poisoned wine without being injured by it; and the special favor asked is that all who partake of it on that day may be protected from the evil effects of poison, and from all else detrimental to their health, and may also be preserved from sin. To these must be added a blessing for bread and cakes; for cheese and butter; and, finally—peace to the ashes of Father Mathew—one for beer, introduced, no doubt, through the influence of some pious Bavarian.

There are many other blessings in the Ritual which cannot be brought under distinct heads, but which will be treated in some kind of order. Taking, in the first place, those which relate to living creatures, there is one for bees, containing a reference to the mystical use of their wax in the service of the altar, begging that they may be preserved from everything hurtful to them, and that the fruit of their labors may redound to the glory of the three Divine Persons and of the Blessed Virgin Mary; a blessing for herds of cattle and oxen; for horses and other animals; for animals attacked by a plague; and another somewhat similar to it for herds of cattle and oxen afflicted with any disease. Then there is a deprecatory blessing against mice, locusts, grubs, and all noxious vermin. While the worldly-minded may smile at these things, talk about the Pope's bull against the comet, and be joined, tacitly at least, by some nominal Catholics—for it is hard for Catholics to live in the world without some of them becoming contaminated by its sinister influences—the devout child of the Church will ever bear in mind that "every best gift and every perfect gift is from above, coming down from the Father of Lights;"[1] that "the earth is the Lord's and the fulness thereof;"[2] and that all things are under the direction of an all-ruling Providence, by whose command or permission everything takes place, in the irrational and inanimate creation as well as in the angelic spheres.

Among the many other blessings of inanimate things are the blessing of a new ship; of gold, frankincense, and myrrh on the feast of the Epiphany; of chalk for writing the names of the three Magi on the doors of houses; of seeds and sowed fields; two for railroads and the cars to run on them; of a new bridge; of a fountain or spring of water; of a well; of fire; of a limekiln; of a smelting furnace; of seed grain; of a granary and harvested grain; of a bakery; of linen or bandages for the wounded; of every kind of medicine; of salt and vegetables for animals; of a stable for horses, oxen, and other draught animals; of a telegraph; and, lastly, there is one for anything whatever for which no special blessing is given.

Besides these and many others not mentioned—for all could not be introduced—there is a large number reserved to bishops and to the members of religious orders or congregations, which cannot be imparted by any other priest, unless he receives special faculties for that purpose. These faculties are commonly given, or may be easily obtained for certain articles; as, for example, investing with the Brown Scapular, erecting the

---

[1] St. James, i. 17.   [2] Psalms, xxiii. 1.

Way of the Cross, blessing the Beads of St. Dominic, etc.

Not a few of the above blessings might readily and naturally have been made the subject of interesting comments or marginal notes, but it was thought better not to interrupt the course of the essay too much, and only to give what was deemed necessary for a proper understanding of the subject. Such, then, are some, though not all, of the treasures which the Ritual of the Church places at our disposal, kind reader; examine them carefully, and try to avail yourself of them as far as your necessities may require or your piety prompt; remembering that no matter how largely you draw from the treasury of divine grace it can never be exhausted. "Hitherto," says Christ, "you have asked nothing in My name; ask and you shall receive, that your joy may be full."[1]

[1] St. John, xvi. 24.

IV.—THE TREASURES OF THE BREVIARY.

But what, the reader will ask, have I to do with the Breviary? Only priests are concerned with it. Let us see. Perhaps you have more to do with it than you imagine. Is it a small matter that in this country alone more than eight thousand priests daily spend from an hour to an hour and a half in its recitation? Surely some others also must be benefited by so holy an exercise. But when it is remembered that the clergy of the United States form but a small fraction of those of the universal Church, the importance of this good work will be still more apparent.

Any attempt to explain the Breviary, the arrangement of its parts, and the changes for the different seasons, feasts, etc., would tend to confuse the reader rather than enlighten him, and will not, for that reason, be undertaken. But inasmuch as essays have been given on the treasures of the Missal and the Ritual, it seems fitting that something should also be said of the Breviary; and it is believed the reader will find that it is far from being an uninteresting volume.

The Breviary, it is unnecessary to state, is a book containing the offices which all priests and others in Holy Orders are obliged, under pain of mortal sin, to recite daily, unless exempted by a grave reason. It is divided into four volumes, similar to one another in general outline, and adapted to the four seasons of the year, as the whole in one volume would be too unwieldy for general use. The Office is known by several names. It is called the Divine Office, because it is recited in the divine honor ; the Ecclesiastical or Church Office, because it is recited in the name and by the command of the Church ; the Canonical Office, because it is said according to the sacred canons or laws of the Church ; and the Breviary, for reasons that will appear in the sequel. But by far the most common name by which it is known among both the clergy and laity is simply the Office. It is composed of psalms, canticles, hymns ; lessons from the Scripture, the lives of the saints, and the homilies or sermons of the Fathers ; prayers, versicles and responses, with the frequent repetition of the Lord's Prayer, the Hail Mary, and the Apostles' Creed ; and it is divided into seven parts called the canonical hours. These are Matins, with Lauds, so named from the Latin word *matutinum* (morning), because in the primitive Church, and still with some religious orders, this part of the Office was said early in the morning ; and it is required to be recited by all priests before Mass, unless hindered by a sufficient cause. Then come Prime—that is, *first*, because it was said at the first hour, or sunrise ; Tierce, or *third*, from its being recited at the third hour, or nine o'clock ; Sext, or *sixth*, which was said at the sixth hour, or noon ; None, or *nine*, recited at the ninth hour, or three o'clock ; Vespers, from the Latin word *vespera* (evening), because it was said in the evening ; and Compline, or *the completion*, which was recited at bed-time, and served both as a fitting night-prayer and a completion of the Office.

It is to be remarked that the secular clergy and some of the religious orders and congregations are not bound to recite the Office precisely at these hours, being exempted by the nature of their pastoral duties or by their rules. They are permitted to say it at any time within the twenty-four hours of the day, and as much at a time as they may have the opportunity or the desire to recite; with the additional privilege of anticipating Matins and Lauds on the previous day, at any time after the middle of the afternoon, and in some countries after two o'clock. It may be further remarked that in the early days of the Church many of the faithful were accustomed to assist at the whole or a part of the Office, which was recited publicly in the church, — in choir, as it is called,—a custom which is still continued in many of the cathedrals and larger churches of the Old World.

According to the best authorities, the Office is substantially of apostolic origin, although it has undergone a gradual change till it has at length reached its present form. In the beginning it was composed almost entirely of the Psalms of David, which may be called the prayer-book of the early Christians; and they are the groundwork of the Office even at the present day. As time went on the Breviary gradually assumed its present form, the finishing touches being put to it at the recommendation of the Council of Trent. The first Breviary corrected by the Pope at the request of that august assembly was published in the year 1602. All persons obliged to the recitation of the Office were commanded to use this Breviary and no other, except such religious orders or churches as could claim for their own particular Office an antiquity of at least two hundred years. Previous to that time great latitude had been claimed by many bishops and religious communities in the arrangement of their respective Offices and reluctantly accorded by the Holy See.

The reason for adopting the name Breviary for the book containing the Office, and figuratively for the Office itself, has long been a subject of dispute. Some authorities maintain that it was so called from the fact that it is an abridgment, or epitome, of the Sacred Scriptures and the lives of the saints, the Latin word *breviarium* meaning an abstract or abridgment. Others will have it that the name had its origin from the shortening of the Office itself. The name was first used at the end of the eleventh century, when the Office was considerably abbreviated. The book containing the new Office was called the Breviary, or shortened Office, in contradistinction to the longer one. This seems to be the stronger reason for calling it the Breviary, and the true origin of the term; because when the two Offices were in use—as they were for a considerable time—the new one would naturally be distinguished from the other by the name of Breviary, or abridgment.

With regard to the division of the Office into seven parts, or hours, there can be no doubt that, as it was at first composed almost exclusively of the psalms of the Royal Prophet, so it was divided in accordance with his pious custom, as expressed in his own words: "Seven times a day I have given praise to Thee, O God!"[1] And though it was some time before all the several parts were formed, yet traces of some, at least, of the hours are found even in the days of the apostles. Nor is the opinion of some writers improbable, that the apostles, being converts from Judaism, adopted a division of prayer then in vogue among the Jews, the more devout of whom had learned from their great prophet-king to divide the day's devotions into seven parts, or at least to have a certain number of fixed times for prayer.[2] But be that as it may, it is well known that in the times of the apostles the day was divided into certain hours of prayer.[3] Nor did the apostles

[1] Psalms, cxviii. 164.   [2] Daniel, vi. 10.   [3] Acts, iii. 1; x. 9.

permit the most important duties, even those of charity, to interfere with their devotions, so highly did they value communion with God.[1] Tertullian, who flourished in the latter half of the second century, calls the third, sixth, and ninth hours the Apostolic Hours; the Apostolic Constitutions, which date no later at most than the third century, speak of Prime; and St. Cyprian, who lived in the third century, mentions Vespers.[2] According to one authority, Compline was added by St. Benedict, in the sixth century;[3] but another authority,[4] perhaps more deserving of respect, speaks of it as existing as early as the time of St. Ambrose, or in the latter half of the fourth century.

So much for the origin and divisions of the Office; two points yet more interesting remain to be discussed: the excellence of the Office as a form of prayer, and the part the laity have in the fruits of its recitation.

The excellence of the Office is derived from several sources, the first of which is the matter of which it is composed. The greater part of it is the inspired word of God, taken from the Scriptures of both the Old and New Testaments. Besides, there are abridged lives of the most illustrious servants of God in every age; extracts from the homilies and sermons of the Fathers of the primitive Church; hymns as remarkable for their authorship and literary merit as for the sublime truths and pious sentiments which they express; canticles which, for the beauty of their thought and language, have elicited the admiration of the learned of all times; and prayers that will never be equalled for their brevity, and tenderness and comprehensiveness of expression. "Many private prayers," says St. Liguori, "do not

---
[1] Acts, vi. 4.   [2] "Catholic Dictionary," article *Breviary*.
[3] "Kirchen-Lexicon."   [4] Wapelhorst, p. 351.

equal in value only one prayer of the Divine Office, as being offered to God in the name of the whole Church, and in His own appointed words. Hence St. Mary Magdalen of Pazzi says that, in comparison with the Divine Office all other prayers and devotions are of but little merit and efficacy with God. Let us be convinced, then, that after the holy sacrifice of the Mass the Church possesses no source, no treasure, so abundant as the Office, from which we may draw such daily streams of grace." We may say with perfect confidence that the Office is the most efficacious form of prayer ever composed. Nothing approaches it in efficacy but the adorable sacrifice of the Mass, which, though accompanied with prayers, is not itself a prayer, but a sacrifice. The better to be convinced of this important truth, let us glance for a moment at the parts of which an Office is composed; and let us take the Office of a confessor and bishop, which is one of the shortest, and may for other reasons be regarded as one of the best samples. It is composed of thirty-eight psalms, counting the divisions of the one hundred and eighteenth psalm, three canticles, eight hymns, nine prayers, the Lord's Prayer repeated fourteen times, the Hail Mary seven times, the Apostles' Creed three times, and the *Confiteor* once, when recited by one person alone. There are three lessons from the Sacred Scripture, three from the life of the saint whose feast is being celebrated, and three from a homily of one of the Fathers on the gospel read in the Mass of the saint, with an absolution before each three and a blessing before each one. Then there are eight little chapters, the *Te Deum* once, the antiphon of the Blessed Virgin twice, and a great number and variety of versicles and responses, taken for the most part from

[1] "Sacerdos Sanctificatus," pp. 128, 129.

the Scripture. The mere devout recitation of these by any person must call down innumerable graces.

But another source of excellence of the Office is that it is recited by ministers of God, who have been raised to the most exalted dignity on earth, that they may praise God in the name of all mankind, and petition for graces for all His children. Nor is this all. The Office is recited in the name of the Church, and by her authority; and hence it has all the influence with God that the spouse of His divine Son can give it, with the merit, too, of obedience on the part of those who recite it. It is the one great public prayer of the Church, as the Mass is the one great sacrifice of the Church. And here it is well to pause and explain what is meant by a *public* prayer in the language of the Church. It is not necessarily one that is said in public, even by the highest dignitary of the Church, but one that is recited in the name and by the authority of the Church. Hence, for example, if an archbishop were to recite the Rosary in his cathedral, and be responded to by a crowded audience, it would not be public prayer in the meaning of the Church; while it would be a public prayer for a priest, or even a subdeacon, to recite his Office alone in his room: because the one acts in his own name, the other in the name of the Church.

Again, the Office is so excellent a form of prayer that no indulgence is granted for its recitation, as there is none granted for hearing Mass; and this is, perhaps, the best evidence we could have of its surpassing excellence. Much more might be said on this point, but this, it is believed, will be sufficient to impress the reader with the idea that the Office stands alone, and far above all other exercises of devotion. But what benefits do you, kind reader, derive from the recitation of the Office by the clergy? This is a matter in which you are especially interested, and in which it is possible a pleasing revelation may be made to you in the concluding portion of this essay.

From the foundation of the world, as we learn from both sacred and profane history, certain persons were set apart to be, as it were, intermediaries between the people and God, not only to offer sacrifices, which was always the greatest act of divine worship, but also to pray for the people, to present their petitions before the divine presence, and to solicit such spiritual and temporal favors as might be desired. This is true not only of the Church of God in all times—whether patriarchal, Jewish, or Christian—but it is also true of the heathen nations, as is learned from the histories of ancient Egypt, Chaldea, Greece, and Rome; and even from our own aboriginal tribes, that had their medicine-men, whose services were so frequently demanded to propitiate the powers of the unseen world.

As regards the Jewish religion, the passages going to prove that the priests prayed, as well as offered sacrifice for the people, both individually and collectively, are so numerous that quotation is uncalled for; but nowhere is this more pathetically inculcated than in the following passage: "Between the porch and the altar the priests, the Lord's ministers, shall weep, and shall say: Spare, O Lord! spare Thy people; and give not Thy inheritance to reproach, that the heathens should rule over them."[1]

The graces of the Redemption being more numerous, and flowing from more copious fountains, than those of the former dispensation, it is naturally to be expected

[1] Joel, ii. 17.

that the priests of the New Law, the dispensers of the mysteries of God, as St. Paul calls them, should be entrusted with a more high and sacred office, and be vested with more ample powers: as the same apostle writes: "Every high-priest taken from among men is ordained for men in the things that appertain to God."[1] In so far as this relates to the recitation of the Office, we shall again appeal to the authority of St. Liguori, one of the most learned, as well as one of the most holy, men of modern times; and in appealing to him we feel a security seldom accorded by the Holy See to the writings even of a saint—that, namely, that no person can be molested for adhering to an opinion in theological matters advanced by him. Although the little work from which the subjoined extracts are taken was written for priests, and although the extracts themselves are only remotely applicable to the laity, yet, as they go to show both the excellence of the Office, and the fact that it is recited for the benefit of the whole Church, and not for that of the clergy only, as is too generally supposed, they will be given as they stand:

"To those," says the saint, "who are deputed by the Church to recite the Canonical Hours two very great and important offices are entrusted—that of praising and glorifying God and that of imploring the divine mercies upon all Christian people. . . . The Church has appointed her ministers to sing the Divine Office that men on earth may join with the blessed in heaven in honoring their common Creator. . . . As seculars are constantly distracted with the affairs of the world, Holy Church has appointed her ministers to implore for themselves and for all the people of Christ the assistance

[1] Hebrews, v. 1.

of His divine majesty through the different hours of the day. For this end the Office is divided into seven canonical hours, that there may be always some praying for all, and in the best form of prayer; inasmuch as the Divine Office is nothing less than a memorial drawn up for us by God Himself, through which He may more readily hear our prayers, and succor us in our necessities." And, addressing priests, he continues: "Consider that the Church charges you as her ministers to go and praise the Lord, and to implore His divine mercies for all mankind. . . . In a word, think that you are going to speak to Him of your own welfare and of that of the whole Church; and reflect that He then regards you with greater love, and listens more propitiously to your petitions."[1]

Have you not now, kind reader, an answer to your question: What have I to do with the Breviary? When, then, you see a priest recite his Office, whether in the leisure that a limited amount of parochial duties places at his disposal, or in the moments snatched from rest, sleep, or the multifarious and distracting parish work of a large congregation, do not fail to remember that you, without any effort or exertion on your part, are sharing in his prayers; and let your heart well up with sentiments of gratitude to God, whose infinite wisdom has ordered all things with such love for you, and with thankfulness to the good priest, who has perhaps deprived himself of much-needed rest that he might approach the throne of Divine Mercy to present your spiritual and temporal necessities there, wholly unknown to you. Not until the day of the final reckoning will you understand how deeply you may be in-

"Sacerdos Sanctificatus," pp. 126-135.

debted for signal graces to some priest, who perhaps refused your urgent invitation to dinner, tea, or an excursion, that he might say his Office with more leisure and recollection. The recitation of the Breviary is only one more evidence of the truth that priests are not ordained for themselves, but for the people.

V.—THE SIGN OF THE CROSS.

The execution of criminals in the early ages of the world, and until a comparatively recent date, was marked by extreme cruelty and barbarity.¹ A favorite way of inflicting capital punishment among many nations was that of hanging criminals to trees. This practice apparently led to the adoption of crosses for a similar purpose. Execution by crucifixion, of which traces are to be found from the remotest times among the nations of the East and North, was carried into effect in two ways: the sufferer was either bound to a tree or to an upright stake, sometimes after being impaled, and there left to perish; or, again, nails were driven through his hands and feet, and his limbs were also sometimes secured by cords. In time a horizontal bar was fixed to the upright post, and the victim's hands were stretched out upon it. Such, as we learn from the Gospel narrative, was the manner in which our divine Redeemer was crucified.

The earliest mention we have of this manner of executing criminals was at the time of King David, more than a thousand years before the beginning of the Christian era. The Old Testament states that the Gabaonites demanded from the Jewish king seven persons of the house of Saul, that they might be crucified to appease that people for the treacheries and cruelties practised by King Saul against their nation.²

Although the cross was an instrument of torture, there

---

¹ "Manners, Customs, and Dress during the Middle Ages," Lacroix, pp. 407 *et seq.*
² II. Kings, xxi. 6; I. Edsras, vi. 11.

is conclusive evidence, according to certain writers, that it was also honored in almost every nation. The following extract from one of these writers will be given as a sample: "From the dawn of organized paganism in the Eastern world to the final establishment of Christianity in the Western, the cross was undoubtedly one of the commonest and most sacred of symbolical monuments; and, to a remarkable extent, it is still in almost every land where that of Calvary is unrecognized or unknown. Apart from any distinctions of social or intellectual superiority, or caste, color, nationality, or location in either hemisphere, it appears to have been the aboriginal possession of every people of antiquity.... The extraordinary sanctity attaching to the symbol, in every age and under every variety of circumstances, justified any expenditure incurred in its fabrication or embellishment; hence the most persistent labor, the most consummate ingenuity, were lavished upon it. In Egypt, Assyria, and Britain it was emblematic of creative power and eternity; in India, China, and Scandinavia, of heaven and immortality; in the two Americas, rejuvenescence and freedom from physical suffering; while in both hemispheres it was the symbol of the resurrection, or 'the sign of the life to come;' and, finally, in all heathen communities, without exception, it was the emphatic type, the sole enduring evidence, of the divine unity."[1] The early explorers and missionaries of Mexico, Central America, and Peru, found numerous crosses in those countries; and many are still to be seen among the ruins of their cities and temples.[2]

That the crosses found among all the pagan nations of

---

[1] *Edinburgh Review*, July, 1870.
[2] "Conquest of Mexico," Prescott, vol. III. p. 368.

antiquity were nothing more than the Egyptian "*Tau*," or "Symbol of Life," a deification of the productive powers of nature, with different shades of signification attached to it by different peoples, appears certain. But it is a little remarkable that what was the symbol of the earthly life among pagans should be the symbol of the spiritual and heavenly life among Christians. From the dawn of Christianity the cross became the symbol of hope, an object of religious veneration; and, in later times, it has also become one of the most common ornaments.

After the discovery of the true cross in the year 326 by St. Helena, the mother of the Emperor Constantine, that monarch issued a decree forbidding the cross to be used thereafter in the execution of criminals. From that time the veneration which the Christians had shown it in secret from the beginning received a fresh impulse; and since that auspicious day nothing is more characteristic of the followers of Christ than the veneration they entertain for the sacred instrument of man's redemption.

As a religious symbol, the sign of the cross is a sacramental, and the principal one in use among Christians. As made upon the person it is formed in three different ways. That in use in the early ages of the Church was small, and was made with the thumb of the right hand, most commonly on the forehead; but it was also made on any part of the body. The constant use of the sign of the cross by the first Christians, and, much more, the fact that they were surrounded by heathens to whom the sacred sign would have betrayed their faith and put them in danger of persecution, or would have exposed the sign itself to mockery, rendered it necessary for them to make it in such a manner as not to be observed.

Next, there is the triple sign, made with the thumb on the forehead, the mouth, and the breast. At present this form is used more commonly by the Germans than, perhaps, by any other people. It is also prescribed in the Mass at the beginning of each of the gospels, but nowhere else in the liturgy. Lastly, the sign of the cross by excellence is that which is made by putting the right hand to the forehead, then under the breast, then to the left and to the right shoulder. The sign of the cross shall be considered from two points of view: as used by the faithful in their devotions, and as employed in the sacred functions of religion.

The devotion of the early Christians to the sign of the cross was extraordinary, and it attests the power they found to dwell in that sacred emblem. St. Cyprian, Bishop of Carthage, cries out : "O Lord, Thou hast bequeathed to us three imperishable things : the chalice of Thy blood, the sign of the cross, and the example of Thy sufferings!"[1] Tertullian bears witness to the frequent use of the sign of the cross by the Christians of the second century : "At every motion, and every step," he says, "entering in or going out, when dressing, bathing, going to meals, lighting the lamps, sleeping, or sitting, whatever we do, or whithersoever we go, we mark our foreheads with the sign of the cross." St. Basil writes : "To make the sign of the cross over those who place their hope in Jesus Christ is the first and best known thing among us." Not to mention others, St. Gaudentius says : "Let the sign of the cross be continually made on the heart, on the mouth, on the forehead, at table, at the bath, in bed, coming in and going

---

[1] The extracts from the Fathers given in this essay are taken, for the most part, from "The Sign of the Cross in the Nineteenth Century," by Mgr. Gaume.

out, in joy and sadness, sitting, standing, speaking, walking—in short, in all our actions. Let us make it on our breasts and all our members, that we may be entirely covered with this invincible armor of Christians." The writings of the Fathers abound in similar passages; but the following from St. John Chrysostom is worthy of the prince of Christian orators :

"More precious than the universe, the cross glitters on the diadems of emperors. Everywhere it is present to my view. I find it among princes and subjects, men and women, virgins and married people, slaves and freemen. All continually trace it on the noblest part of the body, the forehead, where it shines like a column of glory. At the sacred table, it is there; in the ordination of priests, it is there; in the mystic Supper of Our Saviour, it is there. It is drawn on every part of the horizon—on the tops of houses, on public places, in inhabited parts and in deserts; on roads, on mountains, in woods, on hills, on the sea, on the masts of ships, on islands, on windows, over doors, on the necks of Christians, on beds, on garments, books, arms, and banquet couches, in feasts, on gold and silver vessels, on precious stones, on the pictures of the apartments. It is made over sick animals, over those possessed by the demon; in war, in peace, by day, by night, in pleasant reunions and in penitential assemblies. It is who shall seek first the protection of this admirable sign. What is there surprising in this? The sign of the cross is the type of our deliverance, the monument of the liberation of mankind, the souvenir of the forbearance of Our Lord. When you make it, remember what has been given for your ransom, and you will be the slave of no one. Make it, then, not only with your fingers, but with your faith. If you thus engrave it on your forehead, no impure spirit will dare to stand before you. He sees the blade with which he has been wounded, the sword with which he has received his death-blow."

It was with good reason that the early Christians paid so great reverence to the sign of the cross. They had learned from experience that it is the symbol of power; as St. Cyril of Jerusalem writes: "This sign is a powerful protection. It is gratuitous, because of the poor; easy, because of the weak; a benefit from God, the standard of the faithful, the terror of demons." Armed with this sacred sign the martyrs went forth to battle with the wild beasts of the amphitheatre; walked calmly to the stake to be burned; bowed their necks to the sword, or exposed their bodies to the lash. They braved the terrors of the dungeon, or went willingly into exile. Even tender virgins and children defied the power of the tyrant, and suffered death in its most terrible forms; while thousands sought the lonely deserts to practise a life-long penance, with no companions but the wild beasts, sustained and encouraged by the same never-failing source of supernatural strength.

By the same sign the saints have wrought innumerable miracles. It is related of St. Bernard, to mention no others, that he restored sight to more than thirty blind persons by virtue of the sign of man's redemption. "Such is the power of the sign of the cross," says Origen, "that if we place it before our eyes, if we keep it faithfully in our heart, neither concupiscence, nor voluptuousness, nor anger can resist it; at its appearance the whole army of the flesh and sin takes to flight." The sign of the cross is also a source of knowledge. The form of words uttered in making it, together with the action that accompanies them, teaches the principal mysteries of religion. The words "in the name," instead of "the names," express the fundamental truth of the unity of God; while the mention of the Father, the Son, and the Holy Ghost declares that in this one God there are three Persons, and thus teaches the mystery of the Adorable Trinity. The incarnation, death, and resurrection of Our Saviour are recalled by the form of the cross traced with the hand. No formula could be more comprehensive and, at the same time, more simple. The sign of the cross is no less a prayer. It is an appeal to Heaven, made in the name of Him who in submission to the will of His Father "humbled Himself, becoming obedient unto death, even to the death of the cross";[1] of Him who declared that, "if you ask the Father anything in My name He will give it you."[2] Hence Christians have learned to begin and end their devotions with the sign of the cross, to render their petitions more acceptable at the throne of grace.

But especially is the sign of the cross a shield and safeguard against the temptations and dangers that threaten the life of the soul. The Fathers of the Church have insisted very strongly on this point, and a few extracts will be given from their writings. And here I shall pause to remark that I have drawn, and shall continue to draw, freely from the Fathers, preferring their own words to their ideas clothed in the language of another. Their voices, echoing down through the vista of ages, instruct, encourage, admonish, and at times rebuke us for the coldness of our devotion to the sign which they cherished as a priceless inheritance. Prudentius instructs the Christians of his day in these words: "When, at the call of sleep, you go to your chaste couch, make the sign of the cross on your forehead and heart. The cross will preserve you from all sin; before

[1] Philippians, ii. 8.   [2] St. John, xvi. 23.

it will fly the powers of darkness ; the soul, sanctified by this sign, cannot waver." St. Chrysostom continues in the same strain : "Do you feel your heart inflamed? Make the sign of the cross on your breast, and your anger will be dissipated like smoke." And St. Maximus of Turin : "It is from the sign of the cross we must expect the cure of all our wounds. If the venom of avarice be diffused through our veins, let us make the sign of the cross, and the venom will be expelled. If the scorpion of voluptuousness sting us, let us have recourse to the same means, and we shall be healed. If grossly terrestrial thoughts seek to defile us, let us again have recourse to the sign of the cross, and we shall live the divine life." St. Bernard adds : "Who is the man so completely master of his thoughts as never to have impure ones? But it is necessary to repress their attacks immediately, that we may vanquish the enemy where he hoped to triumph. The infallible means of success is to make the sign of the cross." St. Gregory of Tours says : "Whatever may be the temptations that oppress us, we must repulse them. For this end we should make, not carelessly, but carefully, the sign of the cross, either on our forehead or on our breast." St. Gregory Nazianzen thus defied the demon : "If you dare to attack me at the moment of my death, beware ; for I shall put you shamefully to flight by the sign of the cross."

At the risk of heaping up unnecessary proofs of the efficacy of the sign of the cross, a few more extracts will be given from the Fathers. We are their successors in the faith and in the world : let their devotion to the consoling emblem of man's redemption stimulate us to be truly their successors in our constant and confiding use of the same sacred panoply. Says St. Cyril of Jerusalem : "Let us make the sign of the cross boldly and courageously. When the demons see it they are reminded of the Crucified ; they take to flight ; they hide themselves and leave us." Origen continues : "Let us bear on our foreheads the immortal standard. The sight of it makes the demons tremble. They who fear not the gilded capitols tremble at the sign of the cross." St. Augustine answers for the Western Church in these words: "It is with the symbol and sign of the cross that we must march to meet the enemy. Clothed with this armor, the Christian will easily triumph over this proud and ancient tyrant. The cross is sufficient to cause all the machinations of the spirit of darkness to perish." St. Jerome, the illustrious hermit of Bethlehem, expresses his confidence in the cross in these terms : "The sign of the cross is a buckler which shields us from the burning arrows of the demon." Finally, Lactantius remarks : "Whoever wishes to know the power of the sign of the cross has only to consider how formidable it is to the demons. When adjured in the name of Jesus Christ, it forces them to leave the bodies of the possessed. What is there in this to wonder at? When the Son of God was on earth, with one word He put the demons to flight, and restored peace and health to their unfortunate victims. To-day His disciples expel those same unclean spirits in the name of their Master and by the sign of the cross." Let this suffice, where much more might be said, regarding the use of the sacred emblem of man's redemption among Christians. Turn we now to the employment of it in the august ceremonies of religion.

The sign of the cross is met with everywhere in the liturgy of the Church. No ceremony is performed without it. The hands of the priest are consecrated with the holy oil to enable them to confer blessings by the sign of the cross. In the course of the ceremony of ordination the bishop anoints the interior of his hands with the Oil of Catechumens, reciting at the same time the prayer: " Vouchsafe, O Lord, to consecrate these hands by this unction and our blessing, that whatsoever they bless may be blessed, and whatsoever they consecrate may be consecrated and sanctified, in the name of Our Lord Jesus Christ."

With these words is conferred on the priest such power over material objects, no matter what they may be, that he can bless them by simply making the sign of the cross over them, without it being necessary for him to utter any form of words, except, of course, in such cases as the Holy See requires a particular form for the blessing of certain things. He can, by merely making the sign of the cross, confer on beads, medals, statues, crucifixes, etc., the Papal indulgences, so that a person who is rightly disposed can gain all these indulgences by having one of those blessed objects in his possession

The number of times in which the sign of the cross is made in the ritual blessings of the Church is all but countless. In the blessing of holy water, for example, it is made twelve times. All the sacraments are administered with the use of the sign of the cross at least once, while in some of them it is employed a number of times. In baptism it is made fourteen times; in extreme unction, seventeen times. In the recitation of the Divine Office it is prescribed a great number of times. But these last crosses, unlike those of the Mass and the sacraments, are not of obligation, except when the Office is said in choir; and hence they may be dispensed with for sufficient cause, at the discretion of the person reciting the Office. It is related of St. Patrick that while reciting the Office he signed himself almost constantly with the sign of the cross.

It is superfluous to state that the sign of the cross is made very frequently in the adorable sacrifice of the Mass ; but it may not be generally known that during an ordinary Mass the celebrant makes it in the various ceremonies no less than forty-five times, besides the little triple crosses, already mentioned, at the beginning of the gospels. There is one point, however, with regard to the sign of the cross made in the Mass that seems to call for an explanation. " It is natural that the Church, accustomed to bless everything with the sign of the cross, should so bless the unconsecrated bread and wine. But it is surprising at first sight that the sign of the cross should frequently be made over the body and blood of Christ. Many explanations have been given, but the truth seems to be that no single explanation meets all difficulties, and that the sign of the cross is made over the consecrated species for several reasons. Usually the rite is made to indicate the blessing which flows from the body and blood of Christ." The sign of the cross at the words immediately preceding the *Pater Noster*—" Through whom, O Lord, Thou dost ever create all those good things, sanctifiest them, givest them life, blessest them, and bestowest them upon us" —were originally meant to be made over the *eulogia*, or blessed bread, placed on the altar and then given to those who did not communicate. And here an explanation of the *eulogia* may not be out of place.

One of the great characteristics of the Church is the unity of its members in one body, with Christ as the head. This unity is admirably expressed in both the elements from which the Holy Eucharist is consecrated : bread being made from a countless number of wheat grains, and wine being pressed from myriads of grapes. The Blessed Sacrament is, then—both from its matter before consecration and from Him whose flesh and blood it becomes by consecration—the special bond of union among the faithful. As the Apostle says: "We being many are one bread."[1] "However, when many of the faithful no longer communicated as a matter of course at every Mass, the need was felt of showing by some outward sign that they were in full communion with the Church. Accordingly, the celebrant consecrated so much only of the bread placed on the altar as was needed for the communicants; the rest was merely blessed, and distributed to those who did not actually communicate, though they had the right to do so. The *eulogia* (something blessed) then was a substitute, though, of course, a most imperfect one, for the Holy Communion; whence the Greek name *antidolon*—'that which is given instead.' The custom could scarcely have risen before the third century. In the fourth it was well known throughout the East; in the West we find it mentioned by Gregory of Tours in the sixth century. The bread used was sometimes the same as that which was set aside for consecration; sometimes ordinary bread was placed on the altar, and used for the *eulogia*. Usually the latter bread was blessed after the Offertory; but sometimes, as Honorius of Autun tells us, at the end of Mass. The Council of Nantes gives a form of benediction which the Church still employs in the blessing of the bread at Easter." Traces of this custom still exist in some French and Canadian churches, as well as among the Greeks.

"The signs of the cross made with the Host in the Mass, immediately after those referred to above, at the

[1] I. Cor. x. 17.

words, 'Through Him, and with Him, and in Him, is unto Thee, God the Father Almighty in the unity of the Holy Ghost, all honor and glory,' probably arose from the custom of making the sign of the cross in naming the persons of the Blessed Trinity. Such, at least, is the result of Bishop Hefele's careful investigation of the subject. The mystical interpretations of Gavantus and Merati deserve all respect, but scarcely explain the actual origin of the practice."[1] To return from this digression: so frequent is the use of the sign of the cross in the sacred functions of religion that one can hardly look for a moment at a priest performing any of the sacred ceremonies of his ministry without seeing him make the sign of our redemption.

A very important inquiry for all here presents itself. It is: Has the Church granted any indulgences to the use of the sign of the cross? and, if so, what are they? They are these: Pope Pius IX., by a brief of July 28, 1863, granted to all the faithful every time that with at least contrite heart they shall make the sign of the cross, invoking at the same time the Blessed Trinity with the words, "In the name of the Father, and of the Son, and of the Holy Ghost," an indulgence of fifty days. And by another brief of March 23, 1876, the same Sovereign Pontiff granted an indulgence of one hundred days to those who make the sign of the cross with holy water, with the same conditions and the same form of words.[2] It is well to note that the words to be used in making the sign of the cross with holy water are not, "Glory be to the Father," etc., as some persons imagine, but the formula, "In the name," etc.

When we are assured by the Christians of all ages, but especially by those of the first centuries, that we have

[1] "Catholic Dictionary." pp. 236, 322, 323. [2] *Raccolta*, p. 4.

so powerful a weapon as the sign of the cross at our command, it is much to be regretted that we should make so little use of it. Never did the world array before the child of God enemies so numerous or so insidious as at the present time. They assail him on every side; and not with the sword or with fire, but with false philosophy, with pride of intellect, with religious indifference, with materialism; against which it is more difficult to combat for a lifetime than it would be to gain the martyr's crown in a momentary struggle in the amphitheatre. If the first Christians, trained in the school of the apostles and their immediate successors, regarded as necessary the frequent use of the sign of the cross, why should we all but abandon it? Are we stronger than they? Is not the very opposite the truth? Why, then, do we not return to the pious custom of our fathers in the faith? Why disarm ourselves in the very presence of the enemy?

Still more deserving of censure are those who indeed make the sign of the cross, but make it carelessly. If a person were to stand fifteen minutes at the door of almost any of our churches on a Sunday morning, and look at the motions gone through by not a few of those who enter, he would be safe in concluding that if they were reproduced on paper they might as readily be taken for a Chinese manuscript as for anything else; but it would require a stretch of the imagination to see in many of them what they were intended to represent. It may be seriously doubted whether such careless persons receive the graces or gain the indulgences attached to a proper use of this sacred sign. It is indeed true that there is a tendency to do mechanically what a person has to do often; but for that very reason, if for no other, particular attention should be bestowed on such things. A careful examination of the manner in which they make the sign of the cross would be productive of good to many persons.

But what shall be said of those who are ashamed to make the sign of the cross? We should not, on the one hand, parade what is sacred unnecessarily before the world, on account of the disposition there is in so many persons to scoff at whatever others regard as holy; but, when circumstances require it, we should not, on the other hand, hesitate to sign ourselves with the symbol of man's redemption. The sign of the cross inspires us with respect for ourselves by teaching us our true dignity. It reminds us that we are the brothers of Jesus Christ. It sanctifies our members with the sanctification which it derived from His. It stamps the unity of God on our forehead, the seat of the mind; it seals our heart and breast with the remembrance of the love of the Father; it strengthens our shoulders to bear the cross of the Son; aud it maintains an unbroken union of love with the three Divine Persons by means of the Holy Ghost.

"In making the sign of the cross," says Mgr. Gaume, "we have behind us, around us, with us, all the great men and grand ages of the East and West—all the immortal Catholic nation. . . . In making the sign of the cross we cover ourselves and creatures with an invincible armor. In not making it we disarm ourselves, and expose both ourselves and creatures to the gravest perils."[1]

All this being true, what opinion are we to form of non-Catholics, not a few of whom have an almost fiendish hatred of the sign of the cross? Yet, were they to use it, it would be the marking upon themselves of the

[1] "The Sign of the Cross in the Nineteenth Century," p 296

instrument upon which the salvation of mankind, and their own, if they are to be saved, was wrought. And, withal, how illogical they are! Witness with what respect the Liberty Bell is cherished, and how it was almost worshipped during its recent trip to New Orleans. Witness the care with which the relics of Liberty Hall, Philadelphia, are guarded. Witness the enthusiasm of the people to have some souvenir of the place where the late General Grant died; how people went so far as to carry away branches of the trees that grew near the cottage in which he breathed his last. Witness, finally, how almost every person has some highly-prized relic of a departed parent or ancestor. And why all this? Because it is natural to man, and because it is ennobling in him, although his enthusiasm frequently carries it to excess. Must Catholics, then, be maligned and called idolators for following the promptings of nature in the worship of nature's God? Must we be asked to honor the sword of George Washington because it achieved our liberation from the tyranny of England, and then censured for venerating the cross of Jesus Christ that freed us from the thraldom of Satan? The man who should be so heartless as to insult his mother's picture would be justly censured by all the world as an inhuman wretch. Let the same world decide whether he is less deserving of censure—to put it in a very mild form—who insults the cross of Christ. Of such so-called Christians let St. Paul be the judge, who cried out: "God forbid that I should glory, save in the cross of Our Lord Jesus Christ!"[1]

I shall conclude with two extracts from the Fathers. Says St. Ephraim: "The sign of the cross is the invincible armor of the Christian. Soldier of Christ, let this

[1] Gal. vi. 14.

armor never leave you, either by day or by night, at any moment, or in any place; without it undertake nothing. Whether you be asleep or awake, watching or walking, eating or drinking, sailing on sea or crossing rivers, have this breastplate ever on you. Adorn and protect each of your members with this victorious sign, and nothing can injure you. There is no buckler so powerful against the darts of the enemy. At the sign of this the infernal powers, affrighted and trembling, take to flight." And St. John Chrysostom adds: "Never leave your house without making the sign of the cross. It will be to you a staff, a weapon, an impregnable fortress. Neither man nor demon will dare to attack you, seeing you covered with such powerful armor. Let this sign teach you that you are a soldier, ready to combat against the demons, and ready to fight for the crown of justice. Are you ignorant of what the cross has done? It has vanquished death, destroyed sin, emptied hell, dethroned Satan, and resuscitated the universe. Would you, then, doubt its power?"

VI.—THE STATIONS OR WAY OF THE CROSS.

THE times change, and we change in them; and one of the saddest of these changes is that which makes us averse to the practice of corporal mortification, on the one hand, and, on the other, prompts too many among us to harmonize with the pernicious principle of Protestantism by desiring to take the interpretation of the laws of the Church as of all other law into our own hands. Yet, notwithstanding this, our Holy Mother the Church tempers her laws as far as possible to the weakness of her children, and instead of exacting the rigorous penances of former ages, to which we are almost entire strangers, permits us to satisfy for temporal punishment on the easier condition of gaining indulgences. Not only so, but she mitigates the conditions of many of these from time to time, so much so that she would almost appear to have lost sight of her former rigorous discipline. While this should humble us, by reminding us that we lack the masculine energy of the Christians of other days, it should also be a strong inducement for us to gain as many indulgences as possible. It is easier to gain indulgences here than it will be to burn in purgatory hereafter.

The Way of the Cross is a devotional exercise, which, while most profitable in itself, is also more liberally enriched with indulgences than any other in the entire range of approved devotions. It is called, indiscriminately, "The Way of the Cross" and "The Stations of the Cross;" and, although the former is the more correct, both are perfectly intelligible to Christians. How noble the origin of this holy exercise! Jesus Christ it was who first performed the devout exercise of the Way of the Cross, carrying the instrument of man's redemption on His mangled and bleeding shoulders, and marking each step of the painful journey with His most precious blood—blood which the thoughtless crowd trod ruthlessly into the dust and mire, regardless of its infinite value and of the myriads of angels who bent before its every drop in profoundest adoration. Nothing need be said here of this first Way of the Cross; it is indelibly engraven on the minds and hearts of all reflecting Christians. But let us ask, To whom do we owe the exercise of the Stations of the Cross? This beautiful and inspiring devotion is due, beyond all doubt, to none other than the august Mother of God, the Queen of martyrs. From the moment the Archangel Gabriel saluted Mary as the Mother of the long-expected Messias, she knew, both from the Scriptures of the Old Testament, which doubtless she had read and heard explained during her stay in the temple, and also from her more than seraphic contemplation of the mission of the Man of sorrows, that His Mother must of necessity be the Dolorous Mother. But after the presentation of her divine Infant in the temple, when holy Simeon foretold that her Child was set for the ruin as well as for the redemption of many in Israel, and for a sign that should be contradicted, and that a sword of sorrow should pierce her own soul on account of Him, the sorrowful way was ever present to her mind. Whether an exile in distant and inhospitable Egypt, or at home in her quiet retreat at Nazareth, or accompanying her divine Son during His public ministry, this sorrowful way was never lost sight of. But when it came to be made in the reality, it far exceeded all ideas of it that even the mind of

Mary was capable of forming. And once past, it could not be forgotten. The different places that marked the more than common sufferings of her Son and her God were indelibly engraven on her memory; and when His mission on earth was accomplished she would visit these sad scenes either alone or accompanied by other holy women, and there devoutly meditate on the love of God for man. It was thus she became the founder of one of the most fruitful devotions of holy Church.

Of the stations some are referred to in the Sacred Scriptures, as the first, second, fifth, etc.; while the others have been handed down by the constant tradition of the Church, as the third, fourth, seventh, etc. The number of the stations, although generally fourteen or fifteen, was not at first authoritatively fixed; and we learn from a statute of the Archdiocese of Vienna, as late as February 25, 1799, that the number of stations there was but eleven.[1] This, however, must have been a local custom, approved by the proper ecclesiastical authority; for according to the rules laid down by Pope Clement XII., April 3, 1731, the number of the stations was fixed for all future time at fourteen. It may be remarked, as is learned from the same decree, that little chapels were sometimes erected for the stations when they were set up outside the church.

No better idea of the high character and inestimable value of the Way of the Cross can be conveyed to the mind of the reader than that contained in the following quotation from the *Raccolta* (pp. 102, 103): "Among the devotional exercises which have for their object meditation on the Passion, Cross, and Death of Our Lord and Saviour Jesus Christ, the sovereign means for the conversion of sinners, for the renovation of the

---

[1] "Kirchen-Lexicon," vol. vi. p. 274.

tepid, and for the sanctification of the just, one of the chief has ever been the exercise of the Way of the Cross. This devotion, continued in an unbroken tradition from the time Jesus Christ ascended into heaven, arose first in Jerusalem, amongst the Christians who dwelt there, out of veneration for those sacred spots which were sanctified by the sufferings of our divine Redeemer. From that time, as we learn from St. Jerome, Christians were wont to visit the holy places in crowds; and the gathering of the faithful, he says, even from the farthest corners of the earth, to visit the holy places, continued to his own time. From Jerusalem this devout exercise began to be introduced into Europe by various pious and holy persons who had travelled to the Holy Land to satisfy their devotion. Amongst others, we read of the Blessed Alvarez, of the Order of Friar Preachers, who, after he returned to his own convent of St. Dominic, in Cordova, built some little chapels, in which he represented, station by station, the principal events which took place on Our Lord's way to Mount Calvary. Afterward, more formally, the Fathers Minorite Observants of the Order of St. Francis, as soon as ever, on the foundation of their Order, they were introduced into the Holy Land, and more especially from the time when, in the year 1342, they had their house in Jerusalem, and the custody of the sacred places, began, both in Italy and elsewhere, in short, throughout the whole Catholic world, to spread the devotion of the Way of the Cross. This they effected by erecting, in all their own churches, fourteen separate stations, in visiting which the faithful, like the devout pilgrims who go to visit the holy places in Jerusalem, do themselves also make this journey in spirit, whilst they meditate on all that Our Lord Jesus Christ vouchsafed to suffer for our eternal salvation at those holy places in the last hours of His life. This excellent devotion has met with the repeated approvals of holy Church : in the constitutions, for instance, of the venerable Pontiff Innocent XI. . . . and of Clement XII. By this last Pope it was extended to the whole world." This extension was made by his constitution *Exponi Nobis*, of January 16, 1731.

The reader may form an idea of the zeal with which some saintly missionaries have labored for the propagation of this devotion—which is at the same time the strongest evidence of the value they set upon it—from the single instance of St. Leonard of Port Maurice, who erected no less than five hundred and seventy-two sets of stations. It was he, too, who induced Pope Benedict XIV. to have them erected in the Colosseum at Rome, the spot which had been so frequently bedewed with the blood of martyrs ; and the saint himself preached on the occasion. It was here that Archbishop Hughes, of New York, during one of his visits to the Holy City, performed the Way of the Cross, accompanied by five thousand people.

One of the first questions that will present itself to the minds of those who read this essay will be : What are the indulgences granted by the Holy See to the devout performance of the Way of the Cross? Here something extraordinary confronts us : it is that no preacher or catechist is permitted to state from the pulpit or in writing what precisely are the indulgences gained by the performance of the Way of the Cross ![1] "One of the reasons for this may have been the loss of many of the ancient briefs by which the Holy See had applied several rich indulgences to that pious practice, and

---

[1] *Raccolta*, p. 104.

which, it is said, were destroyed at Jerusalem on the occasion of the burning of the archives belonging to the Franciscan Friars there. The instructions, however, assign a different reason. For in the rule referred to, it is expressly stated as having been ascertained, on more occasions than one, that, either through malice, negligence, or excessive zeal, the truth of the indulgences had been so altered as to render them altogether obscure and uncertain."[1] It is only permitted, and it is sufficient, to state in general terms that whoever performs devoutly the holy Way of the Cross will gain the same indulgences as he would if he were to visit the actual Way of the Cross in Jerusalem.[2] What some at least of these indulgences are may be learned from Father Vitromile's "Travels in Europe and the Holy Land." All the indulgences granted to the Way of the Cross may be gained by those who perform the devotion, either in public or in private, by day or by night (D. March 1, 1819). They can also be applied to the souls in purgatory. Father Maurel states (p. 147) that, "should a person perform the Way of the Cross repeatedly on the same day, he can gain the indulgences each time." This has been modified, however, by a more recent decree, and it cannot now be maintained. The question having been put to the Sacred Congregation, the response was, that: "From the documents in the possession of the Congregation it is not certain (*non constat*) that a person will gain the indulgences as often as he performs the holy exercise" (D. September 10 1883).

[1] Maurel on Indulgences, pp. 144, 145.
[2] Decree of the Sacred Congregation of Indulgences and Holy Relics, April 13, 1731. In the rest of this essay the decrees of this Congregation, which will frequently be quoted, will be given in the text as "D," with date

The Stations or Way of the Cross. 77

It is needless to state that, in order to gain these indulgences, whether a person performs the devotion in public or in private, he must strictly comply with all the conditions prescribed by the Holy See. These conditions may be divided into (1) such as refer to the stations themselves; (2) such as refer to the person who erects them; and (3) such as refer to the person or persons performing the holy Way of the Cross. And first as to the stations themselves. The stations may be erected either inside or outside the church or chapel; but when erected outside they should either begin or end in the church or in some other holy place; the place they occupy should be properly guarded against profanation, and there should also be a set of stations in the church to be used in inclement weather (D. April 3, 1731). The indulgences are attached to the crosses only which surmount the pictures or reliefs representing the various scenes in the sorrowful journey of our divine Redeemer. Hence the pictures or reliefs need not be blessed (D. January 30, 1839); but they may be blessed.[1] If the pictures become defaced, or if it is desirable to change them for others, and the first crosses are retained, it is not necessary to bless the latter anew; they are simply to be placed over the new pictures or reliefs, and the indulgences are not lost (D. August 22, 1842). But it is carefully to be borne in mind that the crosses must, under penalty of forfeiting all the indulgences, be of wood, in the strict acceptation of the word, and must be large enough and so placed as to be visible to the people (DD. June 2, 1838, and November 23, 1878). Nor should the crosses have the image of our divine Saviour upon them.[2] If the stations are taken from the church or place in which they were first

[1] Maurel, p. 148.   [2] Ibid., p. 149.

erected, and placed in another location, with the intention that it shall be in future their permanent place, they lose the indulgences, and require a new erection (D. January 30, 1839). But if they are only taken out of the church or place for a time, in order that the church may be repaired or frescoed, and are then restored to their places, the indulgences are not lost and no new erection is necessary. The same is true if they are arranged differently in the same church or place. But a person who performs the Way of the Cross before the places where the stations were before their removal, or who performs it before the stations in the place to which they are temporarily removed, will not gain the indulgences (D. December 16, 1760). From all this we are to understand that when the stations are erected in a certain place, it is in that place only that the indulgences can be gained before them.

It must have struck persons who are accustomed to perform the Way of the Cross in different churches that the stations do not always begin on the same side of the altar. In one they will be found to start on the Gospel side, in another on the Epistle side. Indeed, it would appear to be left rather to the caprice of the artist, if such he can always be called, who paints the stations than to any legislative enactment of the Church to determine the direction in which the Way of the Cross is to be made. There is no positive enactment in the matter; and so far as the indulgences are concerned, it is perfectly indifferent whether they begin on the one side of the altar or the other. Maurel says (p. 150) that "general usage, grounded on the basis of piety and congruity, would have the first station commence on the Gospel side of the church. But this arrangement is not strictly required." And he quotes a decree of March 13, 1837.

Next, as regards the conditions to be observed by the person who erects the stations, few remarks need be made, because it will naturally be taken for granted that the essential conditions have been complied with. It may not, however, be amiss to venture the following observations. By *erecting* the Stations or Way of the Cross is meant the blessing and placing of them in the position they are destined afterwards to occupy, and doing so in such a manner and by such authority that persons performing the exercise of the Way of the Cross before them, with the proper dispositions, will gain all the indulgences granted by the Holy See to this salutary devotion. It is not necessary that there should be a fixed or an equal distance between the different stations, much less that they should be as far apart as the stations of the way of Calvary in Jerusalem (D. December 3, 1736). But yet there must be some distance between them (D. August 28, 1752).

According to the rules for the erecting of the stations, the privilege was reserved to the Minor Observantine Fathers, under penalty of forfeiting the indulgences; and others who wanted the stations erected were required to have the ceremony performed by one of these fathers, or obtain the privilege from the Superior-General of that Order (D. April 3, 1731). But many bishops have now received the faculty from the Holy See, not only of erecting the stations themselves, but also of delegating such of their priests to perform the same function as they see fit. As regards the validity of the erection, it is not necessary that the priest who performs the ceremony should personally set up the different stations. He can employ another, even a laic, to do this (D. March 20, 1846); or he may himself place them privately on an occasion different from that of their blessing, and without any ceremony (DD. August 22, 1842, March 20, 1846). By a decree of September 25, 1841, it was made obligatory that the request for faculties, or permission, to erect the stations in a church or other place, the granting of the request, and all the papers relating to the erection, should be in writing, and should be kept in the diocesan archives, and that at least a brief account of the whole proceeding should also be kept in the church itself; and all this under pain of nullity as regards the gaining of the indulgences. These documents, too, were to be executed with as little delay as possible, lest a doubt might afterwards arise regarding the validity of the erection; although it was not required, as some persons imagined, that this should be done within twenty-four hours (D. February 10, 1844). Maurel is of opinion that this was not required under the penalty of forfeiting the indulgences, and says (p. 151): "Looking at the decisions issued by the Sacred Congregation, January 27, 1838, it does not appear that these different formalities are exacted under pain of nullity. This may be inferred from the very words which I took at the *Segretaria* of the Sacred Congregation of Indulgences." This decree is not found in the Decrees of this Congregation lately published by order of the Holy Father. But a later decree (June 21, 1879) requires the written permission of the bishop for each case under pain of nullity. And Schneider (p. 269) makes no reference to the above remarks of Maurel, although translating and editing his work; and since he wrote after the date of the last decree, and yet insists upon all that is contained in the former one, he seems clearly to be of the opinion that all these conditions are required by the Holy See. From other authorities and the present practice there remains no doubt in the matter.

With regard to those who perform the devout exercise of the Way of the Cross, they may be divided into three classes: those who perform it in public with a leader; those who perform it in private; and those who, through infirmity or for any other sufficient reason, are not able to make the Stations in the church, but use a crucifix, blessed for that purpose, at home. The conditions for gaining the indulgences are but two in number: First, to go from one station to another around the entire fourteen, without omitting any. "Hence it is necessary to rise at each station, change one's place, and go from one to another, unless a person be prevented from doing so by reason of some infirmity, the narrowness of the place, or a crowd of people; because, in that case, it would be enough to make some slight movement, and turn toward the following station. By this pious exercise the faithful reproduce, on a small scale, the pilgrimage of the Way of the Cross of Jerusalem. But bear in mind that wherever it is impossible to pass from one station to another the decrees invariably require some motion of the body" (DD. September 30, 1837, February 26, 1841). Again: "When the devotion is gone through publicly, to avoid all confusion, it is permitted by a decree dated July 23, 1757, to adopt the method observed by St. Leonard of Port Maurice: 'that all the people remain in their respective places, while the priest, accompanied by two chanters, goes around the different stations, and, stopping before each of them, recites there the usual prayers, to which the faithful answer in their turn.'"[1] No vocal prayers are required to be said as a condition for gaining the indulgences, when the Stations are performed either in public or in private, except by those who constitute the third class named above; and of those further on. Says the *Raccolta* (p. 104): "The recitation at each of the stations of the words: 'We adore Thee, Christ,' etc., the 'Our Father,' the 'Hail Mary,' and the 'Have mercy on us, O Lord,' is nothing more than a pious and praiseworthy custom, introduced by devout persons in the devotion of the Way of the Cross. This the Sacred Congregation of Indulgences declared in the Instructions for performing the exercise of the Way of the Cross, Nos. vi. and xi., published by the order and with the approbation of Clement XII. (April 3, 1731) and Benedict XIV. (May 10, 1742)."

The second condition for gaining the indulgences of the stations is contained in these words of the *Raccolta* (p. 103): "All who wish to gain the indulgences by means of this devotion must bear in mind that it is indispensably required of them to meditate, according to their ability, on the Passion of Our Lord Jesus Christ." "Mind, it does not lay down that a special meditation ought to be made on each of the fourteen stations. It suffices to meditate on the Passion in general, for nowhere in the Constitutions of the Holy See is it enjoined to meditate on each individually. True, the Sacred Congregation of Indulgences, having been consulted on the matter, replied that one should meditate on the mysteries represented by the fourteen stations (February 16, 1839). But at Rome this declaration is regarded as a counsel, and not as an essential condition for sharing in the indulgences, especially since the

[1] Maurel, pp 144, 145.

same decree, No. 3, even expressly states that a short meditation on the Passion of Our Lord is what is prescribed for participating in these favors. I give the very words of the Instruction: 'Any short meditation on Our Saviour's Passion suffices, which is the work enjoined for obtaining the holy indulgences' (D. April 3, 1731). Persons not knowing how to meditate may content themselves with pious thoughts on some circumstances of the Passion, according to their capacities. . . . Confession and Communion are not required; it is enough to be in the state of grace, and to have a sincere sorrow for one's sins."[1]

Another important inquiry is that regarding the interruptions that are or are not permitted those who perform this devotion. The rule which applies here is similar to that which obtains in the case of any other devotion, such as the Rosary; that is, that a person who should interrupt the Way of the Cross to hear Mass, go to Holy Communion, confession, etc., would not lose the indulgences, provided there was not a notable or moral interruption (D. December 16, 1760).

The second class of persons, or those who perform the Stations in private in the church, are not required to fulfil any other conditions than those imposed on the first class, except that they must pass from one station to another. They should not perform them during Mass or Vespers, nor when any other public devotion is going on in the church (D. April 3, 1731).

As to the third class, the infirm and others hindered from performing the Way of the Cross before stations erected in a church or chapel, the Church, in her maternal solicitude for their spiritual welfare, is unwilling to deprive them, through no fault of theirs, of the ad-

[1] Maurel, pp. 145, 146.

vantages of this devotion. Accordingly, Pope Clement XIV. (D. January 26, 1773) granted the following privileges to such persons, which were confirmed by Pius IX. (D. August 8, 1859): " All who are sick, all who are in prison, or at sea, or in heathen lands, or are prevented in any other way from visiting the Stations of the Way of the Cross erected in churches or public oratories, may gain these indulgences by saying, with at least contrite heart and devotion, the ' Our Father,' the ' Hail Mary,' and the ' Glory be to the Father,' each fourteen times, and, at the end of these, the ' Our Father,' the ' Hail Mary,' and the ' Glory be to the Father,' each five times ; and, again, one ' Our Father,' ' Hail Mary,' and ' Glory be to the Father ' for the Sovereign Pontiff, holding in their hands the while a crucifix of brass, or of any other solid substance, which has been blessed by the Father General of the Order of the Friars Minor Observants, or else by the Father Provincial, or by any Father Guardian subject to said Father General." [1] It may be added that any other priest can be, and frequently is, authorized to bless such crucifixes. As to the reasons that would be deemed sufficient to justify a person in performing the Way of the Cross with one of these crucifixes, " a moral impossibility suffices. . . . Thus a person on a journey, or in the country, at a considerable distance from the parish church, may be constituted in a moral impossibility of visiting the Stations. So, too, as regards a priest or religious who, on account of his multiplied duties, or for other grave reasons, is unable to visit a church to go through the Stations. Accordingly, all such persons may perform the Stations privately by means of the crucifix. It may be well to note that the person possessing the crucifix indulgenced

[1] *Raccolta*, p. 104.

for the Way of the Cross can alone gain the indulgence: the privilege is personal (D. May 29, 1841). Again, conformably to recent decrees, the crucifix can never be sold, or given away, or lent to others with the intention of communicating to them the indulgences. Though, strictly speaking, all crucifixes, no matter how diminutive, can be blessed for this end, it would not be becoming to apply the indulgences to very small ones, which would scarcely be visible in the hands of those using them. In fine, recollect that, pursuant to the late decree quoted above, the twenty 'Our Fathers' and 'Hail Marys,' and 'Glory be to the Fathers' should be said without, at least, any notable interruption which might break the moral connection or unity of the prayer."[1]

I may remark that I have seen small pictures of the fourteen stations so joined together as to fold up, but which had no crosses whatever surmounting them; yet the persons having them believed they could gain the indulgences of the Way of the Cross by using them. This is certainly erroneous, inasmuch as the decrees above cited require, in all cases, the cross or crosses—fourteen of wood when the stations are erected in a church or chapel, and one of brass or some other solid material when blessed for the use of the infirm or of such as are hindered from performing the devotion before duly erected stations. It is never to be forgotten that in matters relating to indulgences we must in all cases conform strictly to the conditions laid down by the Holy See in granting them; for nothing is left to our free choice. Part may be, and is, sometimes, left to the discretion of our spiritual director, but not to our discretion.

[1] Maurel, pp. 153, 154.

II.—THE HOLY OILS.

AFTER the Most Holy Sacrament of the Altar, the Church possesses nothing more sacred than the Holy Oils used in the administration of certain of the sacraments and in certain other functions of religion. It must, therefore, prove interesting and instructive to treat of the Holy Oils; for whether they are used in elevating a bishop or a priest to his sacred dignity, in consecrating an altar, a chalice, or a bell, or in blessing a baptismal font, they always conduce either directly or indirectly to the spiritual benefit of the individual Christian. Yet here, as with regard to the Missal, the Ritual, and the Breviary, the opportunities afforded the people for obtaining full and accurate information are limited.

It is to be remarked that wherever the word *oil* is used in the Sacred Scriptures, the Fathers, or the liturgy of the Church, olive oil is meant. It is pre-eminently *oil*. The olive and the cedar were the most important trees of the East; and the inhabitants of those countries being an imaginative people, both of these trees were extensively used in supplying writers and speakers with rhetorical figures. A glance at the Scriptures will be sufficient to establish this fact. The latter tree was the symbol of majesty and strength; the former, of fecundity, utility, beauty, and perennial life.[1] The first symbolical use of the olive in sacred history was that of the branch brought to Noe by the dove, as the emblem of peace, after the waters of the deluge had subsided; and

---

[1] Psalms, li. 10; cxxvii. 3; Osee, xiv. 7.

from that time the olive-branch has been regarded in art and literature as the emblem of peace, as the palm has been of victory. The time of pressing oil as well as wine was a season of festivity among the Orientals.

The natural uses of oil, in contradistinction to its mystical uses, are: for food, for light, for medicine, and for anointing, with a view of increasing beauty or strength. Of the first three uses nothing need be said; they are known and admitted by all; the last named, too, is almost as well known. Not only those who wished to improve their appearance used oil upon their hair, to which Our Saviour alludes when He says, "When thou fastest, anoint thy head," but the athletes of classic times anointed their bodies to strengthen them for the contests in which they were to engage. In the mystic sense, oil is the symbol of grace and charity, of mercy and alms, of spiritual consolation and joy.[1] But how, it may be asked, did oil come to have a mystic signification? And the answer to this question is the more important and necessary as we live in a material age, when all things are judged by the testimony of the senses. We of this age, and especially of the Western World, are not naturally so imaginative as the Orientals, and, as a consequence, the mystic signification of anything will not be so likely to impress us, even if brought to our notice, as it would them; while we would seldom dream of seeking a mystic signification, although it would be their first study. It was natural for the early Christians to attach symbolical meanings to many of the sacred functions of religion, and this for three reasons. In the first place, it was in harmony with the genius of the people themselves; again, it was taught them by the example of those of the Jewish Dis-

[1] Cornelius à Lapide, vol. vi. p. 117.

pensation whom they regarded as their fathers both in the flesh and in the faith; and, finally, it was in a measure necessary, since they worshipped an invisible God, in whose service they were constrained to make use of visible creatures to aid them in giving expression to their faith and devotion. They recognized the work of the hand of God in the visible world, and learned from it to make use of that creation to express their homage and to solicit His aid. The Church, then, adopted mystic significations both on account of their appropriateness and from necessity; and she could not have found in all creation anything better calculated than oil, by its nature and its various uses, to become a symbolical exponent of her feelings and desires.

The first person who used oil in the worship of God of which any record is preserved was Jacob, who, when he was fleeing into Mesopotamia from his brother Esau, as related in the 29th chapter of the Book of Genesis, slept one night in the open air, and was favored by God with the vision of a ladder reaching from earth to heaven, upon which angels were ascending and descending, while the Almighty rested on the top. Filled with a holy fear, on awakening he set up the stone upon which his head had rested during the night, and poured oil upon it as a memorial of the vision with which he had been favored.

When the Mosaic law was promulgated, the use of oil was prescribed for the fourfold purpose of anointing priests, prophets, and kings, and the sacred vessels and vestments used in the service of religion. The 29th chapter of the Book of Exodus prescribes the manner in which Aaron and his sons, their vestments, the altar of incense and holocausts, and the sacred vessels were to be consecrated. Numerous passages of the Old Testament show that oil was used in the consecration of kings, who were commonly said to be "anointed" kings. And that it was used in setting aside persons for the prophetic office is seen from III. Kings, xix. 16, not to mention other passages.

The only places in which the use of oil for religious purposes is mentioned in the New Testament are in the Gospel of St. Mark and the Epistle of St. James. The former relates how Our Saviour sent His apostles two and two throughout Judea and Galilee to teach the people and to heal the sick; and it is said of them that they "anointed with oil many that were sick, and healed them." This anointing was not, however, the administration of a sacrament, both because the sacraments were not as yet instituted, and also because the apostles were not then priests, and priests only can administer the sacrament of Extreme Unction; but, as the Council of Trent[1] teaches, the ceremony performed by them foreshadowed that sacrament. The reference to oil in the administration of the sacrament of Extreme Unction made by St. James (v. 14) is the only one found in the Scriptures of its use in connection with the ritual of the New Law.

It is not the intention to enter in this place into an inquiry as to the early use of oil in the various rites and sacraments in which it is now employed, nor when or how it came to be so used, but rather to take it as we find it, and, after speaking of the way in which it is consecrated and kept. to treat of its present uses, and the lessons they are calculated to teach us.

Three kinds of oil are used in the ritual of the Church; or, to speak more correctly, there is only one kind, but it is blessed for three different purposes, and is called in

---

[1] Session xiv., chapter i., *de Extrema Unctione.*

the language of the Church by three different names: the Oil of Catechumens, Holy Chrism, and the Oil of the Sick. The first of these, which is simply olive oil, derives its name from its being used principally in the ceremony of baptism to anoint the catechumens—that is, those who are undergoing instruction preparatory to being baptized —before the infusion of water changes them from catechumens to Christians. The second is composed of a mixture of olive oil and balsam, or balm, and derives its name from its being used to anoint; chrism being derived from the Greek word *chrisma*, which means anything smeared or spread on. Mystically it signifies the fulness of grace; and our divine Saviour, being anointed Priest, Prophet, and King, is by pre-eminence the Anointed, and hence His name Christ.[1] The balsam used in Holy Chrism is a kind of odoriferous resin which exudes from a tree that grows in Judea and Arabia. This species was always used in the West till the sixteenth century, when Popes Paul III. and Pius IV. permitted the use of a better kind brought from the West Indies. The Oil of the Sick is so named from its principal use being to anoint the sick in the sacrament of Extreme Unction.

With regard to the time when the oils are consecrated, and the person by whom the solemn ceremony is performed, it is to be remarked that they are consecrated by bishops only, and that the ceremony takes place during Mass on Holy Thursday. The consecration of the oils during the Mass dates from the earliest times, and St. Basil attributes the origin of it to apostolic tradition. In the Western, or Latin, Church it was always performed by the bishops, but in the Eastern Church it was reserved to the patriarchs, who consecrated the oils for their entire patriarchates. At first the oils were blessed

[1] Isaias, lxi. 1; St. Luke, iv. 18; Acts, x. 38.

on any day at Mass; but in a letter of Pope Leo the Great to the Emperor of the same name, in the synod of Toledo, in the year 490, Holy Thursday was permanently fixed as the day upon which the ceremony must take place. France did not, however, adopt this ruling until the Council of Meaux, in 845. Barry thus accounts for the selection of Holy Thursday as the day upon which the consecration should take place: "It was customary among the Jews for guests invited to a banquet to anoint themselves with oil. From this we may understand why the Church consecrates her oils in the last week of Lent. Two spiritual banquets are preparing. Many that were without the pale of truth are to be brought into it by baptism during Easter time, and made to sit down with the children of the household at the banquet of Christ's holy faith. The Holy Ghost, too, is getting ready a feast of sevenfold gifts and twelve precious fruits of holiness. For the happy guests called to these two divine banquets Mother Church prepares the fragrant oils of gladness wherewith they may be anointed."[1]

The ceremony of the blessing of the oils is very interesting and impressive, and the time and manner are indicative of the reverence with which the Church regards them and requires her children to treat them. Besides the sacred ministers necessary to assist the bishop, as at every solemn Pontifical Mass, there must be seven subdeacons, seven deacons, and twelve priests, each clothed in the vestments of his order; or rather, as it almost universally happens, so many of the neighboring priests vested as subdeacons, deacons, and priests; for it is seldom that so many subdeacons and deacons are found in any of our dioceses at the same time. In places where it is impossible to have so large a number of the

[1] "The Sacramentals," pp. 114. 115

reverend clergy assist, the Holy See permits a bishop to consecrate the oils with a smaller number. For the ceremony a table is placed in the sanctuary, between the foot of the altar steps and the communion rail, with a white cover, a book-stand, and a number of candles on it, and with seats placed by it so as to face the altar. When the bishop, who must celebrate the Holy Sacrifice himself, comes to the part of the Mass immediately before the *Pater Noster*, he leaves the altar and goes to the table, where he seats himself with his ministers. The assistant priest then calls out in an audible tone, in Latin, of course, "The Oil of the Sick!" Immediately one of the subdeacons, with an acolyte at each hand, goes to the sacristy where the oil is, and carries the vessel containing it to the bishop. The latter then reads an exorcism and recites a prayer over it, which constitute the blessing of this oil. It is then taken back to the sacristy in the same manner in which it was brought; and the Mass proceeds till the bishop has communicated and received the ablutions. He then returns with his ministers to the table, and seats himself; and the assistant priest calls for the other oils with the words, "The Oil for the Holy Chrism," and "The Oil of Catechumens." These are brought to the bishop with greater ceremony than was the Oil of the Sick—partly, it may be because they are destined to serve more important purposes; and partly, perhaps, because the manner in which the Oil of the Sick is brought and blessed typifies the silence of death. A subdeacon with a processional cross, an acolyte at either hand, carrying a lighted candle, and the censer-bearer, leading the procession, are followed by the seven subdeacons, the seven deacons, and the twelve priests, who proceed to the sacristy, where one of the subdeacons takes the little vessel containing the balsam, while two of the deacons take those containing the oils—the latter vessels being covered with veils. Forming a procession they return to the sanctuary, chanting an appropriate hymn. On arriving all take their places, except those who hold the vessels, who stand at a convenient distance from the table, where they deliver up the vessels as the ceremony proceeds. The bishop first blesses the balsam with three prayers, mixing it in the meantime with some of the oil from that which is to be, after consecration, the Holy Chrism. The bishop, and, after him, the twelve priests then breathe over the vessel of oil three times in the form of a cross, but say nothing, while the vessel is still covered, except the top, with the veil. This done, the bishop reads an exorcism, and then sings a very beautiful preface, at the conclusion of which he puts into the oil the mixture of balsam, reciting at the same time an appropriate prayer. He next sings thrice, raising his voice a tone each time, the words *Ave, Sanctum Chrisma!*—"Hail, Holy Chrism!"—and kisses the lip of the vessel, in which he is followed by the twelve priests, who go in turn to the foot of the altar, genuflect to the Blessed Sacrament, and turning toward the vessel of oil on the table, repeat the same words thrice, raising their voices and genuflecting to the vessel each time.

At the conclusion of this ceremony the vessel is set aside, its blessing being concluded, and that containing the Oil of Catechumens is taken from the deacon and presented to the bishop. The blessing of this oil begins with the bishop and, after him, the twelve priests breathing on it thrice in the form of a cross, after which the bishop reads over it an exorcism and a prayer. He then sings thrice, as he did over the Holy Chrism, *Ave, Sanctum Oleum!* — "Hail, Holy Oil!" — and kisses the lip of the vessel; and the same is done by the twelve priests. With this ends the blessing of the oils, and they are taken back to the sacristy in procession as they were brought out, with the chanting of a hymn, the bishop returning in the meantime to the altar to finish Mass. This brief account affords but a faint idea of the solemnity of the ceremony, and the beauty and expressiveness of the prayers that accompany it.

The holy oils must be blessed every year, and it is not permitted to mix any of the oil of the previous year with what has been newly consecrated. What, then, is done with it? It is burned in the sanctuary lamp, if there is enough for that purpose; but if not, it must be burned in some other way. As soon as possible, and generally on Holy Thursday, immediately after the conclusion of the Mass, the clergy of the diocese, as far as possible, procure their supply of the new oils for the ensuing year, which they keep in three small vessels, that must be of some substantial and proper material for the reception of so holy an article, and which must be duly marked to prevent mistakes afterward in the use of the oils. They should be kept in a receptacle in the wall of the sanctuary, at the side of the main altar; but if for a sufficient reason this cannot be done, they must be kept in some other becoming place under lock and key, but not with the Blessed Sacrament in the tabernacle. As much as may be necessary for present use is kept by the priest in the oil-stocks — a small cylindrical vessel, which screws apart, forming three little compartments, one for each of the oils, which are absorbed in cotton, the whole being enclosed in a leathern case convenient for carrying.

It is to be remarked with regard to the numerous anointings with the Holy Oils in the administration of sacraments or the conferring of blessings that they are always performed with the thumb of the right hand. And first, of anointings in the administration of sacraments. Of such as are performed by a bishop, there are those that take place in the consecration of a bishop; the first of which is that of the tonsure, or top of the head, which is performed early in the ceremony and with holy chrism, the officiating prelate reciting at the same time these words over the bishop-elect: "May thy head be anointed and consecrated with celestial benediction in the pontifical order: In the name of the Father, and of the Son, and of the Holy Ghost. Amen. Peace be to thee." It may be remarked, once for all, that whenever, in performing any unction, the word "bless," "sanctify," or "consecrate" occurs, as a rule the sign of the cross is made, whether it be a bishop or a priest who is officiating; and that, when the anointing is followed by the name of the three Divine Persons, as above, a bishop makes the sign of the cross with his hand on or over the person or article blessed, at the mention of each of the Divine Persons, while a priest makes it but once for all three Persons. Later on in the ceremony of consecration is the anointing of the hands of the bishop-elect with holy chrism, the consecrating prelate saying the while, "May these hands be anointed with the consecrated oil and the chrism of salvation; as Samuel anointed David king and prophet, so may they be anointed and consecrated: In the name of the Father, and of the Son, and of the Holy Ghost, making the holy sign of the cross of Our Saviour Jesus Christ, who hath redeemed us from death, and led us to the kingdom of heaven," etc. These are the only unctions in the consecration of a bishop.

There is but one unction in the ordination of a priest,

which is that of the inside of his hands with the Oil of Catechumens, to consecrate them for the conferring of blessings, as the words used express, and for touching the Most Blessed Sacrament. While anointing the hands the bishop says: "Vouchsafe, O Lord, to consecrate and sanctify these hands by this unction and our blessing. Amen." And joining them together palm to palm, and making the sign of the cross over them, he continues: "That whatsoever they bless may be blessed, and whatsoever they consecrate may be consecrated and sanctified: In the name of Our Lord Jesus Christ." By virtue of this consecration the priest is empowered not only to touch and handle what is most holy, even the sacred Body of Jesus Christ in the Adorable Sacrament, but also to bless any proper article by merely making the sign of the cross over it.

Another sacrament in the administration of which the bishop uses the holy oils is Confirmation. While conferring this sacrament he makes the sign of the cross with holy chrism on the forehead of each one confirmed, saying at the same time: *N.*, I sign thee with the sign of the cross, and I confirm thee with the chrism of salvation: In the name of the Father, and of the Son, and of the Holy Ghost. Amen." The bishop anoints the forehead of the person confirmed, that he may become a valiant soldier of Christ, carrying before him, as it were, in the face of the world, the sign of Him under whose standard he has enlisted and is doing battle, in imitation of those whom St. John saw in the Apocalypse (vi. 3), who were marked with the sign of the Son of man, in contradistinction to those who bore the mark of the infernal beast (xix. 20); and in imitation of the courageous Apostle of the Gentiles, who gloried in the cross of Christ.[1]

[1] Galatians. vi. 14

Of the sacraments administered by a priest, there are two in which the holy oils are used — Baptism and Extreme Unction. In Baptism there are two unctions, the former of which takes place before the pouring of the water, when the priest anoints the person with the Oil of Catechumens, first on the breast and then on the back between the shoulders, saying while performing the ceremony, "I anoint thee with the oil of salvation in Christ Jesus Our Lord, that thou mayest have eternal life. Amen." These unctions, like all the other ceremonies of the Church, have a mystic signification, and one which should be very interesting to us, since every one of us has had this ceremony performed for him, and that, too, at a time when he was incapable of receiving an explanation of it. The baptized person, as an athlete of Jesus Christ, in entering on the struggle for faith and piety, is anointed.[1] By the anointing on the breast the Christian is reminded that he should carry Christ in his heart by faith, love, and the frequent remembrance of His holy presence, and, like St. Paul, should desire to know nothing but Jesus Christ, and Him crucified. The anointing between the shoulders reminds him that he must be prepared to carry the cross, according to the words of Christ: "If anyone will come after Me, let him deny himself, and take up his cross and follow Me."[2] Another anointing takes place immediately after the pouring of the water, and this time with holy chrism, in the form of a cross, on the top of the head. While performing it the priest says: "May Almighty God, the Father of Our Lord Jesus Christ, who has regenerated thee by water and the Holy Ghost, and who has granted thee the pardon of all thy sins, Himself anoint thee with the chrism of salvation, in the same Jesus Christ Our Lord, unto life everlasting.

[1] Cornelius à Lapide, vol. xviii., p. 334. [2] St. Matthew xvi. 24.

Amen." Allusion is here made to the words of Our
Saviour to Nicodemus : " Unless a man be born again of
water and the Holy Ghost, he cannot enter into the
kingdom of God."[1] Regarding this unction the "Cate-
chism of the Council of Trent" remarks : " The person
being now baptized, the priest anoints with chrism the
crown of his head, to give him to understand that from
that day he is united as a member to Christ, his head,
and engrafted on His body, and that therefore is he
called a Christian from Christ, but Christ from chrism."[2]
O'Kane gives the following explanation of this unction:
" With respect to the unction with chrism after baptism,
we may observe that in the beginning the bishop was
usually the minister of baptism, and he signed the neophytes on the forehead with chrism immediately after
baptizing them, so that the chrism used by the bishop
was in reality for the sacrament of Confirmation. The
vertical unction by priests was introduced, according to
Bellarmine, to supply in some way for this when the bishop
was absent, and when, consequently, confirmation could
not be immediately conferred as usual. It is said to have
been instituted by Pope Sylvester I. Innocent I., in a
letter regarding this matter, says that priests may anoint
those whom they baptize with chrism blessed by the bishop;
but they must not apply it to the forehead, as this is reserved to bishops. From the 'Sacramentary' of St.
Gregory it appears that the vertical unction was applied
by priests even when the bishop was present and confirmed the neophytes immediately after. The same may
be also inferred from the 'Sacramentary' of St. Gelasius. . . . It is to be applied even by the bishop when he
baptizes, though he may confer the sacrament of Confir-

[1] St. John iii. 5   [2] Part ii., chapter ii., No. 73.

mation immediately after."[1] Another unction performed by a priest is in Extreme Unction, a sacrament which derives its name from its being the last anointing the Christian receives before departing this life. In the administration of this sacrament the priest, after the sprinkling of holy water, with the customary prayer, recites two other prayers ; then one of the persons present says the *Confiteor*, and the priest recites a third prayer, after which he anoints each sense and the hands and feet with the oil of the sick, in the form of a cross, pronouncing at each the prayer : "Through this holy unction and of His most tender mercy, may the Lord pardon thee whatsoever sins thou hast committed by [here the sense is named]. Amen."

So much for the use of the oils in the administration of the sacraments. The thoughtful and devout reader cannot but recognize the important part which they play, whether they affect the Christian directly, as in Baptism, Confirmation, and Extreme Unction, or indirectly, as in the consecration of a bishop and the ordination of a priest, in Holy Orders. If we turn to their uses apart from the sacraments, we shall find that they are only of less importance then these, but are still of immense benefit to the faithful.

I shall not pause to speak of the use of the holy oils in the consecration of kings and queens, both because it does not affect us, and also because in these unhappy times it is seldom or never that rulers ascend their thrones with the solemn ceremonies prescribed by the Church.

Foremost among the blessings of inanimate objects in which the holy oils are used must be placed that of an

[1] Notes on the Rubrics of the Roman Ritual, No 248.

altar or an altar-stone. As there is but slight difference between these two, mention will be made only of an altar. From the nature and dignity of the Divine Victim offered in sacrifice in the New Law, we are prepared to expect a more solemn consecration of our altars than of those of the Jewish Dispensation, upon which the sacrifice of animals or of inanimate things was offered. Yet even those altars were consecrated with great ceremony. From the beginning of the Christian era great attention was paid to whatever related to the altar. But during the ages of persecution and before the Christians were permitted to build churches, little attention, as a rule, could be devoted to the material and location of altars. The faithful were then compelled by stern necessity to do the best they could, and await happier days. But when freedom began to be enjoyed, disciplinary laws were enacted, and a new order of things was inaugurated. Churches were built, generally with the altar to the east — which is called in liturgical language the *orientation* of churches, as Christ is called " the Orient from on high," who, like the sun rising in the east, diffused the light of truth on those who sat in darkness and in the shadow of death. The altar was then required to be of stone; and if not the whole altar, at least the table of it must be of stone. But for the convenience of missionaries who had frequently to offer the Holy Sacrifice outside a church, as well as for churches too poor to afford an entire stone altar, an altar-stone, large enough to place the chalice and host upon, was and still is permitted.

Five crosses, one near each corner and one in the centre, are cut in the altar-table; and in front of the one in the centre is also cut a little cavity, called the "confession" or "sepulchre," into which the relics of martyrs are placed at the time of consecration. The ceremony of consecrating an altar is very long, and is one of the functions reserved to a bishop, or to a priest having special faculties from him. It consists of the recitation of prayers and psalms, and the performance of ceremonies, such as signing with the cross, sprinkling with holy water, blessed especially for that purpose, incensing, etc. But we are concerned only with the anointings, of which there is a considerable number. In the course of the blessing the bishop anoints the interior of the four corners of the sepulchre with holy chrism, before depositing the relics in it, repeating at each unction the words: "May this sepulchre be consecrated and sanctified: In the name of the Father, and of the Son, and of the Holy Ghost. Peace be to this house." After the placing of the relics in the sepulchre and the recitation of a psalm, he takes the diminutive stone that is to cover the sepulchre, and, while signing it with holy chrism in the form of a cross, he says: "May this table (or stone) be consecrated and sanctified with this unction and the blessing of God: In the name of the Father, and of the Son, and of the Holy Ghost. Peace be to thee." When the cover of the sepulchre has been put in its place, and cemented there, he again signs it with holy chrism with the words: "May this altar be signed and sanctified: In the name of the Father, and of the Son, and of the Holy Ghost. Peace be to thee." Proceeding with the ceremony, he anoints with the Oil of Catechumens the five crosses cut in the altar, repeating at each unction the formula: "May this stone be sanctified and consecrated, in the name of the Father, and of the Son, and of the Holy Ghost, in honor of God and of the glorious Virgin Mary, and of all the saints, to the name and memory of St. N. Peace be to thee." Soon the bishop anoints the same places with the Oil of Catechumens in the same manner, and with the same form of words. As the ceremony proceeds he repeats the anointings, but this time with Holy Chrism, with the same ceremony and form of words as before. Having intoned an antiphon, those in attendance recite a psalm while he pours Oil of Catechumens and holy chrism on the altar, and anoints its entire surface. A number of prayers follows, after which the bishop forms with Holy Chrism a cross at each corner of the altar-table, at the points where it rests on the substructure, as it were joining them together; and during each unction he repeats the words: "In the name of the Father, and of the Son, and of the Holy Ghost." With this ends the anointings of the altar.

The altar is now ready for the offering of the Adorable Sacrifice. But vessels must also be consecrated for its use, and this, too, by a bishop; for in them are to rest the sacred body and blood of Jesus Christ. The ceremony of consecrating these is short. The paten, or small plate upon which the Sacred Host is placed, is first consecrated with three short prayers, and while the bishop makes the sign of the cross on its inner surface with Holy Chrism, and afterward anoints the entire inside, he repeats the words: "Vouchsafe, O Lord God, to consecrate and sanctify this paten by this unction and our blessing, in Jesus Christ Our Lord, who liveth and reigneth with Thee in the unity of the Holy Ghost, God forever and ever. Amen." The chalice is then consecrated with the same number of prayers, and is anointed in the interior, first in the form of a cross, and afterward in the whole interior surface, the bishop reciting the while the same form as in the case of the paten, only substituting the word *chalice* for *paten*.

But it is not enough to have an altar upon which

sacrifice is to be offered, and the vessels necessary for its use; there should also be a means of calling the people to assist at the Holy Sacrifice, and the more so as this assisting is of obligation. Hence from the beginning of our era various means were employed, but all have long since given place to bells, which will be treated of in another essay.

"Unless a man be born again of water and of the Holy Ghost, he cannot enter into the kingdom of God;"[1] nor, as a preliminary step to that, can he enter into the Church, which is the kingdom of God upon earth. But that the water by which he is to be regenerated may be fitted for so holy a purpose, it should first receive the blessing of the Church. For this a very beautiful and appropriate ceremony is arranged to be performed by priests, in every church that has a baptismal font, on Holy Saturday and the eve of Pentecost, immediately before Mass, because on those days the baptism of the catechumens took place in the primitive Church. A shorter form of blessing, that can be performed at any time, is arranged for the use of priests in missionary countries; but as it is special, we shall not pause to speak of it. The blessing for the days named consists of two short prayers and a beautiful preface, interspersed with a number of ceremonies; and toward the end of it the oils are mingled with the water in the following manner. The Oil of Catechumens is first poured into the water in the form of a cross, the priest at the same time saying: "May this font be sanctified and fructified with the oil of salvation, for those regenerated out of it, unto everlasting life." After this he pours in the Holy Chrism, also in the form of a cross, reciting the words, "May the infusion of the chrism of

[1] St. John, iii. 5.

Our Lord Jesus Christ and of the Holy Ghost the Paraclete be effected in the name of the Most Holy Trinity." Next, taking in each hand one of the small vessels containing the oils, he pours them together thrice into the font in the form of a cross, saying: "May the mingling of the chrism of salvation and the oil of unction and the water of baptism be at the same time effected. In the name of the Father, and of the Son, and of the Holy Ghost." With this ends the ceremony, and with the mingling of the oils with the water by the priest ends the blessing of the font, and the employment of the holy oils in the functions of religion. In all these uses the reader has seen how holy Mother Church manifests her solicitude for the spiritual welfare of her devoted children. Whatever she does must, after the honor and glory of God, redound to their advantage. Our gratitude to her should increase with our increased knowledge.

VIII.—HOLY WATER.

KIND reader, as you sometimes stand at the church door, and see people enter and depart, taking holy water as they do so, and some making a well-defined sign of the cross, and others a motion that might be taken for the brushing away of an importunate mosquito, or for anything else but what it is intended to represent, did you ever feel a desire to learn anything more about holy water than that it is blessed by a priest as necessity requires, and placed at the church door for the convenience of the people? Or do you, perhaps, belong to the large number of those who are content to practise their religion in a mechanical sort of way without caring to trouble themselves with an inquiry into the history and signification of its numerous sacred rites?

The first point to attract attention is the extensive use of holy water in the sacred functions of religion and among the faithful. From the grand basilica to the hut of the beggar holy water is found, and it enters into the imposing ceremonial of the one as well as into the simple devotions of the other. It is required in almost all the blessings of the Church and in some of the sacraments, and few sacred rites are complete without it. The room in which we are born is sprinkled with it; in one of its three several forms it is poured on our brow in baptism; it accompanies the last sad rites of religion over our remains, and the ground in which we are laid to return to dust is consecrated with its hallowed drops. This is an evidence of the importance the Church attaches to it, as well as of the perfect manner in which the faithful have imbibed her spirit; and it must also be regarded as a proof of its efficacy in conferring blessings and repelling the attacks of the enemy of mankind.

What, then, is holy water? We need not be told that it is water which has been blessed with certain exorcisms and prayers, and into which salt similarly blessed has been mingled.

The better to understand the history of holy water in the Christian Church, it will be well to inquire into the part which water played in the religious ceremonies of both the Jewish and the pagan nations of antiquity. Water being the natural element for the removal of external defilements, it was to be expected that any system of religion, whether true or false, abounding, as all did in ancient times, in symbolical rites, would adopt water as the symbol of interior purity. We do not, however, read of water having been used in the religious ceremonies of the worshippers of the true God before the establishment of the Mosaic Law. Nor need we be surprised at this; for up to that time the ceremonial of divine worship had hardly begun to be developed, but consisted almost wholly of prayers and the offering of sacrifices by the patriarch of the tribe or family. But with the establishment of the Jewish Dispensation, when the ritual prescriptions were defined with the greatest precision, purification by water was made to play an important part.[1]

The student of the Greek and Latin classics need not be reminded that among the Greeks and Romans lustrations and other religious ceremonies, in which the use of water entered largely, formed an important part of the ritual exercises of their temples; and the following will

---

[1] Exodus, xix. 10; xxx. 18, *et seq.*; Leviticus, viii. 6; Numbers, xix *et seq.*; Deuteronomy, xxi. 1 *et seq.*, etc.

suffice for the general reader. "Originally ablution in water was the only rite observed by the Greeks; but afterward sacrifices, etc., were added. They were employed both to purify individuals, cities, fields, armies, or states, and to call down the blessing of the gods. The most celebrated lustration of the Greeks was that performed at Athens, in the days of Solon, by Epimenides of Crete, who purified that city from the defilement incurred by the Cylonian Massacre. A general lustration of the whole Roman people took place, every fifth year, before the censors went out of office. On that occasion the citizens assembled in the Campus Martius, and the sacrifices termed Suovetaurilia, consisting of a sow, a sheep, and an ox, were offered up, after being carried thrice around the multitude. This ceremony, to which the name of *lustrum* was particularly applied, is said to have been instituted by Servius Tullius in 566 B.C., and was celebrated for the last time at Rome in the reign of Vespasian. . . . All Roman armies were lustrated before they commenced military operations. The Roman shepherd at the approach of night adorned his fold with branches and foliage, sprinkled his sheep with water, and offered incense and sacrifices to Pales, the tutelary divinity of shepherds. Whatever was used at lustrations was immediately after the ceremony cast into the river, or some place inaccessible to man, as it was deemed ominous for anyone to tread on it."[1] In the Egyptian pagan worship lustrations were more frequent than among any other people, the priests being required to wash themselves twice every day and twice every night.[2] But it is needless to multiply examples from pagan antiquity; suffice it to say that so universal was the cus-

[1] "American Cyclopedia," article *Lustration*.
[2] Herodotus, book II. No. 37.

tom that it found its way into the New World, the less barbarous tribes of Mexico and Central America having their sacred water, which was used for various religious and medicinal purposes.[1] And among some at least of the pagans, as among Catholics, the custom existed of sprinkling themselves, or having themselves sprinkled by the priests, with water on entering their temples.[2]

The fact that a sort of holy water was in use both among the Jews and pagans might appear to give some plausibility to the statement sometimes made that many Catholic rites and ceremonies are but a reproduction of those of paganism ; or, as one Pittsburg divine charitably put it, "the Romanists are only baptized pagans." Without attempting to defend the Church against these silly attacks, it may be said that several different replies may be made to these accusations. In the first place, water being, as was said above, the most ready and natural element for the cleansing of external defilements, it was to be expected that it would also be used as the symbol of purification from the defilements of sin. as in baptism. Again, the Jews having employed water in certain religious rites, the use of it in the New Dispensation would have a tendency to aid in winning some, at least, of them to the Christian religion. As such an adaptation we have the blessing, or "churching," of women after parturition, as an act of thanksgiving, taking the place of the legal purification enjoined on similar occasions by the Mosaic Law. And a like course of action was sometimes found to be of advantage among pagans who were too strongly attached to some of their pagan rites. According to the principle laid

[1] Hubert Howe Bancroft's "Native Races," vol. ii. p. 611; and vol. iii. p. 370 *et seq.*, etc.
[2] "Kirchen-Lexicon," article *Weihwasser*.

down by St. Paul, missionaries made themselves all to all that they might gain all to Christ.¹ As an instance : when St. Augustine, who had been sent to England to preach the Gospel, found the custom among the pagans of having idols placed in the hollow of trees, and other similar places, he was perplexed as to the best means of winning the people from this idolatry. Knowing, as he did full well, that if the idols were removed not a few of the people would retain a superstitious veneration for the places they had once occupied, he wrote for advice to St. Gregory the Great, who was then ruling the Universal Church. The Pope advised him to substitute for the pagan idols the images of the Blessed Virgin and the saints ; which he did, with the desired effect. Finally, it may be answered that the Church has received from her divine Founder the plenitude of power for the institution of such rites and ceremonies as may seem best to her, enlightened as she is by the indwelling of the Holy Spirit, for the carrying out of her exalted mission. Let us now direct our attention to the history and use of holy water in the Christian Church.

The present rite of blessing water by prayer and an admixture of salt is frequently referred to Pope St. Alexander I., who governed the Church from the year 109 to 119. But from the words which he uses in his decree it would appear that the rite is more ancient than the time of that Pontiff. He says : "We bless, for the use of the people, water mingled with salt." Marcellius Columna attributes the introduction of holy water to the apostle St. Matthew, whose action was approved by the other apostles, and soon became general.² Whether we are disposed to accept this evidence as conclusive or

¹ I. Cor. ix. 20-22.
² "Institutiones Liturgicæ," by J. Fornici, pp. 353, 854.

not, it is all but certain from other proofs that the use of holy water dates from apostolic times, as St. Basil, among others, maintains.[1]

The blessing of water before High Mass on Sundays, and the sprinkling of the people with it by the celebrant, before he commences the offering of the Adorable Sacrifice, are commonly attributed to Pope St. Leo IV., who governed the Church from 847 to 855; but there are also very learned authorities who trace it to a far more remote antiquity.[2] The custom of placing holy water at the door of the church for the use of the faithful entering and departing is still more ancient, as may be inferred from the fact that the idea was evidently suggested by the Jewish custom of requiring purifications before entering the temple to offer or assist at the sacrifices. But it would be impossible to fix the precise date. The custom of Christians sprinkling themselves with water, or even of washing their hands and face before entering the house of God, existed throughout the Church at least from the time of Tertullian, that is, before the end of the second century.[3] Mgr. Barbier has the following in regard to the custom of taking holy water on leaving the church: "The holy-water font, as its name indicates, is a vase intended to contain holy water for the use of the faithful, who bless themselves with it on entering the church, and not when leaving; for they purify themselves to enter the holy place; but when they leave it they should have no further use for that spiritual succor, sanctified as they have been by prayer, the sacraments, and the liturgical offices. Such is the practice universally followed in Rome." While this was, indeed, the original idea with regard to the

---

[1] "Kirchen-Lexicon." [2] See essay on the *Asperges*.
[3] "Kirchen-Lexicon."

use of holy water, it would appear that the custom now generally found of taking it both on entering and departing is to be commended, both because it is so universally in use, because it is certainly beneficial, and because the Church has enriched the pious use of holy water every time it is taken with an indulgence, as will appear further on.

The use of holy water among the faithful at their homes is of still greater antiquity, as may be learned from the Apostolic Constitutions, which contain a formula for the blessing of it, that it may have power "to give health, drive away diseases, put the demons to flight," [1] etc.

Let us now turn to the historical and liturgical view of the question. First, there are three, or, in another sense, four, kinds of holy water. According to the first division, there is, first, baptismal water, which is required to be blessed on every Holy Saturday and eve of Pentecost in all churches that have baptismal fonts. This water, after the holy oils have been mingled with it, is used only in the administration of baptism. In the next place, there is water blessed by a bishop to be used in consecrating churches, or reconciling churches that have been desecrated. This is called Gregorian Water, because Pope Gregory IX. made its use obligatory for the purposes specified. Wine, ashes, and salt are mingled with it. Then there is the common holy water, which, as is well known, is usually blessed by a priest. This blessing may be performed at any t' 'e, and in any suitable place. It is directed to be done every Sunday before Mass, as we shall see, with the exception of Easter and Pentecost, when the water blessed on the previous eve is used for the *Asperges*.

[1] "Catholic Dictionary," article *Holy Water*.

In the Oriental churches there is the custom of solemnly blessing water on the feast of Epiphany, in memory of the baptism of Our Lord in the river Jordan, which event is commemorated by the Church on that day.[1]

According to another division, there may be said to be four kinds of holy water; for when water is being blessed for the baptismal font it is usually put into a larger vessel, and at a certain stage in the ceremony the font is filled, to receive the holy oils and be used in baptism, while the rest is distributed among the people. This is commonly called "Easter Water." It may be remarked, in passing, that the laws of the Church require the holy water to be removed from all the fonts at the church doors during the last three days of Holy Week.

When we examine into the blessing of holy water, it is found to consist of exorcisms, prayers, and the mingling of salt with the water. By the fall of our first parents the spirit of evil obtained an influence not only over man but also over inanimate nature, whence he is called in Scripture "the prince of this world."[2] For this reason, when any material object is to be devoted to the service of God, an exorcism is generally first pronounced over it, to banish the evil spirit and destroy his influence; after which one or more prayers are read over it to call down the blessing of God upon it, and upon those who use it in a spirit of faith. In the exorcism of salt, the priest addresses it, declaring that he exorcises it by the Living God, the True God, the Holy God, by the God who commanded the prophet Eliseus to cast salt into the water to purify it;[3] that it may become exorcised for the use of the faithful; that whoso

---

[1] "Kirchen-Lexicon." [2] St. John, xii. 31; xiv. 30, etc.
[3] IV. Kings, ii. 2.

ever uses it may enjoy health of soul and body; that all phantasms and wickedness and all deceits of the devil may depart from the places where it is sprinkled, and that every evil spirit be adjured by Him who is to come to judge the living and the dead and the world by fire. The salt, having been exorcised, is blessed with the following beautiful prayer: "O almighty and eternal God! we humbly implore Thy boundless clemency that Thou wouldst mercifully deign to bless and sanctify this salt, Thy creature, which Thou hast given for the use of mankind, that it may bring health of mind and body unto all that take it, and that whatever is touched or sprinkled with it may be freed from all uncleanness and from all attacks of the spirit of wickedness." We see from this prayer that the Church begs God to attach a triple efficacy to the blessed salt: 1st, that it may be a means of salvation to the soul; 2d, that it may be a preservative against corporal dangers; 3d; that it may sanctify everything with which it comes in contact. It does not produce these effects of itself, as a sacrament does, but it obtains actual graces for the pious user, which will, if co-operated with, obtain them.[1] The same remark applies to the efficacy of the water.

Then follows the exorcism of the water, in the name of God the Father Almighty, in the name of Jesus Christ, His Son Our Lord, and in the name of the Holy Ghost, for the dispelling of all the power of the enemy of man, and that the same enemy with his apostate angels may be utterly expelled by the power of the same Jesus Christ Our Lord, who is to come to judge the living and the dead and the world by fire. This exorcism is followed by the subjoined prayer: "O God! who, for the salvation of mankind, hast wrought many

---

[1] Barry, p. 60

great mysteries and miracles by means of the substance of water, listen propitiously to our invocations, and infuse into this element, prepared by manifold purifications, the power of Thy benediction: in order that Thy creature (water), being used as an instrument of Thy hidden works, may be efficacious in driving away devils and curing diseases; that whatever in the houses or in the places of the faithful shall have been sprinkled with this water may be freed from all uncleanness and delivered from all guile. Let no pestilential spirit reside there, no infectious air; let all the snares of the hidden enemy be removed; and if there should be anything adverse to the safety or repose of the indwellers, may it be put entirely to flight by the sprinkling of this water, that the welfare which we seek, by the invocation of Thy Holy Name, may be defended from all assaults; through Our Lord Jesus Christ," etc.

"This formula of prayer implores the following effects for the holy water: 1st, to drive away the devils; 2d, to cure diseases; 3d, to free houses and their contents from all evil, particularly from a plague-infected atmosphere. After these prayers the priest puts a little salt into the water three times, in the form of a cross, saying: 'May this commingling of salt and water be made, in the name of the Father, and of the Son, and of the Holy Ghost.'"[1]

A few words on the use of salt in this and certain other solemn rites of the Church. Salt is frequently referred to in both the Old and New Testaments. "The union of water and salt is not without mystery. The property of the first is to cleanse, of the second to preserve. The Church wishes that this sacramental should

[1] Barry, pp. 60, 61.

help to wash away sin from her children, and to preserve them from a relapse. Water quenches fire and fosters the growth of plants; thus, in the spiritual order, water serves to quench the fire of the passions and to promote the growth of virtues. Salt is the symbol of wisdom; it typifies the Eternal Wisdom, the Second Person of the Blessed Trinity. Water represents human nature. Hence the mingling of the two substances is emblematic of the Incarnation—of the assumption of human nature by the Eternal Word. Water represents repentance for past offences; salt, from its preservative properties, represents the care which the true penitent takes to avoid future relapses.

"There is a remarkable instance in the Fourth Book of Kings, 2d chapter,"—to which reference is made in the exorcism of salt, given above,—"of the efficacy which God attaches to salt. The inhabitants of Jericho complained to the prophet Eliseus that the water of their town was bad and the ground barren. The holy man said to them: 'Bring me a new vessel, and put salt into it. And when they had brought it, he went out to the spring of the waters, and cast the salt into it, and said: Thus saith the Lord: I have healed these waters, and there shall be no more in them death or barrenness.'"[1]

The custom of mingling salt with the water when it is blessed is of great antiquity in the Church. One of the Apostolic Canons says: "We bless water mingled with salt, that all who are sprinkled with it may be sanctified and purified."[2]

The importance which Holy Church attaches to indulgences, more especially in modern times, makes it pertinent to inquire, What indulgences, if any, are granted

---

[1] Barry, pp. 58, 59.   [2] "Kirchen-Lexicon."

to the use of holy water? The *Raccolta* says (p. 5): "His Holiness Pope Pius IX., by a brief (March 23, 1876), granted to all the faithful, every time that, with at least contrite heart, they shall make the sign of the cross with holy water, pronouncing at the same time the words 'In the name of the Father, and of the Son, and of the Holy Ghost,' an indulgence of one hundred days."

IX.—THE ASPERGES, OR SPRINKLING OF HOLY WATER BEFORE MASS.

THE self-sacrificing missionaries who first ministered to the scattered Catholic population of the United States encountered, as in many other countries, innumerable difficulties, not the least of which was that of strictly conforming to the ceremonial of the Church in her various sacred functions. At a time when the Adorable Sacrifice was offered up, now under a tree, now in a barn, a house, or a school-house, again in a canal tunnel —as the Very Rev. Prince Gallitzin once celebrated it west of the Alleghany mountains—it is not a matter of surprise that all the ceremonies of the liturgy were not observed. This state of affairs existed for a longer or shorter period in all parts of the country, and it still exists in many places. Few of the older of our missionaries but are able to recall scenes in which it would have been impossible to carry out the ceremonial ; and the poor priest, with the best intentions, found himself in very truth the creature of circumstances. Many of the early missionaries were also at a disadvantage on their own account. Like their people, they were for the most part from Ireland, Germany, or France. The centuries of English oppression, with their restrictions on Catholic education in general, and prohibition, under the severest penalties, of education for the priesthood, were not sufficient to quench the missionary spirit of the Irish people, although they were frequently successful in depriving those who aspired to the sacred ministry of the opportunity of receiving that thorough training which would have better fitted them for the exercise of the noble calling to which, even in their oppressed condition, they heard the divine voice inviting them, and which they had the hereditary courage to obey. The unsettled state of continental Europe, too, a century ago—about the time the Church in this country received permanent organization—was of such a character as to leave the candidates for the sacred ministry a very unfavorable opportunity of preparing themselves to follow the promptings of their heroic zeal. Hence many of them came to this country during that unhappy time with but an imperfect preparation for the fulfilment of their exalted mission. To these difficulties must be added the variety of national customs, both of priests and people, which could not fail to exercise an influence on the rising Church in America.

Coming nearer to our own time, when the indomitable energy of the first American prelates prompted them to found ecclesiastical seminaries for the training of our youth—which was undertaken at a very early day—new elements entered in to render the introduction of the entire ceremonial difficult, if not impossible. The urgent needs of the infant Church forced the greater part of the bishops, much against their will, to ordain and send out priests as soon as they had received the minimum of necessary attainments, in order that bread might be broken for the children who were crying for it. These young priests were generally so much occupied with missionary work that they could find little time for study; they had no brother priests to consult, except at distant intervals; and they were commonly so poor as to be unable to buy the few books suitable for them which the market then afforded. What wonder that their too scanty store of knowledge suffered from the ravages of time, and that the difficulties of their position forced them to encroach somewhat on the domain of ritual requirements? Far be it from us, or from those more favored in our day, to underestimate their difficulties or censure their conduct. Rather should we study to emulate their ardent zeal and heroic spirit of self-sacrifice. These young priests, finding their seniors—with whom they were sometimes placed as assistants, and many of whom had entered the ministry under still less favorable circumstances—omit certain ceremonies, would naturally follow their example, and this for two reasons: first, from fear of being criticised, a fear which was not in every case imaginary; and, secondly, from a reflex conclusion that what was permitted to their elders was also permitted to them. I am accounting for this state of affairs; not approving nor condemning it. People are sometimes perplexed to account for difficulties the solution of which is very simple.

When better times dawned upon the Church here the difficulties by which the priests were surrounded were not entirely removed. The urgent demand for missionaries was, if anything, greater than before, owing to the ceaseless tide of immigration, largely Catholic, which flowed into the country; the professors in our seminaries had for the most part labored on the mission among us and were conversant with the difficulties of the field, and they were not always as familiar, it may be, with the strict requirements of the liturgy as could be desired. Besides, the necessity they were under of crowding a long course of studies into a brief space of time forced them, in spite of themselves, to overlook certain points to which greater attention can be devoted at the present day. With these rather lengthy prefa-

:ory remarks we shall turn to the subject of the *Asperges*. And first of its history.

The introduction of the custom of blessing water before the principal Mass on Sundays, and sprinkling the people with it, is commonly attributed to Pope St. Leo IV. (847-855); but there are not wanting learned writers who trace it to a far more remote antiquity, and regard the words of this Pontiff as referring to an existing custom rather than to the introduction of one not as yet in use. Addressing the clergy on certain of their duties he says : " Bless water every Sunday before Mass, whence the people may be sprinkled, and have a vessel especially for that purpose." [1] The *Asperges* was directed to be given by one of the canons of a synod held at Rheims by Regina and Hincmar, in the ninth century, and Walafrid Strabo (born 806) speaks of it.[2] Hence we may safely conclude that the *Asperges*, substantially as we now have it, dates from at least as early as the beginning of the ninth century. But that it underwent minor changes since that time is more than probable, inasmuch as the rubrics of the Missal were not irrevocably fixed till some seven centuries later.

When St. Pius V., acting in accordance with the recommendation of the Fathers of the Council of Trent, issued a carefully revised edition of the Roman Missal, he commanded all persons of whatever dignity—even the cardinals of the Holy Roman Church--in virtue of holy obedience, to make use of that Missal and no other, unless they had—as in the case of certain churches and religious Orders—a different rite dating back at least two hundred years. The same command, with even severer penalties, was renewed by Popes Clement VIII. and Urban VIII. Among the rubrics of the Missal is

[1] Fornici, p. 356.   [2] "Kirchen-Lexicon."

one directing that the priest who is about to celebrate Mass shall—after the blessing of water, according to the ritual—vest in cope of the proper color for the day or feast, and shall proceed with the servers to the foot of the altar, where he shall sprinkle it, himself, the servers, and the people. The ceremony is also prescribed by the ritual, the Ceremonial of Bishops, the ceremonial prepared by the directions of the several councils of Baltimore and approved by the Pope, and by every work that treats of this subject; so that it is utterly impossible to find any work that even supposes the possibility of its omission. It will suffice to quote Wapelhorst (p. 129) on this point. He says that the *Asperges* is to be given at the conventual or principal Mass, although that Mass is celebrated without singing; and it is not at all to be omitted, but what should otherwise be sung is to be read by the celebrant. In a note he proves it to be the opinion of all liturgicists that the *Asperges* cannot be omitted without fault, since it pertains in a certain sense to the substance of the principal Mass, just as the blessing of the candles does to that of the feast of the Purification, and ashes and palms on their respective days.[1]

The celebrant is the person who must perform the *Asperges*, even though a prelate is present, although another priest may bless the water, as several decrees of the Sacred Congregation have decided. The Ceremonial prescribes the manner in which it is to be given.

In the first synod ever held in the United States, that which convened at Baltimore in November, 1791, it was

---

[1] Ita omnes. "Absque culpa hæc benedictio et populi adspertio omitti nequeunt, cum quasi pertineant ad Missæ principalis substantiam, uti benedictio cereorum in die Purificationis, Cinerum et Palmarum suis respective diebus." Romsée, Bouvry, etc.

decreed that in churches served by more than one priest, or in which there were lay persons able to sing, the solemn sprinkling with holy water should be given as the Missal prescribes.[1]

The mystical signification of the *Asperges* is, that we may renew every Sunday the remembrance of our baptism, which was formerly conferred on Easter and Pentecost—or rather on the eve of those feasts—and also that the holy water by being blessed every Sunday may always be pure. The faithful are sprinkled with holy water that *by* the prayers which are recited in the blessing of it—to the essay on which the reader is referred—they, by being purified from sin, and defended from the wiles of the spirit of evil, may with greater attention and devotion assist at the adorable sacrifice of the Mass.[2]

The following are the words recited by the priest during the *Asperges*, the antiphons and responses being sung by the choir as well as recited by the celebrant: *Ant.* "Thou shalt sprinkle me with hyssop, O Lord, and I shall be cleansed: Thou shalt wash me, and I shall become whiter than snow. *Psalm.* Have mercy on me, O God, according to Thy great mercy. Glory be to the Father, etc. *Ant.* (repeated). Thou shalt sprinkle me, etc. *V.* Show us, O Lord, Thy mercy. *R.* And grant us Thy salvation. *V.* O Lord, hear my prayer. *R.* And let my cry come to Thee. *V.* The Lord be with you. *R.* And with Thy spirit. Let us pray. Hear us, O holy Lord, Father Almighty, everlasting God; and vouchsafe to send Thy holy angel from heaven, to guard, cherish, protect, visit, and defend all those who are assembled together in this house. Through Christ Our Lord. Amen." The antiphon and psalm change in Paschal time, and are: "I saw water flowing from the right side of the

[1] "Concilia Baltimorensia," p. 19.   [2] Wapelhorst, N. 80, ad. 9.

temple, Alleluia; and all unto whom that water came were saved, and they shall say, Alleluia, Alleluia. *Psalm.* Praise the Lord, for He is good; for His mercy endureth forever. Glory be to the Father," etc.

In the *Asperges* the congregation constitutes one whole, and it is not necessary, in order to receive the benefit of it, that the holy water should touch every person, any more than it is necessary for the holy water to touch every candle or palm branch in their respective blessings.

5.—THE FORTY HOURS' ADORATION AND THE BENEDICTION OF THE MOST BLESSED SACRAMENT.

I.

TREATING of the minor rites and offices of the Church, Cardinal Wiseman writes : " No man need hope ever to know, understand, or value worthily the richness and fulness of Catholic devotion, in its many beautiful forms, till he have passed into the interior of its divine sanctuary, and have visited, in its spirit, all its separate, but harmonizing, parts."[1] There are many who have entered this holy of holies ; but they are those who have cultivated a devotion to the Most Holy Sacrament of he Altar, and who have, besides, learned to set a proper value on all the rites of holy Church. They are not the sickly, lukewarm Catholics, who perform the scant service they render to God from a sense of duty, and only so far as strict duty requires, but those who are influenced by love and who deem their service a privilege. As the same eminent writer remarks, those who sustain the Church's noble claim to beauty and loveliness " will be found ever to set the highest value upon the minor observances of the Church—will be found most careful in their use, ever zealous in their defence of them. If then we see, as we always shall, the higher growth in virtue, and the full comeliness of holiness united with these practices, and going hand in hand with their application should we not rather cherish than undervalue them ; increase and encourage, rather than diminish

[1] " Essays," vol. ii. pp. 255, 256.

them; uphold and vindicate rather than abandon them to obliquity and misrepresentation?"[1]

Continuing, he writes: "If the principle of private devotion among Catholics be that of coming as near as possible to the feelings in faith and love of those who lived in our blessed Redeemer's society upon earth, the great idea and principle of public worship in the Catholic Church is to copy, as faithfully as may be permitted, the homage paid to Him and His Father in heaven. With the Church triumphant she is one; and their offices in regard to praise and adoration are the same. Now, if we look up toward that happier sphere, we see the Lamb enthroned to receive eternal and unceasing worship, praise, and benediction."[2] This end is admirably attained in the devotion to the Most Holy Sacrament, especially as exhibited in the Forty Hours' Adoration. And it is not to be the privilege of the few to assist at it; but, as the same writer remarks: "She (the Church) would not even leave this duty of perennial homage to those communities who, distributing the day and night into various portions, some at one hour, some at another, no doubt fill up the entire space with holy services. Through every season, and through every day, she would have ever going on a direct, uninterrupted worship of her Lord and Saviour, as the Adorable Victim on His altar-throne."[3]

It is not the intention to treat in this essay of devotion to the Most Holy Sacrament in general, nor of those processions in which the same Holy Sacrament is carried, whether these take place within or without the church, nor even of those extraordinary expositions that are sometimes ordered by the Sovereign Pontiff, or by bish

---

[1] "Essays," vol. ii. pp. 259, 260.   [2] *Ib.*, vol. ii. p. 266.
[3] *Ib.*, vol. ii. p. 67

ops, as sometimes happens in seasons of great spiritual or temporal necessity. Only the Forty Hours' Adoration, as had in our churches, and the benediction as given then or at other times, will be considered, as the intention is to treat of such matters only as are of practical utility for the general reader. Extraordinary processions or expositions are usually explained when they take place.

The procession of the Blessed Sacrament antedates both the exposition and the benediction, and was, most probably, introduced soon after the institution of the feast of Corpus Christi, a feast that was established by Pope Urban IV. in the year 1264. At first, according to the best evidence at command, it would appear that the Blessed Sacrament was carried in procession in a sacred vessel entirely concealed from view, and that it was afterward placed in the tabernacle without a blessing being given to the faithful present. This latter custom is still continued by the religious of the order of Carthusians. Perhaps the first evidence we have of the Blessed Sacrament being carried in procession exposed to view is found in a work of the learned Thiers, who wrote on the Blessed Sacrament in 1673, and who mentions that he found in a missal, dated 1373, the picture of a bishop carrying a sacred Host in a monstrance or ostensorium—for both mean the same—with one side partly of glass. The imparting of a blessing at the close of the procession was added in time, but for what reason, or at what precise date, has not been ascertained with certainty. The Forty Hours' Adoration—for that is the correct name—grew out of these processions and expositions. The faithful, and the reverend clergy, who were their leaders, seeing by the light of faith that the Real Presence was the source of all good, found their devotion so much enkindled by beholding their Redeemer under the mystic veil of the sacramental species that they both longed for more than a passing glance, as it were, and a continuous exposition was introduced. The mystic number forty was fixed upon to count the hours, a number so conspicuous in the Sacred Scriptures ; and as it was to be a silent adoration, what more natural than that it should be had in honor of the forty hours during which the sacred body of Our Lord remained in the holy sepulchre, in the silent embrace of death ?

At first there were two kinds of Forty Hours' Devotion. The former was celebrated during the Carnival, a festivity held on the two days immediately preceding Ash-Wednesday, during which the people were, and still are, in many places, accustomed to give themselves up to unbridled excesses, in which grievous sins were as a rule committed. Seeing this, many of the saints and other devout servants of God sought by various means to withdraw the people from them, on the one hand, and, on the other, to make reparation to the divine majesty by additional prayers and austerities. One of the means adopted in certain places was the exposition of the Most Holy Sacrament for forty hours preceding the beginning of Lent. But it is not necessary to treat of this exposition, as the other has superseded it.

Although authors are not agreed with regard to the date, place, and circumstances of the establishment of the Forty Hours' Adoration, yet they differ only in minor details, and the following from the *Raccolta* (p. 79) must be accepted as the most reliable account : " The prayer for forty hours together before the Blessed Sacrament, in memory of the forty hours during which the sacred body of Jesus was in the sepulchre, began in Milan, about the year 1534. Thence it spread into other cities of Italy, and was introduced into Rome, for the first Sunday in every month, by the Archconfraternity of the Most Holy Trinity of the Pilgrims (founded by St. Philip Neri in the year 1548), and for the third Sunday in the month, by the Archconfraternity of Our Lady of Prayer, called *La Morte*, in the year 1551. This prayer of the Forty Hours was established forever by Pope Clement VIII., for the whole course of the year, in regular, continuous succession, from one church to another, commencing with the first Sunday in Advent in the chapel of the Apostolic Palace, as appears from the constitution *Graves et Diuternœ*, November 25, 1592. This Pope was moved to establish this devotion by the public troubles of holy Church. in order that day and night the faithful might appease their Lord by prayer before the Blessed Sacrament in solemn exposition."

The first introduction of the devotion seems to have been due to Father Joseph di Fero of Milan, a Capuchin, who died in the year 1556. This beginning seems to have taken place in the year 1537, when Milan was desolated with a plague, and was also torn by civil strife.[1]

The constitution of Pope Clement VIII. referred to is commonly known as the Clementine Instruction, by which the whole matter relating to the Forty Hours' Exposition was regulated for Catholic countries. But there are certain modifications permitted in missionary countries, of which mention will be made as we proceed. There has been, as we have seen, a gradual development in the external devotion to the Most Holy Sacrament, by which it has been brought down to what we have at

[1] "Catholic Dictionary," p. 331 ; "A Manual of Devotion for the Forty Hours," p. 6.

present. First, there was the procession with the sacred Host concealed, which was made on but one or two days in the year; next, the procession with the Blessed Sacrament exposed to view; then the short procession with the long-continued exposition; after that the benediction during and at the close of the Forty Hours; and, finally, the benediction after a short exposition and without the procession, and that once or oftener in the week. But we have only meagre details of the manner in which the gradual development was effected. Many a reader, however, will remember the time when both the Forty Hours' Adoration and the benediction were rare in this country.

Speaking of the Forty Hours' Devotion, Cardinal Wiseman remarks: "In no other time or place is the sublimity of our religion so touchingly felt. No ceremony is going on in the sanctuary, no sound of song is issuing from the choir, no voice of exhortation proceeds from the pulpit, no prayer is uttered aloud at the altar. There are hundreds there, and yet they are engaged in no congregational act of worship. Each heart and soul is alone in the midst of a multitude; each uttering its own thoughts, and each feeling its own grace. Yet are you overpowered, subdued, quelled into a reverential mood, softened into a devotional spirit, forced to meditate, to feel, to pray. The little children who come in, led by a mother's hand, kneel down by her in silence, as she simply points toward the altar, overawed by the still splendor before them: the very babe seems hushed to quiet reverence on her bosom."[1]

I can see no reason why some prayer-books, and some newspapers announcing the Forty Hours' Devotion, continue to call it the "Quarant' Ore." The ex-

[1] "Essays," vol. ii. pp. 269, 270.

pression is not understood by some persons, and it savors of pedantry. The English language in this as in all else is sufficiently expressive. Another abuse, which I have seen condemned somewhere in the *Acta Sanctæ Sedis*, is that of decorating the altar at the Forty Hours more carefully in the evening or at other times when a larger concourse of people is expected, as it were to please them instead of honoring Our Lord. It is true indeed that the Church very wisely makes use of external pomp to excite devotion, since we are greatly influenced by what we receive through the senses ; but this is only a means to an end. The end is the adoration of Our Saviour in the Most Holy Sacrament.

It is not certain who introduced the devotion of the Forty Hours into the United States ; but it was most probably either Archbishop Kenrick of Baltimore or Bishop Neumann of Philadelphia, and about the year 1854. Finding that the Clementine Instruction could not be followed out in this country, so far as keeping the Blessed Sacrament exposed for the forty hours continuously, Archbishop Kenrick applied to the Holy See for such modifications of it for his archdiocese as circumstances demanded ; and Pius IX., by a rescript dated December 10, 1857, granted the following, which were, at the request of the Fathers of the Second Plenary Council of Baltimore, extended to the whole United States in 1868 :

" 1. That, as long as circumstances require it, the Blessed Sacrament may be exposed to public adoration, in the form of the Forty Hours' Prayer, in all the churches and oratories of the diocese of Baltimore once or twice a year, as the archbishop may think best in the Lord, in the daytime only, and that at night it may be replaced in the tabernacle. 2. That the procession may be omitted, even inside the church, if it cannot properly be had. 3. To all the faithful, of either sex, he grants the indulgence of seven years, and as many quarantines to be gained each day that they visit the church where the Blessed Sacrament is exposed and remain there for some time in prayer, and a plenary indulgence to all who, besides visiting the church where the Blessed Sacrament is exposed, and praying there once on each of the three days, also go to confession and receive Holy Communion."[1] But, according to a more recent decree, three visits are not necessary to gain the plenary indulgence."[2]

It is not the intention to speak of local customs, but there is one which it may not be out of place to notice: that of closing the devotion on the evening of the third day, instead of on the morning of the day following, and with the Mass. This does not appear to be in harmony with the spirit of the Church, although the full period of forty hours may have been reached, from the fact that there is a Mass of reposition for the conclusion of the devotion, as well as one of exposition for its commencement; and the rubrics connect the one as intimately with the devotion as the other. Yet if the Mass of reposition is said on the morning before the devotion closes, or on the morning after, it does not fulfil its purpose, and is in no sense a Mass of reposition, being entirely separated from the act of reposing the Blessed Sacrament in the tabernacle and closing the exposition.

This being a silent devotion, as its name indicates, and as its purpose shows, it is not the intention of the Church that sermons should be preached during its continuance. But inasmuch as sermons are under

[1] "Manual of Devotion for the Forty Hours' Prayer," p. 10; "Con cilii Plenar, Baltimoreusis," il. N. 876.
[2] Wapelhorst, p. 339.

certain circumstances likely to be productive of good, and will not interfere with the hearing of confessions, especially in the smaller country parishes, the bishop, should he deem it expedient, may grant permissions; but then the sermon should treat of the Most Holy Sacrament, and a veil should be placed before the monstrance.

It is the custom in some places to open the tabernacle door during Mass. This may be termed a kind of exposition, and is permitted by a decree of March 16, 1876.

II.

According to the learned Thiers, already referred to, the giving of benediction with the Most Holy Sacrament is of recent origin; but just when it was introduced, and the manner in which it extended till it has become so common in the Church, it would be difficult if not impossible to say.

There are three kinds of benediction—that with the pyx, when communicating the sick; that with the ciborium in the church; and that with the monstrance—upon each of which remarks will be made. And first, of benediction when communicating the sick. It is superfluous to state that in Catholic countries the Holy Viaticum is borne in a solemn manner to the house of the sick; and the ritual directs that after the sick person has received, the priest shall make the sign of the cross with the pyx over those present. This is also to be done when the Blessed Sacrament has to be carried secretly to the sick, as among us, so long as there is a sacred Host in the pyx, as when more than one is to receive.

The second kind of blessing is that given with what is called in the language of the ritual the pyx, but which is commonly known among us as the ciborium, or sacred vessel in which the Blessed Sacrament is reserved in the tabernacle on the altar. By a decree of the Sacred Congregation, dated September 11, 1847, this blessing is only to be given where such a custom exists, and with the permission of the bishop on account of the existence of the custom.[1] When imparted it differs from that given with the monstrance, and has the following ceremonial: The tabernacle is opened, but the ciborium is not taken out; the singing and incensing take place as at the ordinary benediction; and the same versicle, response, and prayer are sung; after which the priest takes the ciborium from the tabernacle, envelops it in the extremity of the shoulder veil, and, turning to the people, blesses them. It is seldom, however, that this blessing is given among us.

Little need be said of the third form of benediction— that given with the monstrance; it is so frequently seen in all our churches that the faithful are quite familiar with it. Although the provincial or plenary councils of the various countries fix the times when benediction may be given, the matter is still left to a very great extent to the prudent judgment of the bishops; and both priests and people are accustomed to look to them for guidance in the matter. Late decrees of the Sacred Congregation of Rites permit the singing of hymns and the recitation of prayers in the vernacular during the exposition before the *Tantum Ergo*.[2]

According to several decrees of the same Sacred Congregation, benediction must always be given in silence. When imparted by a priest he makes one sign of the cross with the monstrance; when given by a bishop he makes three. This principle, it will be observed, is also carried out in several other blessings.

[1] Wapelhorst, pp. 348, 349.   [2] Ibid., pp. 168, 338.

The indulgences, plenary and partial, that may be gained by those who devoutly perform the Forty Hours have already been mentioned; but it will be of advantage to make a few remarks upon them. It frequently happens that persons will go to confession on the Saturday preceding the opening of the devotion, and to Holy Communion at an early Mass. Will this confession and Communion suffice for gaining the indulgence? This is an important question. Dr. Smith discusses it at length, and, on the authority of Benedict XIV., answers it in the affirmative.[1] Again, inasmuch as the object of the Forty Hours is not simply to induce people to receive the sacraments of penance and Holy Eucharist, but their reception is made a necessary condition for gaining the plenary indulgence, is it essential that they should be received in the church where the exposition takes place? It is not. They may be received in any church, provided the other conditions are complied with. It may also be remarked that theologians hold that in order to gain a plenary indulgence it is only necessary to be in the state of grace when the last of the conditions enjoined is fulfilled.

As Vespers in the evening takes the place in some sort of the Mass in the morning, and closes the day, as it was begun, by a solemn act of divine worship, so does the benediction by our divine Lord after the one correspond to that given in His name by His minister after the other, and supplies in a measure for the deficiency between the Vespers and the Adorable Sacrifice. And all go to strengthen the claims of holy Church to be called our Mother.

[1] "Notes on the Second Plenary Council of Baltimore," pp. 221-226

XI.—THE ROSARY OF THE BLESSED VIRGIN MARY.

"Who for us men and for our salvation came down from heaven, and became incarnate by the Holy Ghost of the Virgin Mary, and was made man." How profound the mystery honored by the priest of God on bended knees in the adorable sacrifice of the Mass! How full of meaning the words that follow in the symbol of our faith: "He was crucified also for us, suffered under Pontius Pilate, and was buried; and the third day He rose again according to the Scriptures." The Incarnation is the central point of the world's history. The end of the Incarnation was the Redemption, the most stupendous work of divine love. The wisdom of the Church is admirably displayed in uniting these two greatest of her mysteries in a devotion so simple that it is within the range of the most limited intelligence, and so profound as to afford subjects of meditation for the deepest mind. The holy Rosary! What a vast mine of spiritual wealth! what an inexhaustible fountain of grace! The humiliation of the Incarnation and the suffering and ignominy of the Redemption are the remedies which the Eternal Father, in His infinite wisdom, proposed for the pride of poor fallen nature. The remembrance of them, which the Rosary places before our minds, cannot but be a sovereign remedy for the evils of the unhappy times in which we live.

Before entering upon our subject I shall premise by saying that it is the common Rosary of fifteen mysteries that I propose to treat of, and not any of the various other chaplets or rosaries now in use among Christians.[1] Such of them as are approved by the Church are good and to be commended; but they do not enter into the scope of this essay.

Our divine Saviour foretold to His Apostles that they and their followers should be hated by all men for His name's sake; that they were to meet with persecution because they were not of the world, as He was not of the world. But the Church was soon to discover that her enemies were not always to be of the same character, nor were they to wage war against her with the same weapons. Extraordinary trials were to be encountered at intervals, which were to be a test of the constancy, not only of her ordinary children, but also of the elect. She also learned that He who permitted these trials provided also a remedy, as her history in all ages amply testifies. An Arius was to have his Athanasius, an Abelard his Bernard, a Luther his Ignatius, and so of her other enemies. But we are now concerned with the Albigenses, who rose in the southeast of France in the eleventh century, and devastated the Church at the same time that they defied the civil power. But no sooner was His flock threatened than the Good Shepherd came to its relief.

Many efforts having been made both by the civil and

[1] The fifteen decades of the Rosary are divided into the five joyful mysteries, the five sorrowful mysteries, and the five glorious mysteries. The joyful mysteries are: 1. The Annunciation; 2. The Visitation; 3. The Birth of Our Saviour; 4. The Presentation of our Lord in the Temple; 5. The Finding of Jesus in the Temple. The sorrowful mysteries are: 1. The Bloody Sweat of Our Saviour in the Garden; 2. The Scourging at the Pillar; 3. The Crowning with Thorns; 4. Jesus carrying His Cross; 5. The Crucifixion of Our Lord. The glorious mysteries are: 1. The Resurrection of Our Lord; 2. The Ascension of Our Lord; 3. The Descent of the Holy Ghost on the Apostles; 4. The Assumption of the Blessed Virgin into Heaven; 5. The Coronation of the Blessed Virgin in Heaven.

The Rosary of the Blessed Virgin Mary. 137

the religious power to suppress the outbreak of these heretics, but of which it does not enter into our present purpose to give a detailed account, St. Dominic — or Dominic Guzman, as he is called in profane history — entered the field against them with that burning zeal with which only a saint can be animated for the conversion of sinners. Dominic was born at Calarnega, a village of Old Castile, Spain, in the year 1170. He studied for the Church, and was ordained a priest at the age of twenty-three. He entered on the mission of preaching for the conversion of the heretics about the year 1205; founded the Order of St. Dominic, or Friar Preachers, as they are commonly called, on the 15th of August, 1217; and, finally, died at Rome, August 4, 1221. He employed his sanctity and eloquence in endeavoring to stem the tide of evil that had been set in motion by the Albigenses; but his efforts, though heroic, were of comparatively little avail. At length he ventured to complain to the holy Mother of God, for whom he entertained the tenderest devotion, and to ask her to instruct him in the way he could labor most successfully for the conversion of those misguided souls for whom her divine Son had laid down His life. His prayer was acceptable, and Mary revealed to him the devotion of the holy Rosary. He was told to give his time more to the propagation of this devotion than to preaching, and greater success would attend his efforts. This revelation took place about the year 1206, but the precise date cannot be ascertained.

But though we owe the Rosary in its present form to St. Dominic, the idea was not original with him. The custom of repeating the same form of prayer, whether of praise or petition, is of great antiquity, and is natural to man, especially when he is under the influence of strong emotion. The Jews were familiar with it, as may be learned from various passages of the Psalms, but more particularly from the 135th Psalm, in which the same words "for His mercy endureth forever" are repeated twenty-seven times. Influenced no less by the custom of their fathers, the Jews, than by the example of our divine Redeemer, who on a most solemn occasion in the Garden of Gethsemani thrice repeated "the selfsame words,"[1] the Christians early adopted the form of repetition in their private as well as in their public devotions. This would especially be the case with the "Our Father," which Jesus Christ Himself was pleased to teach His children as the most perfect form of praise and petition. The custom of this frequent repetition would naturally lead to the resolution, on the part of the more devout at least, of reciting daily a certain number of these prayers ; and this in its turn would suggest the propriety of adopting some means of counting them. The early Christians, being lovers of poverty, would naturally adopt some simple means, and this is proved from ecclesiastical history. Thus St. Palladius relates that St. Paul, the first hermit, who lived in the fourth century, was accustomed to recite three hundred "Our Fathers" daily, and used little pebbles or grains to count them. These counters were in time strung upon a string for greater convenience, and were called *Pater Nosters*. Beads of different material, varying in value according to the ability, or perhaps in some cases, as at the present day, according to the vanity of those who possessed them, eventually came into use ; but it would be impossible to fix the date ; indeed, from the very nature of things, their introduction must have been gradual. It may be remarked, in passing, that the word

[1] St. Matthew. xxvi. 44.

The Rosary of the Blessed Virgin Mary. 139

bead is of Christian origin, and proves by its derivation the use to which it was first applied. It is simply the Anglo-Saxon word *bead*, which means *prayer*, and which is allied to the German word *beten, to pray*, especially to petition.

Butler informs us that in early times, when many of the faithful were accustomed to assist at the public recitation of the Divine Office, or, if prevented, to perform some devotions at the same hours at their homes, "those who could neither read nor recite the Psalter by heart supplied this by a frequent repetition of the Lord's Prayer; and the many illiterate persons performed, at all the canonical hours of prayer, regular devotions, corresponding to those of the Psalter recited by the clergy and many others. When the number of 'Our Fathers' was told by studs fastened on the belts which people then wore, these prayers were reckoned by so many belts. The ordinary use of the Angelical Salutation in this manner was not so ancient. Erimannus, in the twelfth age, mentions a lady who recited every day sixty Angelical Salutations."[1] From this circumstance the Rosary came to be called the Psaltery of the Blessed Virgin Mary. The name *Rosary* is derived from the title Mystical Rose, by which the Church salutes the holy Mother of God.

St. Albert of Crispin and Peter the Hermit are mentioned long before the time of St. Dominic as having taught the laity who could not read the Psalter to say a certain number of "Our Fathers" and "Hail Marys" in lieu of each canonical hour of the Divine Office; but, says Maurel (p. 223), "in its present form, conformably to repeated testimonies of the Roman Pontiffs, the Rosary has for its author St. Dominic."

[1] "Lives of the Saints," Festival of the Holy Rosary.

From the beginning the devotion of the holy Rosary became very popular with the faithful, and pontiffs and prelates were loud in its praises. A few of these expressions of praise will no doubt be interesting to the reader, and will tend to increase his veneration for a devotion that is so highly commended. And first we have the words of the ever blessed Mother of God to St. Dominic: "Preach the Rosary, which is a shield against the shafts of the enemy, the rampart of the Church of God, and the Book of Life. . . . Exhort everyone to be devout to the Rosary, and thou shalt produce wonderful fruit in souls." Says Pope Leo X.: "The Rosary has been established against the dangers which threaten the world." St. Pius V.: "By the Rosary the darkness of heresy has been dispelled, and the light of the Catholic faith shines out in all its brilliancy." Clement VII.: "The devotion of the Rosary is the salvation of Christians." Adrian VI.: "The Rosary scourges the devil." Sixtus V.: "The Rosary has been established by St. Dominic, under the inspiration of the Holy Ghost, for the utility of the Catholic religion." Gregory XVI. "The Rosary is a wonderful instrument for the destruction of sin, the recovery of God's grace, and the advancement of His glory." The well-known devotion of Pius IX. to the Blessed Virgin, and the extraordinary importance which Leo XIII. attaches to the Rosary, are too recent to require comment.

A number of important questions relating to the holy Rosary will present themselves to the mind of the thoughtful reader, the first of which would naturally be, What are the essential parts of the Rosary? This question is all the more important owing to the numerous indulgences with which the Church has enriched this devotion, and also on account of the various customs of different countries. Inasmuch as these customs are an expression of the devotion of different peoples to the holy Mother of God, a few of them will be placed before the reader. In Rome and in many other places it is customary to begin the Rosary with the versicle and response: "Incline unto my aid, O God! O Lord, make haste to help me." This is followed by the "Glory be to the Father," after which the mysteries are simply announced or named, as the "Annunciation," the "Prayer in the Garden," the "Resurrection," etc., followed by the recitation of the "Our Father," ten "Hail Marys," and "Glory be to the Father." The devotion concludes either with the "Hail, holy Queen," or the Litany of the Blessed Virgin. In other places, and generally among us, the custom is to begin with the Apostles' Creed, the "Our Father," three "Hail Marys," and the "Glory be to the Father," after which follow the mysteries in order, with the "Hail, holy Queen," in the end. Instead of the mere names of the mysteries, some books of devotion have prayers before and after each mystery; these being intended to assist persons who may find it difficult to meditate or place the scene of the mystery vividly before their minds. Still another custom, more general, perhaps, among the Germans than among others, is that of adding a few words, explanatory of the mystery then being meditated upon, after the holy Name of Jesus in the "Hail Mary"; as, "Whom thou, O Virgin, didst conceive of the Holy Ghost," "Who for us didst sweat blood in the Garden," "Who didst rise from the dead," etc. Now, the question arises, How much of this—which is all very good in itself—is necessary to gain the indulgences attached to the recitation of the Rosary? or, in other words, what are the essential parts of the Rosary?

All that is essential is the recitation of the fifteen

decades — or, where the Papal Briefs granting the indulgences permit, the recitation of only five decades— of one "Our Father," and ten "Hail Marys" each, and meditating during the recitation on some mystery in the life of Christ, where the same Papal Briefs require meditation as a necessary condition. It is to be observed, however, that the indulgences granted for the recitation of the whole Rosary are also granted for the recitation of only one-third part of it, or five decades, except where the opposite is expressly declared, as is proven by the decrees of September 23, 1775, and February 25, 1877. The Creed, "Our Father," three "Hail Marys," and "Glory be to the Father," at the beginning of the Rosary ; the announcement of the different mysteries, or the prayers before and after them ; the "Glory be to the Father" at the end of each decade ; the "Hail, holy Queen," or the Litany at the conclusion, are not essential parts, and may all be omitted without forfeiting the indulgences. The essential parts of the holy Rosary are, then, one "Our Father" and ten "Hail Marys" repeated five times, and nothing more.

Inasmuch as the Rosary in a measure takes the place among the laity which the Divine Office occupies among the clergy, the question arises, Is it permitted to interrupt the Rosary between the decades as it is to interrupt the Office between the different parts or "hours" ? The Office must be recited within the twenty-four hours of the day ; does the same privilege extend to the Rosary ? This question having been proposed for solution to the Sacred Congregation of Indulgences, it was decided by a decree dated January 22, 1858, that the whole Rosary cannot be divided into more than three parts, and that each such part must be said without interruption. "It is not sufficient, then, to recite the entire chaplet on the same day; there must be, moreover, between the different parts of the five decades no notable interruption which would destroy the moral unity of the prayer." The whole question, then, turns on the point, What is a "notable interruption"?

An interruption of the Rosary, or of any other devotion, may be viewed in a twofold light: either with reference to the actual length of time over which the interruption extends, or with reference to the withdrawal of the mind from the devotion. If a person is called, for example, from the recitation of the beads to transact some secular business, which by its very nature withdraws the mind from prayer, it is different from interrupting the Rosary to take part in any other devotion; for while the one by its nature stifles the spirit of prayer for the time, the other only withdraws the mind from one kind of prayer to turn it to another, and leaves the spirit of prayer undisturbed. Says Konings of the Stations of the Cross, which he afterward applies to the Rosary: "An interruption which would be made to hear Mass, to go to confession, or to receive Holy Communion is not morally an interruption, because it does not divert the mind to extraneous things."[2] Hence, according to him, this would not constitute a "notable interruption," and would not forfeit the indulgences.

It may be further inquired, What *omissions* in the recitation of the beads would be sufficient to lose the indulgences? All authorities agree that if a person were to omit a "notable part" he would lose these graces, and the same is true in regard to the conditions prescribed for the gaining of any other indulgence; but if the

[1] Maurel, p. 227.
[2] "Theologia Moralis," N. 1788, 3.

omission is of only a small part the indulgence is not thereby endangered. But it is difficult to determine what precisely constitutes a "notable part." In general it may be safely concluded, with Konings and other theologians, that the omission of the fifth part of the prayers or other good works prescribed would be enough to forfeit the indulgence. Whether less would suffice or not they do not say.

Still another inquiry is rendered necessary owing to the fact that human ingenuity has found means of manufacturing beads from an almost endless variety of materials. Of what materials must beads be made in order that the Church will permit them to be indulgenced, and what materials are forbidden? Indulgences may be attached in general to beads—and the same is true of statues and crucifixes—made of any solid material, or such as is not easily broken; and although it was formerly forbidden to indulgence beads, etc., made of wood or iron, that prohibition has been withdrawn. Even glass beads may be indulgenced, if the beads are solid, and not hollow.[1]

What are we to conclude with regard to giving our beads away or lending them to another?

"1. Beads are indulgenced for one person only. When a number of beads are blessed together it is understood that each of them is blessed for the person who, being the owner of it, or one to whom the owner has given it gratuitously, is the first to use it with the intention of gaining the Rosary indulgences.

"2. If a person lend his indulgenced beads to a friend merely to accommodate him to count his beads, and not for the purpose of enabling him to gain the

[1] Decree of February 29, 1820.

The Rosary of the Blessed Virgin Mary.

indulgences attached to them, the beads do not in this case cease to be indulgenced for him who lent them.

"3. If the beads are lent or given with the intention of enabling another to gain the indulgences, the beads simply cease to be indulgenced at all, as well for the lender as for the receiver. They must be blessed again to become indulgenced.

"4. If one took the beads without the knowledge or consent of the owner, they do not in this case, we believe, cease to be indulgenced. The Congregation has decided that the loss of the indulgence applies to the case where the owner lends or gives them for the purpose of enabling another to gain the indulgence."[1]

If beads that have been indulgenced are lost they have no indulgence for the one who finds them, but he may have them indulgenced for himself. The same is true of beads which a person inherits from a parent or friend. It is also to be remembered that a person is not permitted to sell beads that have been indulgenced, even though he charge no more for them than they would sell for before they were blessed. Such sale would cause the beads to lose their indulgence altogether.[2] To charge a higher price for them because they are blessed would not only forfeit the indulgence, but would also be the sin of simony.

Once more: the holy Rosary to some extent takes the place of the Little Office of the Blessed Virgin; the question thence arose: "That Office is divided in such a manner that the first Nocturn is recited on Mondays and Thursdays, the second on Tuesdays and Fridays, and the third on Wednesdays and Saturdays. Now,

---

[1] *Irish Ecclesiastical Record*, 1883, pp. 195, 196; decrees of January 10, 1839; March 12, 1855; and February 13, 1845.

[2] Decree of June 4, 1821; Maurel, pp. 257, 258.

can or should the three different series of the Joyful, the Sorrowful, and the Glorious Mysteries of the Rosary be recited on these days of the week in the same manner? When this question was proposed to the Sacred Congregation the response was that, although everyone is free to select whichever five mysteries he prefers to recite, yet the custom of dividing off the whole Rosary in the same manner as the Little Office is coming into use, and meets with the approbation of the Holy See. According to this arrangement, the five Joyful Mysteries are recited on Mondays and Thursdays, the five Sorrowful Mysteries on Tuesdays and Fridays, and the five Glorious Mysteries on Sundays, Wednesdays, and Saturdays.[1]

It may be further remarked that, where the Papal Briefs granting indulgences for the recitation require meditation as one of the conditions, it is not enough to meditate on any pious subject; the meditation must always be on some mystery in the life of our divine Redeemer. If this point is neglected the indulgences are not gained.[2]

There are three forms of blessing by which indulgences are attached to beads: the Dominican, the Bridgetine, and the Papal or Apostolic. And first of the Dominican. The holy Rosary having been revealed to St. Dominic by the Mother of God, it is natural to expect that the Dominicans should have special privileges in the matter of blessing rosaries. And so it is, according to the decrees of several Sovereign Pontiffs. To impart these indulgences a certain form of words and the use of holy water are necessary in blessing the beads.[3]

So numerous are the indulgences attached to the reci-

---

[1] Decree, July 1, 1839.   [2] Decree, August 13, 1726.
[3] Decree, February 29, 1864.

tation of the Rosary that no attempt will be made to state them in this place; the reader is simply recommended to form an intention, when reciting the beads, to gain all the indulgences within his reach.

The conditions required for gaining the Dominican indulgences are stated in the *Raccolta* (pp. 170, 171) in these words: "To gain these indulgences it is required that the rosaries should be blessed by the religious of the Order of Friar Preachers, and that while the prayers are being said meditation be made on the mysteries of the birth, passion, death, resurrection, etc., of Our Lord Jesus Christ, according to the decree of the Sacred Congregation of Indulgences, August 12, 1726, approved by Benedict XIII. This Pope declared, moreover, in his Constitution *Pretiosus*, May 26, 1727, § 4, that those who cannot meditate may gain the indulgence by merely saying the Rosary devoutly." These indulgences are applicable to the souls in purgatory. It is also to be remembered that in order to gain the Dominican indulgences it is sufficient, when the Rosary is said in common by a number of persons, that one of the company have a string of beads that has been indulgenced, and that he use it in the recitation, in order that all the company may gain the indulgences attached to it; provided, as the decree states, that all those who unite in the recitation withdraw their minds from all other affairs, and apply them to the devotion in which they are engaged.[1]

As to the Bridgetine indulgence, "this chaplet is so called because we are indebted for it to St. Bridget (of Sweden), who first conceived the notion of circulating its use. She intended by means of the devotion to honor the sixty-three years which, in the opinion of many, the Blessed Virgin spent upon earth. Consequently it is

[1] Decree, January 22, 1858.

composed of six decades, each containing one 'Our Father,' ten 'Hail Marys,' and a Creed instead of the 'Glory be to the Father.' To make up the number seven, an 'Our Father' is added in honor of the Seven Dolors and Seven Joys of Mary, together with three 'Hail Marys' to complete the sixty-three years.

"Nevertheless, the indulgences of this chaplet can be applied as well to rosaries as to the ordinary beads of five decades. But for this application a special faculty is requisite, since, agreeably to a decree of January 28, 1842, the ordinary power of indulgencing chaplets is not sufficient. At the same time the Briefs from Rome to bless and indulgence chaplets, medals, etc., generally contain that faculty. Bear in mind also that, in according the power to apply the Bridgetine indulgence to rosaries, the Briefs do not by that act give power to bless the real chaplets of St. Bridget, constituted of six decades, as above. The faculty was reserved to the Superior of the Order of St. Saviour, or of St. Bridget, or to the priests of the same Order deputed for that object. Hence, as this Order does not exist at present, the popes grant permission to annex to ordinary chaplets the indulgences of St. Bridget. Yet, as already stated, this delegation exclusively regards chaplets of five decades, without any reference to the chaplets of St. Bridget made up of six decades. This has been repeatedly declared by the Sacred Congregation, particularly in the decrees of January 15, 1839, September 25, 1841, and January 28, 1842.

". . . To participate in the indulgences of the chaplet of St. Bridget it is not necessary to meditate on the mysteries of Our Lord and the Blessed Virgin."[1] No formula is required for blessing the beads; it is sufficient

[1] Maurel, pp. 273, 275.

that the priest merely make the sign of the cross over them, without saying a word, and without sprinkling them with holy water.[1]

Turning, finally, to the Papal or Apostolic blessing, the history of its origin is given in the *Raccolta* (p. 444) in these words: "However ancient may have been the custom of the Sovereign Pontiffs to bless and distribute to the faithful sacred articles of gold, silver, or other metals (whence originated the pontifical blessing and distribution of crosses, crucifixes, rosaries, medals, etc.), yet it would seem that previous to the sixteenth century no indulgences were annexed to such articles. Pope Sixtus V., on the rebuilding of the patriarchal Lateran arch-basilica (when by the falling of the walls of the former building in various places were found many medals of gold, on which were impressed the holy cross, and other figures bearing the cross), caused a distribution to be made of them, and granted many indulgences to those who had any of these medals in their possession, provided they fulfilled certain works enjoined them, as we learn from the Constitution *Laudemus viros*, December 1, 1587. From that time the popes, his successors, annexed indulgences to other objects besides medals blessed by them, — such as chaplets, rosaries, crosses, crucifixes, etc., — persuaded that the usage of these sacred objects excites in the minds of the faithful faith and acts of adoration toward God and reverence for the Blessed Virgin and the saints."

In order to gain these indulgences it is necessary that the beads—for we are treating of them only—should be blessed by the Sovereign Pontiff, or by a priest having the requisite faculties from him. The bishops of this and other missionary countries are as a rule empowered

[1] *Irish Eccl. Record,* 1882, p. 753.

to grant this faculty to their priests; and for that reason the priests of the United States are able to attach the Apostolic indulgences to rosaries, and thus place these indulgences within the reach of such of the faithful as may wish to gain them. No particular formula is required for this blessing: it is sufficient to make the sign of the cross over the objects, without saying a word, or sprinkling them with holy water.

It is further to be noted that these indulgences are not attached to the beads themselves, or to their recital, as those of St. Dominic and St. Bridget are; on the contrary, the beads in this case hold the place of some other blessed object—as a cross, a medal, etc. Hence, without reciting the beads, the person may gain the Apostolic indulgences, provided he fulfil the conditions prescribed. "To gain these indulgences it is necessary for one to carry about him the blessed object, or, at any event, to have it in his possession. Moreover, the pious considerations or prayers assigned as conditions for sharing in the indulgences must be made either while carrying the articles, or at least when kept in one's room, or other suitable place in the house, so that the prayers be recited before them." [1] From this the reader will perceive that actual ownership and possession of the beads, or any other object to which these indulgences have been attached, are necessary conditions for partaking of these spiritual favors, and that, consequently, it is not enough, as in the case of the Dominican indulgences, that one person of the company, when a number of persons recite the Rosary together, should have an indulgenced string of beads. The Apostolic indulgences are applicable to the souls in purgatory.[2]

The Bridgetine, the Apostolic, and the Dominican in-

[1] Maurel, pp. 259, 264, note.   [2] *Raccolta*, p. 448

dulgences may all be attached to the same string of beads, and may all be gained by the person who recites them, provided he fulfils the conditions required for each.

Considering the excellence of the holy Rosary in itself and the numerous indulgences, both plenary and partial, with which it has been enriched by the Holy See, need we wonder that the spirit of evil should make it the object of his most violent and insidious attacks, and that he should succeed in making it unpopular with many persons? Poor, deluded mortals ! Let them learn from those who were real lights in the Church, real servants of the Mother of God, the mistake they are making. St. Dominic, to whom the Rosary was revealed, and whose Order is justly regarded as one of the most learned in the Church, was not ashamed to recite the beads, and with all his energy, eloquence, and zeal recommended the devotion to all who came within his reach. St. Alphonsus Liguori was most devoted to the Rosary, and we read in his Life that it was revealed to him that his eternal salvation depended upon his daily performance of this devotion. Of St. Francis of Sales it is related that he spent an hour every day in the recitation of the holy Rosary. Yet these were men as remarkable for their learning as they were for their sanctity. No; to underestimate the holy Rosary is not an evidence of learning, but a sign of ignorance and pride, and of a very low standard of piety. I can have no patience with such people ; let us have no more of them.

XII.—THE SCAPULAR OF OUR LADY OF MOUNT CARMEL, OR BROWN SCAPULAR.

The purpose of this essay is to give a brief account of the origin, the graces, and the indulgences of the Brown Scapular, with the conditions upon which these spiritual favors may be gained. Since the introduction of this scapular into general use among the faithful, so many questions have been proposed to the Sacred Congregation of Rites or to the Superior-General of the Carmelites relating to it that it is difficult for many to know what precisely is necessary to be done in order to reap all the spiritual advantages which the Church in her liberality has granted to the devout wearers of this livery of Mary. Some persons may do more than is necessary, while others may do less; and while the members of the one class err by imposing unnecessary obligations upon themselves, those of the other commit a greater mistake in failing to fulfil what is prescribed, and hence reap little advantage. Another difficulty which priests too often meet with in propagating devotions of this kind is that in almost every congregation one or more devout persons are found who are looked upon by the rest as authorities in matters relating to devotions which pious Catholics are accustomed to practise, whether such persons are learned or not; and here, as elsewhere, it generally turns out that a little learning is a bad thing. Such pious souls, being anxious to extend the devotion to which they are particularly attached, will recommend it to others, and, either from the very excess of their unenlightened piety, or from the desire of making the gaining of indulgences doubly sure, are not infrequently prompted to make unwarranted additions to the conditions which the Church has laid down for the securing of these spiritual treasures, or to interpret them more strictly than the letter of the grant warrants, which amounts to about the same thing. And, to increase the difficulty, it will too often be found that people will take the word of these persons in preference to that of the priest ; at least such has been my experience. It is much to be desired that these pious souls were either more enlightened or more diffident.

But all this aside, we owe the scapular to the direct intervention of the holy Mother of God, who in this new proof of her love for man chose St. Simon Stock as her instrument. This devout servant of Mary was a native of England, who had attached himself to the Order of Our Lady of Mount Carmel soon after its introduction into his native land, had made such progress in the science of the saints, and had displayed such prudence, that he was ere long elected Superior-General of the Carmelites of the West. The scapular was revealed to him in a celebrated vision with which the Mother of God favored him on the 16th of July, 1251, at Cambridge. Holding the scapular in her hand, she said : "Receive, my beloved son, this scapular of thy Order ; it is the special sign of my favor, which I have obtained for thee and for thy children of Mount Carmel. He who dies clothed with this habit shall be preserved from eternal fire. It is the badge of salvation, a shield in time of danger, and a pledge of special peace and protection." This address of the Mother of God is given in different words by different writers, but all agree substantially. The vision has been called in question by certain writers ; but when it is stated that it has been confirmed by many well-authenticated miracles, that Pope Benedict XIV., among others, accepted it as genuine, and that the indulgences granted by several Sovereign Pontiffs also suppose its genuineness, there is little room left for cavilling.

It is not the intention to pause to inquire into the manner in which this devotion became, in a very short time, extended not only among the members of the Order to which it had been granted, but also among such of the faithful—and they were many—who wished to place themselves under the special protection of the august Mother of God. Nor shall any of the miracles be adduced by which it pleased Almighty God from time to time to confirm the belief and confidence of the faithful in the promises of the Mother of His divine Son. It will be more profitable to turn to the various questions that have arisen in the lapse of years in connection with the devotion of the scapular.

The word *scapular* is derived, like many others, from the Latin, and means the shoulder-blade, or, in the plural, in which it is more commonly found, the shoulders. As a garment, the scapular is a broad piece of cloth, with an aperture in it for the head, which hangs down in front and at the back almost to the ground, as may be seen in the habits of the Carmelites, the Benedictines, and some other religious Orders. The scapular worn by the faithful is a symbol of that worn by the religious of the Order of Mount Carmel. In form it is essential that it should consist of two parts, each oblong or square,—in accordance with the custom that has long been observed and is sanctioned by the Church,—fastened together with two strings, so that one part may hang on the breast and the other on the back. When the Sacred Congregation was consulted as to whether it was lawful to make scapulars of an oval, round, or polygonal form, the response was that no innovation should be made; in other words, that the form up to that time in use should be retained as the only proper one.[1] As regards the material of which it is lawful to make scapulars, it must be woollen cloth; cotton, silk, or other material is strictly forbidden; and by the word *cloth* is meant woven cloth, so that if threads of woollen were knit or worked with the needle into the form of a scapular it would not do. In color the scapular must be brown or black. The habit of the Carmelites, of which it is a symbol, is brown, and hence that has always been regarded as the proper color for the scapular; but it was maintained by some that the wool of a black sheep, inasmuch as it was the natural color of the wool, and not dyed, would also be permitted. When the question was brought before the Sacred Congregation it replied that the members of the confraternity gained the indulgences although the scapular was not exactly brown, provided the color substituted for brown was something similar to it, or black.[2] It is permitted, although it is not necessary, to ornament the scapular with needle-work, even though the ornamentation is of a different color from that of the scapular; nor need such ornament be worked with woollen thread; silk, cotton, or other thread may be used. But it is essential that the necessary color of the scapular should predominate. It is not necessary to work any image or picture on the scapular; it may, however, be done if the color of the scapular is left to predominate.[3]

Who may be invested with the scapular? The Church

[1] Decree of August 18, 1868; Schneider, p. 686, No. 9.
[2] Decree of February 12, 1840; Schneider, p. 686, No. 8.
[3] Decree of August 18, 1868; Schneider, p. 686, No. 12.

not only permits, but also wishes that all the faithful should enroll themselves among the devout servants of Mary, as she wishes them to make use of all the means of grace which in her liberality she places within their reach ; and hence all Catholics may be lawfully and validly invested with the scapular, there being nothing in the bulls or briefs of the Sovereign Pontiffs to forbid it. Even infants who have not yet come to the use of reason may be invested ; and when they attain to the years of discretion it is not necessary for them to be again invested, or to do anything more than simply to comply with the necessary conditions for gaining the indulgences, and immediately they will begin to reap these spiritual advantages.[1]

By whom can a person be invested ? By a priest of the Carmelite Order, or by any other priest duly authorized to invest with it. In this country it is customary for bishops to give all their priests the faculty of investing with the scapular. A priest who has power to invest others may also invest himself. Whatever formulas were heretofore permitted for investing, the priest must now use the one prescribed by Pope Leo XIII., July 24, 1888. But one priest cannot bless the scapular, and another invest a person with it ; the blessing and investing must both be done by the same priest. The practice which obtained in some places of giving blessed scapulars to pious laymen for distribution among the faithful is also forbidden under penalty of forfeiting all the graces and indulgences attached to the scapular. If the first enrolment of any person was invalid for any reason whatever, such as the scapular not being of the required material or form, or both parts being at one end of the strings, it is not sufficient

[1] Decree of August 29, 1864 ; Schneider, p. 6.

for the person so enrolled to get a scapular and have it blessed; he must be again invested, as if he had never gone through the ceremony at all.[1]

As to the place and manner of receiving the scapular, a person may receive it in any becoming place; and the sick may receive it in their beds. It is not necessary for the person being invested to hold the scapular in his hands; it is sufficient that it be placed near him; nor is a lighted candle necessary. But the priest who invests must himself, under penalty of nullity, place the scapular on the neck of the person whom he invests. But when the first scapular is worn out or lost, or got rid of in any other way, all that is necessary is for the person to get another, and put it on without blessing or ceremony. When a number of persons are invested at the same time, all the scapulars may be blessed at once; but the form of investment must be repeated as each scapular is placed on the neck of the person who is to wear it, except in the case of some missionaries, who have special faculties for investing differently. But if a number of persons are to be invested at the same time, and there are not scapulars enough for all, the same one may be successively placed on several persons one after another, and each can afterward procure a scapular for himself; but the first that each one wears must be blessed.[2] It was formerly necessary that persons receiving the scapular should have their names enrolled with the Carmelite Fathers at Rome; but Pope Gregory XVI. dispensed with this obligation, April 30, 1838, which dispensation was confirmed by a decree of the Sacred Congregation of September 17, 1845. This priv-

---

[1] Decrees of March 7, 1840, August 24, 1844, June 16, 1872, and September 18, 1862.
[2] Schneider, pp. 686-688; decree of August 18, 1868.

ilege of dispensing with the enrolment was, however, withdrawn by Pope Leo XIII. by a decree of April 27, 1887; and by another decree of the same date he forbade the investing with the brown scapular in connection with others. It must be blessed and imposed by itself.[1] If a person puts off his scapular for a longer or shorter time, either through indifference, forgetfulness, or even contempt, and afterward resolves to commence wearing it, it is not necessary for him to be invested anew; it is sufficient for him to put on the scapular again, and wear it, trusting in the mercy of God that he will again be made partaker of the spiritual favors attached to the pious confraternity.[2]

What are the spiritual advantages of wearing the scapular? First let us clearly understand what precisely is meant by *wearing* it, for on this depends the participation in those graces. By wearing the scapular is meant that it be so adjusted upon the person that one part hangs on the breast and the other on the back, one of the strings passing over each shoulder. If both parts be carried on the breast, or both on the back, it is not wearing it, in the sense of the Church, and the person so acting would not be entitled to any of the graces or indulgences. Much less would a person be entitled to them who carried the scapular in his pocket. To keep the scapular about him in any way might indeed be a sign of devotion to the Mother of God and of confidence in her protection, and as such would receive a fitting reward; but it would not in any sense be regarded as *wearing* it. It is not necessary that the scapular should be worn next the person; it may be worn over or under any part of the clothing. The religious who wear the

---

[1] *Irish Ecclesiastical Record*, July, 1887, and May, 1889.
[2] Schneider, p. 688, Nos. 22, 23.

large scapular are accustomed, as we know, to have it outside their habit.[1]

The spiritual advantages of wearing the scapular are fivefold: those which are received during life; those received at the approach of death; those after death; the Sabbatine indulgence or privilege; and the other indulgences granted to those who wear the scapular. And, first, as regards the advantages that may be received during life, it is to be remarked that the members of the Confraternity of the Scapular are associated with the religious Order represented by that scapular, which means that they participate in the fruit of all the good works of the religious belonging to that Order; that is, in the fruit of their prayers, meditations, Masses, fasting, penances, alms, and all else that goes to form the spiritual treasures of the Order. Now, the brown scapular represents the Order of Our Lady of Mount Carmel. But the devout wearers of this scapular enjoy favors not granted to those who wear the other scapulars; for Popes Clement VII. and Clement X. declared that the associates participated in a special manner in the fruit not only of the spiritual works of the Carmelites, to whom they are united as a confraternity, but also in all the good done throughout the whole Catholic Church. The associates of this scapular have received, as we have seen, the promise of the Blessed Virgin, according to the revelation made to St. Simon Stock, to be adopted as her favorite and privileged children, and to enjoy during life her special protection both for soul and body.

Secondly, the favors granted at the approach of death to those who devoutly wear the scapular are that there is for them, like for those who wear the other scapulars,

[1] Schneider, p. 686, No. 11.

a formula for a general absolution at the moment of death, independent of the ordinary "Last Blessing," which all the faithful are privileged to receive at their departing hour, as may be seen in another part of this work. Persons wearing the scapular are also encouraged to hope for the special assistance of the Mother of God at the moment of death, as she promised to St. Simon Stock: "He who dies clothed with this scapular shall not suffer eternal fire." This is what is called the "privilege of preservation." It means that the Blessed Virgin, by her powerful intercession, will draw from the divine treasury in favor of the associates special graces to help the good to persevere to the end and to move sinners to avail themselves of favorable opportunities of conversion before death seizes on them. This privilege may also mean that sometimes, owing to the influence of the Blessed Virgin, the hour of death is postponed, to give an associate who is in sin a further opportunity of conversion; and writers add that this privilege may sometimes be exemplified in the case of obstinate and obdurate sinners when God permits death to come upon them when they are not wearing the scapular, either as the result of forethought or from indifference or neglect.

In the third place, as regards the graces after death, the deceased members of the confraternity have a special share in the fruit of the daily prayers of the Order of the Carmelites and of the Holy Sacrifice, which they offer once a week, and occasionally at other times during the year, for the deceased Carmelites and associates of the Carmelite Confraternity.

Fourthly, the meaning of the "Sabbatine indulgence" is this: the associates of the Scapular of Carmel enjoy, on certain conditions, however, which we will mention later on, the remarkable privilege known as the "privilege of delivery," or the "Sabbatine indulgence." This privilege refers to, and is grounded on, the promise of the Blessed Virgin, made to Pope John XXII., to withdraw promptly from purgatory, and especially on the first Saturday after death, associates of the Scapular of Carmel. The account of this revelation to Pope John XXII. is embodied in his famous Bull *Sacratissimo uticulmine*, more commonly called the Sabbatine Bull, on account of the promise of deliverance on the first Saturday after death. The genuineness of this bull has been questioned on the ground of internal evidences of the absence of authenticity, and also because it is not found in the Roman bullarium. It is, however, printed in the bullarium of the Carmelites and in many other works. It may be further stated that Pope Benedict XIV. admits its authenticity.[1] "Leaving the discussion of the authenticity of this bull to others whom it concerns more directly, it is enough for us to know that the privilege of deliverance has been explained and sanctioned by succeeding Popes. Paul V., when giving permission to the Carmelite Fathers to preach this indulgence to the faithful, explains the nature of it in this way: 'The Carmelite Fathers,' he says, ' are allowed to preach that the people can believe that the Blessed Virgin will help, by her continual assistance, her merits, and her special protection, after death, and particularly on Saturdays—the day consecrated by the Church to the Blessed Virgin—the souls of the members of the Confraternity of Mount Carmel who have died in the grace.

---

[1] This question is ably discussed, with a conclusion in the affirmative, against certain doubts in an article on the scapular in the "Catholic Dictionary," by a writer in the *Irish Ecclesiastical Record* for September and November, 1887.

of God, and who have in life worn her habit, observed chastity according to their state, and recited the Office of the Blessed Virgin, or, if they are not able to recite the Office, who have observed the fasts of the Church, and abstained from meat on Wednesdays and Saturdays, except when Christmas falls on either of these days.'"[1] In the Second Nocturn of the Office of the feast of Our Lady of Mount Carmel, given in the Roman Breviary, mention is made of this privilege in much the same language. We read in this Office: "It is piously believed, since her power and mercy have everywhere great efficacy, that the Most Blessed Virgin consoles with special maternal affection the associates of this scapular, when detained in the fire of purgatory, who have practised certain light abstinences, repeated certain prescribed prayers, and observed chastity according to their state in life, and that she will endeavor to bring them to heaven sooner than would otherwise happen."

To recapitulate. The conditions necessary for participating in the spiritual advantages of the scapular are the following: to observe exactly all that has been prescribed regarding the material, color, and form of the scapular; to receive it from a priest duly authorized to invest with it; and to wear it constantly in the manner prescribed. These are the only conditions for membership in the confraternity of the scapular. No prayers or good works are necessary, if we except the special advantages of the "privilege of deliverance" or "Sabbatine indulgence," for which the following conditions in addition to those necessary for membership in the confraternity are required: 1. Chastity according to one's state of life; 2. The daily recitation of the Little Office of the Blessed Virgin, or the abstinence on Wednes-

[1] *Irish Ecclesiastical Record*, 1883, pp. 329, 330.

days and Saturdays, as remarked above. Those who say the Divine Office, on which an essay will be found elsewhere in this work, comply by means of it with this condition, even though the Office is already, as in the case of priests, a work of obligation.[1]

Although the wearing of the scapular and the conditions prescribed for gaining the indulgences and other supernatural favors do not, absolutely speaking, induce any obligation binding in conscience, yet the person invested with the scapular, who through his own indifference or neglect should fail to fulfil the obligations of the confraternity, could not be regarded as free from at least some venial fault before God.[2] To gain the plenary and partial indulgences that are granted in addition to the favors enumerated, it is necessary to fulfil the conditions prescribed for each of those particular indulgences.

I shall not give all the indulgences that are granted to those who devoutly wear the scapular and comply with the conditions, but shall quote from the *Irish Ecclesiastical Record*, from which much of the last few pages is taken.[3] The writer says: "It is no small advantage to have numerous indulgences specially granted on easy conditions in favor of those who wear the scapular. These conditions vary a good deal, and to know exactly what are the conditions required for a particular indulgence we must examine the terms of the grant, or consult some approved book on indulgences that treats of it. To illustrate what we say we will mention a few of the indulgences granted in favor of those who wear the brown scapular, with the conditions attached. (1) A plenary indulgence on the day of receiving the scapu-

---

[1] Decree of February 12, 1840; Schneider, p. 689, No. 27.
[2] Schneider, p. 689, No. 26.   [3] 1883, pp. 326–333.

lar Conditions: confession and communion. (2) **Plen-**ary indulgence at the moment of death. Conditions: confession and communion, and the devout invocation with the lips, or at least with the heart, of the holy Name of Jesus. (3) 100 days' indulgence. Conditions devout recital of the Office of the Blessed Virgin. Thus each indulgence is granted on certain conditions, which can be known with accuracy only by investigating the particular case." Schneider (p. 380) further states that by a decree of the Sacred Congregation of Indulgences, June 22, 1865, all Masses said for the repose of the souls of deceased members enjoy the advantage of a privileged altar; that is, a plenary indulgence is gained for the repose of the soul of the person for whom the Holy Sacrifice is offered. The same author gives all the other indulgences granted to the scapular, and the conditions upon which they may be gained.

When the Superior-General of the Carmelites was asked whether the laying aside of the scapular for a day would forfeit the indulgences and other favors or not, he replied that, as one day was but a small part of the year, there was no reason why we should conclude that the indulgences would be forfeited.[1] The reader cannot but conclude from what has been said that we possess in the Scapular of Our Lady one of the richest fountains of grace the Church in her liberality has opened to us.

[1] Schneider, p. 688, No. 20.

XIII.—THE ANGELUS.

WE cannot but admire the wisdom of the Church in summarizing so many of her principal doctrines in popular devotions. It both makes the devotions more attractive and intelligible and it impresses the doctrines more indelibly on the memory. When to this is added the performance of these devotions at stated times, the children of God are made to live and act more perfectly in harmony with the spirit of the ecclesiastical year. In the devotion of the holy Rosary, for example, is presented a succinct history of the Blessed Virgin Mary; the central mystery of the Incarnation, with the life, passion, death, resurrection, and ascension of our divine Redeemer; the coming of the Holy Ghost, and the glorious assumption of the Mother of God, with her coronation as Queen of heaven. In the Way of the Cross are represented the particulars of the dread drama of man's redemption. When performed on the Fridays of Lent, in the afternoon, it not only brings the Christian into harmony with the spirit of the Church, but it moves his heart to conceive those sentiments of sorrow for his sins and that purpose of amendment which, though fitting at all times, are especially so at the season when the Church invites her children to repentance. The sign of the cross, too, is a lesson in our holy faith, recalling to our minds some of the principal mysteries of religion. But still more happy, in many respects, was the Church in instituting the devotion of the *Angelus*.

When God called Abraham from Ur of the Chaldees

He said to him: "Walk before Me, and be perfect."[1] When Christ came upon earth He bade His followers pray always; and when the Apostle of the Gentiles would instruct his faithful disciple he admonished him to meditate continually on the great truths which he had taught him, and which he in turn was required to communicate to others. The exercise of frequently calling to mind the presence of God is one of the most conducive to perfection, and this is admirably effected by means of the *Angelus*, which raises our thoughts to God at morning, noon, and night, revives our remembrance of the principal mysteries of religion, enlivens our faith in them, increases our hope, enkindles our love, and awakens our gratitude.

The history of the *Angelus* is, to some extent, involved in mystery; for while certain points are known, others are disputed, and still others are unknown. Nothing in either Jewish or pagan antiquity resembled it. The former had indeed certain hours of prayer and fixed times for offering sacrifice, as may be learned from numerous passages of the Old Testament, and the latter also observed a degree of regularity in the performance of some religious rites; but the *Angelus* is purely Christian in its origin, its character, and its scope. It originated in the custom of ringing church bells at sunset. As early as the beginning of the thirteenth century the custom arose of ringing church bells at that hour.[2] It is most probable that the ringing of the church bells was introduced into different countries at different times; and if this be true, the discrepancies of different authorities on the subject may perhaps be reconciled. Among the Latin nations this bell was

---

[1] Genesis, xvii. 1.
[2] "Kirchen-Lexicon," article *Angelus Domini*.

called the *ignitegium* or the *pyrotegium*, among the French the *couvrefeu*; and among the English the *curfew*, which have all the same signification—a signal for the covering or extinguishing of all fires or lights, and retiring of the inmates of the house to rest. This custom existed throughout all Europe during the Middle Ages, especially in cities taken in war. It was also a precautionary measure against fire, rendered to some extent necessary, owing to the peculiar construction of the houses in those times.'

It is not probable that the Holy See ordered the recitation of certain prayers simultaneously with the introduction of the custom of ringing the church bells; for while, on the one hand, the greater number of devotions are introduced by some pious person or community, and extend until they have gained a fair hold on the people of at least one diocese or country, or on the members of one religious Order, when application is made to the Holy See, and they are formally approved, and not infrequently enriched with indulgences; on the other hand, nothing would be more natural than that persons who were accustomed, as all good Christians are, to the regular performance of their daily devotions, would ere long fix upon the ringing of the bell as the signal for doing so.

Devotion to the great mystery of the Incarnation, and to her through whom it pleased Almighty God to effect it, must ever be leading characteristics of the spiritual life of every Christian. But there were special reasons why this should be so about the time that the recitation of the *Angelus* was first introduced. The attention of the Christian world was then turned to the Holy Land, where the mystery of the Incarnation had been accom-

[1] " Encyclopædia Britannica," article *Curfew*

plished, and where the supereminent virtues of Mary had shown in all the richness of living splendor. Add to these circumstances the fact that so eminent a servant of Mary as St. Bernard was one of the most active in arousing the enthusiasm of the people to take up arms for the expulsion of the Mussulman from the holy places and their re-occupation by the Christians—a man whose love for Mary was only equalled by his eloquence in proclaiming her praises. Not only were his stirring appeals heard from the pulpit and the platform, but also in the assemblies of his religious brethren his fervid discourses and inspiring example infused his own spirit into them, and made them also so many advocates of the Mother of God. The same may be said of St. Bonaventure, who a little later proclaimed the praises of Mary in his own masterly way from the pulpit, the professor's chair, and as head of his devoted and simple-minded Franciscans. All things considered, it may be said that the date, as nearly as it can be fixed, of the introduction of the *Angelus* was a time when the Christian world was ripe for such a devotion.

The lapse of time and the imperfection of records render it difficult to collect all the facts regarding the institution of the *Angelus*, but such as are to be met with will be given. Says the Rev. John Evangelist Zollner: "According to the testimony of many historians, Pope Urban II. (1088) ordained that the bell should be rung in the morning and evening and the *Angelus Domini* recited, in order to obtain of God the possession of the Holy Land. Gregory IX. renewed this ordinance in the year 1239; Calixtus III. (1456) required it to be observed also at noon."[1] The statements of this author do not harmonize with those of other reliable writers:

[1] "The Pulpit Orator." vol. vi. p. 147.

but they are supported by some authorities, and may tend to throw light on a disputed question. St. Bonaventure, in the general chapter of his Order held in Paris in 1226, and in the next held at Assisium, ordered the triple salutation of the Blessed Virgin, called the *Angelus*, to be recited every evening at six o'clock in honor of the incomprehensible mystery of the Incarnation.[1] From this it is safe to infer that the *Angelus* had already been introduced, to some extent at least, among Christians. Pope John XXII. issued a bull dated May 7, 1327, commanding that at the sound of the bell the "Hail Mary" should be said three times. A council held in 1346 by William, Archbishop of Sens, decreed that, in accordance with the command of Pope John XXII., of blessed memory, the three "Hail Marys" should be recited; and it granted an indulgence of thirty days to those who did so. This is the first indulgence of which there is authentic record in connection with the *Angelus*. The statutes of Simon, Bishop of Nantes, of about the same date, direct pastors of souls to have the evening bell rung, and to instruct their people to recite three "Hail Marys" on bended knees, by doing which they can gain an indulgence of ten days.

Up to that time the custom had existed of reciting the *Angelus* only in the evening; but in the year 1368 the Council of Lavaur issued a decree requiring all pastors and curates, under penalty of excommunication, to have the bell rung at sunset, and to recite five "Our Fathers" in honor of the Five Wounds of our divine Redeemer, and seven "Hail Marys" in honor of the Seven Joys of the holy Mother of God. In the following year the Synod of Bessiers decreed that at the break of day the great bell of the church be rung three times, and that

[1] Butler's "Lives of the Saints," July 14th.

whoever heard it should recite three times the "Our Father" and "Hail Mary," to which recitation an indulgence of twenty days was granted. According to some writers, it was Calixtus III. who, in 1456, introduced the custom of reciting the "Hail Marys," or *Angelus*, at noon. But Fleury and Du Cange ascribe it to King Louis XI. of France, in the year 1472; and Mabillon declares that the custom spread from France throughout Europe, and in the beginning of the sixteenth century received the approval of the Holy See.[1]

It would be difficult, if not impossible, to determine when and by whom the versicles and responses, together with the concluding prayer, were introduced, or, in other words, who reduced the *Angelus* to its present form. We have seen, however, the various changes through which the devotion passed in the Middle Ages, and that its perfection was not the work of one, but of several hands.

If, turning from the history of its origin, we examine the parts of which it is composed, its surpassing excellence will be readily seen. The purpose of the devotion, as has been remarked, is the commemorating of the great mystery of the Incarnation of the Second Person of the ever blessed Trinity and the virginal maternity of the Blessed Mary. The Gospel narrative, which so admirably summarizes it, is found in the 1st chapter of St. Luke, from the 26th to the 42d verse, from which the first half of the "Hail Mary" and the first and second versicles and responses are taken, while the third versicle and response are from the 14th verse of the 1st chapter of the Gospel of St. John. From this it will be seen that the *Angelus* holds a place in the front rank of Catholic devotions. What could be more salutary than

---

[1] "Kirchen-Lexicon," as above.

the recitation at morning, noon, and night of this beautiful prayer, which reminds us of Him whose name is the only one under heaven given to men whereby they may be saved, and the dignity of her whom the Church bids us salute as "our life, our sweetness, and our hope"?

Inasmuch as the *Regina Cœli* has been made to take the place of the *Angelus* during Easter time, it will be proper for us to pause and inquire into the origin of that devotion. I shall premise by saying that at the end of Lauds and Compline in the Divine Office, and at the end of Vespers, as they are commonly sung in churches, an antiphon of the Blessed Virgin is added. These antiphons are four in number, are named from the Latin words with which they begin, and vary according to the season. The only one, however, with which we are now concerned is that which takes the place of the *Angelus* in the Office during Paschal time.

The origin of the *Regina Cœli* is thus accounted for by a writer of note: "In 596, during Paschal time, a horrible pestilence was ravaging Rome, and the Pope, St. Gregory, called the people to penance and appointed a procession. The day having come, he himself repaired at dawn to the church of Ara Cœli, and, taking in his hands a picture of the Blessed Virgin, said to have been painted by St. Luke, he proceeded to St. Peter's, followed by the clergy and a numerous crowd. But all of a sudden, while passing the Castle of Adrian, voices were heard in the air singing the *Regina Cœli*. The Pontiff, astonished and enraptured, replied with the people: '*Ora pro nobis Deum, alleluia.*' At the same moment an angel, brilliant with light, was seen replacing his sword in the scabbard, and the plague ceased from that day."[1] "After the disappearance of the plague the

[1] "The Divine Office," Bacquez, p. 564; Feraris, "Verbum Antiphona."

anthem *Regina Cœli* was introduced into the Church service, to thank the Blessed Virgin, whose intercession was believed to have stayed the disease."[1] But it must be said of the *Regina Cœli*, as of the *Angelus*, that it did not at once assume its present form.

Not content with approving and recommending so appropriate a devotion as the *Angelus*, the Church, anxious to encourage its recitation still further, has enriched it with indulgences. Into this point we must now inquire. It has already been seen that a number of bishops and local councils granted indulgences to certain devotions corresponding more or less closely to the *Angelus*. These indulgences have long since been abrogated even in the narrow territories for which they were originally granted, and it is to the Holy See alone that we must now look for indulgences of the *Angelus*. The following are those granted at various times by the Vicar of Christ: "The Sovereign Pontiff Benedict XIII., by a brief of September 24, 1724, granted a plenary indulgence once a month to all the faithful who every day at the sound of the bell, in the morning, or at noon, or in the evening at sunset, shall say devoutly on their knees the *Angelus Domini*, with the 'Hail Mary' three times, on any day when, being truly penitent, they shall pray for peace and union among Christian princes, for the extirpation of heresy, and for the triumph of holy mother Church." Also "an indulgence of one hundred days, on all the other days of the year, every time that, with at least contrite heart and devotion, they shall say these prayers."[2]

Certain points are here to be noted, as they have

---

[1] Darras' "General History of the Catholic Church," vol. ii. p 176, note.

[2] *Raccolta*, p. 170

The Angelus. 173

since been somewhat modified. The first is that the devotion was to be performed at the sound of the bell; in the second place, that it was not necessary to recite the *Angelus* three times in the day in order to gain the indulgence, as some persons imagine, but only once; thirdly, that it had to be said kneeling; and, finally, that the prayer, "Pour forth," etc., did not constitute an essential part of the devotion. Benedict XIV. confirmed the above indulgences April 20, 1742; but he at the same time introduced certain new features, which were, that the *Angelus* should be said standing on Saturday evening and all Sunday; and that the *Regina Cœli*, with the versicle, response, and prayer, should be said instead of it during Paschal time—that is, from Holy Saturday evening to the eve of Trinity Sunday, both included. To the latter he granted the same indulgences as to the *Angelus;* and he, moreover, permitted those who did not know it by heart to continue the recitation of the *Angelus* in its place. "The Sovereign Pontiff Pius VI., by a rescript dated March 18, 1781, granted that, in those places where no bell is rung at the times stated above, the faithful may gain the indulgences if, at or about the hours specified, they say, with at least contrite heart and devotion, the *Angelus*, or the *Regina Cœli* in the Paschal season."[1] When it was asked of the Sacred Congregation of Indulgences whether persons unable to kneel, or those on a journey at the time the bell rang, could gain the indulgences of the devotion without complying with those conditions, a reply was given under date of February 18, 1835, that the devotion must be performed according to the decree of Benedict XIII. To the inquiry, put by Canon Falisé of the cathedral of Tournay, whether or not the

[1] *Raccolta*, pp. 179, 180.

bell for ringing the *Angelus* must be blessed, the Sacred Congregation of Indulgences replied, August 24, 1865, that it was not necessary.[1] Thus matters rested till April 3, 1884, when a decree was issued still further lessening the conditions for gaining the indulgences. In the words of that decree : " Recently many pious men implored the Sacred Congregation of Indulgences to mitigate to some extent those two conditions " (of reciting the devotion at the sound of the bell, and on bended knees), " for the *Angelus* bell is not rung in all places, nor three times a day, nor at the same hours ; and if rung, it is not always heard ; and if heard, the faithful may be prevented by reasonable cause from kneeling down just at that moment to say the prayers. Besides, there are any number of the faithful who know neither the *Angelus* nor the *Regina Cœli* by heart, and cannot even read them in print. Wherefore His Holiness Pope Leo XIII., in order not to have so many of the faithful deprived of these spiritual favors, and in order to stir up an abiding and grateful remembrance of the mysteries of Our Lord's Incarnation and Resurrection, . . . graciously granted that all the faithful who say the *Angelus*, with the three ' Hail Marys,' the ' Pray for us, O holy Mother of God,' and the prayer ' Pour forth,' etc., though for reasonable cause they do not say them on bended knees nor at the sound of the bell ; or who recite during Paschal time the *Regina Cœli*, with the versicle and prayer ; or who in the morning, or about midday, or in the evening,[2] say five ' Hail Marys ' in a becoming manner, with attention and devotion—in case they do not know the *Angelus*

---

[1] Schneider, pp. 75 and 200, note.
[2] Sive mane, sive circiter meridiem, sive sub vespere.

or the *Regina Cœli*, and cannot read them—may gain the indulgences."[1]

It is here to be noted that, although in some points the Holy Father mitigated the conditions for gaining the indulgences, he at the same time added an obligation which had not previously existed—that of reciting the versicles and prayer after the three "Hail Marys."

To sum up: in order to gain the indulgences of the *Angelus* given above, it is necessary at the present time, first, to recite the three "Hail Marys," with the versicle and response that precede each one, and the versicle and response with the prayer after them—that is, the *Angelus* as it is found in prayer-books; or, secondly, to recite in place of it the *Regina Cœli*, with its versicle, response, and prayer, in its proper season; or, thirdly, for those who do not know these by heart and cannot read, to recite five "Hail Marys"—one of which devotions must be performed in the morning, about midday, or in the evening. The obligations of reciting at the sound of the bell and of kneeling are not essential when the fulfilment of them is prevented by any reasonable cause.

Instances might be given of the devotion of the saints to the *Angelus*, such as that of St. Charles Borromeo, who, though a cardinal, was accustomed to alight from his carriage at the sound of the bell, and kneel on the street, or wherever he chanced to be, to recite it. St. Francis of Sales had the same devotion. But examples are not necessary. What has been said with regard to the devotion will, it is believed, be sufficient to stimulate the zeal and piety of the reader to a higher appreciation and a more careful practice of this excellent devotion.

[1] *The Pastor*, vol. iii. pp. 13, 14.

XIV.—THE MIRACULOUS MEDAL.

THERE is no Christian amulet so generally worn by all ages, classes, and conditions as the Miraculous Medal of the Blessed Virgin Mary. So well known is it and so universally worn that it is called by excellence *the medal;* and it is difficult to find any man, woman, or child who lays any claim to leading a good Christian life that does not wear it. There are many other medals approved and blessed by the Church, the efficacy of which has been frequently attested by the supernatural favors they have obtained for those who wear them in the spirit of faith; but there is none to compare with this little symbol of our confidence in our Immaculate Mother.

Much of what appears in this essay is taken from the excellent work of the Abbé Aladel, C. M., "The Miraculous Medal." This pious and learned religious was for many years the spiritual director of the favored soul through whom it pleased the Mother of mercy to bestow so signal a favor upon her children; and it was at his command tnat she reluctantly committed to writing an account of the visions accorded her regarding the Miraculous Medal. It will, then, be of interest to cast a hasty glance at the life of this favored servant of Mary.

Zoe Labouré, for such was her name in the world, was born May 2, 1806, in a village of the Cote-d'Or Mountains, called Fain-les Moutièrs, of the parish of Moutièrs-Saint-Jean, France. The locality was rendered holy by the presence and labors at an earlier day of such eminent servants of God as SS. Bernard, Vincent of Paul, and Jane Frances de Chantal. Zoe's parents were a pious rural couple of limited means; and her mother died when she was but eight years of age. But holy souls were not wanting to continue the good work which her mother had begun in her Christian training; and God soon began to give unmistakable proofs that even in childhood she was one of His favored children. At an early age she began to be favored with supernatural visions, among which was, several times, that of a venerable man, whom her confessor told her was doubtless St. Vincent of Paul, who wanted her to become a Daughter of Charity. After persevering prayer and careful examination, she followed this advice, and the event proved that her confessor had been enlightened from on high. Zoe became a postulant in the house of the Sisters at Chatillon, a town of France, about a hundred miles south-east of Paris, in the beginning of the year 1830. Her visions continued; and in January, 1831, she was clothed with the habit of religion under the name of Sister Catharine. She was characterized by her superiors as a person of a somewhat reserved, but calm, positive character, cold, and even pathetic. After having been for more than forty-five years a favored child of Mary and a shining example of every virtue for her companions, she closed her mortal career on the last day of the year 1876, in the House of Providence, near the spot where she had spent her life in religion. Such, then, was the person whom it pleased God and Our Lady to make the instrument of the divine mercy in giving to the faithful on earth the Miraculous Medal. Let us pause and examine into the circumstances attending this important event, and the spread of the devotion to which it immediately gave rise.

Sister Catharine was favored with many visions, but the one with which we are principally concerned took place November 27, 1830. It was not, however, till 1856 that, at the command of her spiritual director, the Abbé Aladel, she committed the account of it to writing. Again, in 1876, a short time before her death, she wrote another account of it. A third copy, without a date, was found among her papers after her death, that was probably only a draft from which one of the other copies had been made.

The circumstances which led immediately to the vision in which the medal was shown were these: Sister Catharine, having been favored with so many celestial visions, ardently desired to see the Blessed Virgin herself, whose voice, it would seem, she had frequently heard; and with the childlike simplicity so much insisted on by our divine Saviour, and so distinguishing a feature of the true servants of God, she prayed long and devoutly for this favor. On July 18, 1830, the feast of St. Vincent of Paul, the directress of the novices gave a very touching instruction on devotion to the saints, which affected Sister Catharine very much and increased her desire to look upon the Queen of saints. That night about half-past eleven o'clock she heard her name distinctly called three times, and looking out through the curtains she saw a child of ravishing beauty, and apparently about three or four years of age, who said to her: "Come to the chapel, where the Blessed Virgin awaits you." Accompanied by the child, whom she confidently believed to be her guardian angel, she obeyed, and soon after entering the chapel the holy Mother of God appeared, and spoke of the trials which were in store for the Sister and which were to befall the Church. Some of these she described in detail, while the tears flowed from her eyes, and she appeared very sad. At the conclusion of this vision her celestial companion conducted Sister Catharine back to her place in the convent. This was but the preparation for the more important manifestation that was to be made to her.

In the month of November Sister Catharine communicated to her spiritual director an account of another vision with which she had been favored, and which he related to the Promoter of the diocese, February 16, 1836, in these words: "At half-past five in the evening, while the Sisters were in the chapel making their meditation, the Blessed Virgin appeared to a young Sister as if in an oval picture; she was standing on a globe, only half of which was visible; she was clothed in a white robe and a mantle of shining blue, having her hands covered, as it were, with diamonds, whence emanated luminous rays falling upon the earth, but more abundantly upon one part of it. A voice seemed to say: 'These rays are symbolic of the graces Mary obtains for men, and the point upon which they fall most abundantly is France.' Around the picture, written in golden letters, were these words: 'O Mary! conceived without sin, pray for us who have recourse to thee!' This prayer, traced in a semicircle, began at the Blessed Virgin's right hand, and, passing over her head, terminated at her left hand. The reverse of the picture bore the letter "M" surmounted by a cross, having a bar at its base, and beneath the monogram of Mary were the hearts of Jesus and Mary, the first surrounded with a crown of thorns, the other transpierced with a sword. Then she seemed to hear these words: 'A medal must be struck upon this model; those who wear it indulgenced, and repeat this prayer with devotion, will be in a special manner under the protection of the Mother of God.' At that instant the vision disappeared." [1]

According to the testimony of Sister Catharine this

[1] "The Miraculous Medal," pp. 57, 58.

vision appeared several times in the course of a few months. Her own account of what may be called the final vision, which resulted in the striking of the medal as we now have it, will be of special interest. It is related in the following words, and the length of the quotation will be more than compensated for by the importance of the subject. The Sister writes: "The 27th of November, 1830, which was a Saturday, and the eve of the first Sunday in Advent, while making my meditation in profound silence, at half-past five in the evening, I seemed to hear on the right-hand side of the sanctuary something like the rustling of a silk dress, and, glancing in that direction, I perceived the Blessed Virgin standing near St. Joseph's picture; her height was medium, and her countenance so beautiful that it would be impossible for me to describe it. She was standing, clothed in a robe the color of auroral light, the style that is usually called *à la vierge*—that is, high neck and plain sleeves. Her head was covered with a white veil, which descended on each side to her feet. Her hair was smooth on the forehead, and above was a coil ornamented with a little lace and fitting close to the head. Her face was only partially covered, and her feet rested on a globe, or rather a hemisphere (at least I saw but half a globe). Her hands were raised about as high as her waist, and she held in a graceful attitude another globe (a figure of the universe). Her eyes were lifted up to heaven, and her countenance was radiant as she offered the globe to Our Lord. Suddenly her fingers were filled with rings and most beautiful precious stones; the rays gleaming forth and reflecting on all sides enveloped her in such dazzling light that I could see neither her feet nor her robe. The stones were of different sizes, and the rays emanating from them were more or less brilliant in proportion to the size. I could not express what I felt, nor what I learned in these few moments.

"While occupied in contemplating this vision, the Blessed Virgin cast her eyes upon me, and a voice said in the depths of my heart: 'The globe that you see represents the entire world, and particularly France, and each person in particular.' . . . And the Blessed Virgin added: 'Behold the symbol of the graces I shed upon those who ask me for them,' thus making me understand how generous she is to all who implore her intercession. . . .

"There now formed around the Blessed Virgin a frame slightly oval, upon which appeared, in golden letters, these words: 'O Mary! conceived without sin, pray for us who have recourse to thee!' Then I heard a voice which said: 'Have a medal struck upon this model; persons who wear it indulgenced will receive many graces, especially if they wear it around the neck; graces will be abundantly bestowed upon those who have confidence.' 'Suddenly,' says the Sister, 'the picture seemed to turn,' and she saw the reverse, such as has already been described." [1]

Although the twelve stars surrounding the monogram and the two hearts are not mentioned in the Sister's notes, it would appear certain that she spoke of them at the time she related the vision; otherwise they would hardly have been added.

It is only proper to state that there are certain discrepancies between the accounts of the vision as given by Sister Catharine and her spiritual director; but these are only regarding minor details, and do not affect the narrative as a whole.

The Abbé Aladel was very slow to credit the Sister's

[1] "The Miraculous Medal," pp. 57-60.

accounts of her visions, and told her to pay no attention to them, but to dismiss them from her mind. But the Blessed Virgin, in the goodness of her tender heart, was resolved to afford her faithful servants on earth another proof of her maternal care and protection, and to make this humble religious the instrument of her mercy. So, in the month of December of the same year, she favored the Sister with another vision. "But," says the Abbé Aladel, "there was a striking difference between this and the previous one; the Blessed Virgin, instead of stopping at St. Joseph's picture, passed on, and rested above the tabernacle, a little behind. . . . The Blessed Virgin appeared to be about forty years of age, according to the Sister's judgment. The apparition was, as it were, framed from the hands in the invocation: 'O Mary! conceived without sin, pray for us who have recourse to thee! traced in golden letters. The reverse presented the monogram of the Blessed Virgin, surmounted by a cross, and beneath were the divine hearts of Jesus and Mary. Sister Labouré was again directed to have the medal struck upon this model. She terminates her account in these words:

"To tell you what I understood at the moment that the Blessed Virgin offered the globe to Our Lord would be impossible, or what my feelings were while gazing on her. A voice in the depths of my heart said to me: 'These graces are symbolic of the graces the Blessed Virgin obtains for those who ask for them.'" When Sister Labouré related the third apparition of the medal, M. Aladel asked her if she had seen anything written on the reverse. The Sister answered that she had not. The father then told her to ask the Blessed Virgin what should be put there. The Sister obeyed, and, after persevering prayer, she was told one day at meditation that "M" and the two hearts expressed enough.¹

None of the accounts of the apparition mentions the serpent under the feet of the Blessed Virgin; and the Sister, being asked in confidence by her superior, long after Father Aladel had passed to his reward, about it, said that there was a serpent of a greenish color, with yellow spots. She remarked at the same time that the globe in the hands of the Mother of God was surmounted by a little cross.

Two years after the apparition of the Blessed Virgin to Sister Catharine, Mgr. de Quélen, Archbishop of Paris, had the medal struck, and with this important event dates the beginning of the extraordinary devotion that has since been paid to it. It is not necessary to remark on the rapid spread of this devotion among all classes of Christians, first in France and then in other countries, nor upon the many well-authenticated supernatural favors with which God Himself has attested the efficacy of the Miraculous Medal. The smallness of its size and the manner in which it is worn place it in the power of everyone to keep a medal about him, and to have a share in the protection of which the holy Mother of God makes it the instrument.

Such, then, was the origin of the Miraculous Medal. At first it was received with mistrust by the Sister's spiritual director, as spiritual directors are always accustomed to receive such communications; and when the account was narrated to the Archbishop of Paris, the same and even greater precautions were observed; for the hierarchy of the Church are not so precipitate nor so enthusiastic in matters of this kind as our ill-informed

¹ "The Miraculous Medal," pp. 63, 64.

separated brethren would fain have the world believe. They well know that if these things are from God He will, in His own good time and way, give unmistakable evidence of His divine approval, and if not, He will ere long doom them to an eternal oblivion. Hence the ecclesiastical authorities know they can leave all to the workings of His providence, and await the result. That there have been delusions in matters of this kind no one will deny; but that all such manifestations are not delusions is equally certain. Matters of this kind must stand or fall by the ordinary laws of evidence ; and it is as great a folly to reject all evidence as it is to accept all evidence.

The indulgences attached to the Miraculous Medal are those known as the Papal or Apostolic indulgences, mentioned in the *Raccolta*, pp. 444-450.

XV.—THE LITTLE OFFICE OF THE BLESSED VIRGIN MARY.

THE Little Office of the Blessed Virgin is based on the Divine Office, which the reverend clergy and some religious Orders are bound to recite daily; and an acquaintance with the latter will throw considerable light on the former.[1] The compilation of the Little Office has been attributed to St. Peter Damian; but Cardinal Bona, a very reliable authority on the subject, holds that it existed in the beginning of the eighth century, and that St. Peter Damian only restored its use. The Council of Clermont, held under Pope Urban II. in 1096, made the recitation of the Little Office obligatory on the clergy; but secular priests have been freed from that obligation by the bull of Pope St. Pius V., *Quod a Nobis*, of July 9, 1568. It is not the intention to speak in this essay of the obligation of those who are bound by rule to the recitation of the Little Office,—their several constitutions regulate that matter for them,—but only of what is required of those who recite the Office out of devotion. While the latter do not sin in omitting it, or any part of it, they may sustain spiritual loss in not complying with all that the Church requires in its recitation.

With regard to the language in which the Little Office is to be recited, we must distinguish between the general law of the Church and the special indults that have been granted by the Holy See to certain places or religious communities. This question is one of considerable importance, inasmuch as it affects the indulgences granted

[1] See "The Treasures of the Breviary," pp. 47 *et seq.*

to the recitation. After much discussion on both sides,[1] it has been finally settled by a decision of the Sacred Congregation of Rites of September 13, 1888, in reply to two doubts proposed to that learned body. The first of these was whether the faithful reciting the Little Office in the vernacular gain the indulgences granted by the Sovereign Pontiffs, especially by the decrees of April 30, 1852, and December 29, 1864, provided the translation has the approbation of the ordinary of the diocese. And the second doubt was that, in case the first were answered in the negative, would it be advisable to have these indulgences extended to the recitation of the Office in the vernacular. Both questions were answered in the negative. This settles the matter, and renders it certain that the indulgences granted to the Little Office can be gained by those only who recite it in Latin.

We are here reminded of the importance which many of the saints, and notably St. Francis of Sales, attached to the recitation of prayers in the liturgical language of the Church. Only a special indult from the Holy See can secure the indulgences in any other than the language of the Church, which is equivalent to saying that the Church desires all her liturgical prayers to be recited in her liturgical language--the Latin. Such indults have been seldom granted, and only two have come under my notice. A custom existed in Chili, and probably still exists, of reciting the Little Office in Spanish, the language of the country; and the bishop of the diocese of the Immaculate Conception presented certain doubts to the Sacred Congregation of Rites, because books containing the Office in Spanish were printed and in use among the people, and others were offered for sale. For these

[1] See *The Pastor*, vol. vi. pp. 307-313, for a summary of this discussion.

The Little Office of the Blessed Virgin Mary. 187

reasons he asked to know whether the Spanish Offices could be used without losing the indulgences. The reply of the Sacred Congregation, dated August 20, 1870, was that the custom could be tolerated, provided the bishop saw that the Office in Latin was printed on parallel columns with the Spanish. The question regarded the tertiaries ; and it was further asked whether they would sin by reciting the Office in the vernacular, since they were bound to the recitation. Again, a Redemptorist Father in Belgium, the better to encourage devotion to the Blessed Virgin, had the Little Office translated into French, and printed side by side with the Latin text. But, having some doubt as to the licitness of his action, he had recourse to the Sacred Congregation of Rites for advice in the matter. That august body referred the question back to the bishop, by a decree of September 4, 1875, charging his conscience with seeing that the Office was that approved by the Church, on which condition the book was permitted to be printed and used.

The rubrics, or rules, for the recitation of the Little Office do not state definitely at what precise hours the different parts are to be said ; but we can learn this from analogy, by examining the rules laid down for the recitation of the Divine Office ; for the Little Office, which does not bind under pain of sin, cannot have a stricter law for its recitation than the Divine Office, which does bind under pain of sin, and of mortal sin. And the several Papal decrees granting indulgences to the recitation of the Little Office have added no new obligations regarding its recital. The different times at which the Divine Office was formerly recited, and is yet by those who are bound to its recitation in choir, have given names to the several parts, or "hours," as they are called ; but this imposes no obligation as to time on those who say the Office out of choir, whether they are bound to its recitation or not. The Divine Office must be recited every day by those on whom that obligation is binding ; and this day is calculated mathematically—that is, exactly from midnight to midnight, with the privilege of anticipating Matins and Lauds the previous afternoon or evening, beginning at any time after half the time has elapsed between midday and sunset. But the bishops of this and some other countries have faculties for granting permission to those who are bound to the recitation of the Office to begin Matins and Lauds at two o'clock in the afternoon. Hence the same can be done by those who are bound to the recitation of the Little Office ; and if by those upon whom it is an obligation, much more by those who recite it out of devotion. As to the recitation of the rest of the Divine Office, St. Liguori says—and all theologians agree with him—that the Little Hours of Prime, Tierce, Sext, and None may be recited at any time in the forenoon, and Vespers and Complin any time after midday. Anyone who finishes the recitation of the Office before midnight does not sin ; and anyone who says the Office at any time within the twenty-four hours, with the additional privilege of anticipating Matins and Lauds the previous evening, even though he anticipates or postpones the hours without any reason whatever, commits no more than a venial sin, no matter how early or how late the recitation may be ; and he is not bound to repeat any part. Hence if a person were to rise at midnight and recite the whole Office, including Complin, without any reason, he would be guilty of only a venial sin ; and if he had any valid reason for doing so, he would commit no fault whatever. On this point St. Liguori says that, in order to recite the Office earlier or later than the times indicated by the names of the several hours, any cause of either utility or propriety will suffice—*sufficit quævis causa utilis vel honesta*. What is true of the Divine Office is, for a greater reason, true of the Little Office, when said out of devotion. It is superfluous, however, to say that, inasmuch as the Church has appointed particular times for the recitation of the Office for those who are bound to it, it is desirable, though not of obligation, for all who say it to conform as near as may be to that order.

Inasmuch as God is everywhere, any place or posture that is proper or becoming for the recitation of other prayers will suffice also for the Little Office, though it is needless to remark that some places and postures are more becoming than others, and less exposed to distractions. On these points the general good sense of pious Christians will serve as a safe enough guide.

Attention is required for the performance of every human act, and this is more especially true of such as have an immediate relation to the supernatural. This attention is manifestly of two kinds: external and internal. External attention consists, as is self-evident, in avoiding whatever might interfere with the pious exercise on hand, as talking, writing, etc. Internal attention is threefold: *spiritual*, by which the mind is directed to God as the end and object of all adoration and praise; *literal*, which consists in fixing the mind on the meaning of the words read; and *material*, which regards the mere correct pronunciation of the words. Any of these forms of attention will suffice for the fulfilment of the obligation of reciting the Office; but spiritual attention, for obvious reasons, is the most perfect and the most to be desired.[1]

Although in the recitation of the Little Office the

[1] Konings, "Theologia Moralis," N. 1126.

several parts or "hours" should follow one another in the order in which they are placed, this is not essentially necessary for the fulfilment of the obligation of reciting it; and any reasonable cause will justify an inversion of the order. For example, a person has not the office-book at hand, and knows certain parts by heart; or he is asked by another to recite it with him, and begin at an hour which he has not yet reached. Even if the order were inverted without any reason, a person would not be bound to repeat any part of the Office, though he were obliged to its recitation.

With regard to the interruptions permitted in the recitation of the Little Office, the rule holds good which is laid down for the Divine Office. Any reasonable cause—advantage to self or others which cannot conveniently be deferred to another time; civility, charity, making a note of anything that might be on the mind and that might otherwise be forgotten, making ejaculations—though not a meditation and the like—suffices. A person is not bound to repeat any part of the Office he has gone over, no matter where he interrupts it, if the sense be complete.[1] Hence he may interrupt it in the middle of a psalm or a lesson. But since these are short in the Little Office, it is better to begin them again. Persons should be careful to avoid scruples in this matter, as those who laid down these rules understood their responsibility, and the rules can be followed with absolute safety.

It remains to speak of the indulgences granted to the recitation of the Little Office. I shall premise by saying that these indulgences are granted only to the recitation of the Office in Latin, and as it is found in the Roman Breviary, unless there is a special indult from

---

[1] Konings, "Theol. Mor.," NN., 1118 et 1122.

the Holy See.¹ And though an Office should be modelled after that in the Breviary, and approved by the bishop of the diocese where it is recited, the indulgences are not attached to it.² The following are the indulgences with the conditions that have not been already mentioned. Pope St. Pius V., by a bull of July 9, 1568, granted to all the faithful who are bound to the recitation of the Little Office, on the days prescribed by the rubrics of the Roman Breviary, provided they say it with devotion, an indulgence of one hundred days. The same Pontiff, by a bull of April 5, 1571, granted to all who shall say this Office through devotion an indulgence of fifty days; and to those who shall say any prayers contained in the same Office, with devotion, an indulgence of fifteen days.³

In order to still further increase devotion to the holy Mother of God, His Holiness Pope Leo XIII., by a decree dated November 17, 1887, granted to all the faithful of both sexes, who shall have recited the Little Office —with only one nocturn in Matins, and the rest complete—for an entire month, a plenary indulgence, to be gained on any day of the month which each person may select, provided that, being truly penitent, he shall on that day go to confession and receive Holy Communion, and shall pray according to the intention of the Holy Father. And, secondly, he granted an indulgence of seven years and seven quarantines,⁴ to be gained once

---

¹ Beringer, "Die Ablässe" (the German Raccolta), p. 81.
² *Decreta Authentica S. Cong. Ind. et Rel.*, N. 367, ad 3.
³ *Raccolta*, N. 88.
⁴ The quarantines have reference to the Lenten fast. Accordingly, an indulgence of seven years and as many quarantines, for example, means the remission of a temporal penalty corresponding to seven years of canonical penances, joined to the special austerities of seven Lents.—Maurel, p. 52, note.

a day by all who shall, with at least contrite heart, recite the Little Office. Also an indulgence of three hundred days, to be gained once a day by all who shall, with the same pious dispositions, recite Matins and Lauds daily. These indulgences are granted in perpetuity, and are applicable to the souls in purgatory.[1]

[1] *The Pastor*, vol. vi. pp. 309, 310.

XVI.—THE LITANIES.

AFTER the holy Rosary, perhaps the most popular form of devotion, and the one best suited to an assembly of Christians, is the litanies, both on account of their intrinsic worth and because they arrest and secure the attention of those engaged in prayer much better than devotions that are performed alone or are led by one of a number. The word "litany" is of Greek origin, and signifies an humble supplication and devout or fervent prayer. But the term applies rather to each petition than to the form of prayer as a whole; and hence, we may remark, the word is always in the plural in the liturgical language of the Church, and not in the singular, as it is in English.

Ecclesiastical writers reckon four litanies: that of the Old Testament, that of All Saints, that of the Blessed Virgin, and that of the Holy Name of Jesus. And first of

THE LITANY OF THE OLD TESTAMENT.

From the beginning it was natural for man to invent terms of praise to express the admiration he had for those whom he regarded as great, or who had conferred any special favor upon him or his country or his fellow-men; and much more was it natural for him to invent terms of praise of God, whose mercies, like Himself, are infinite. And it is equally natural for man to make supplication in the time of need to those who he knows are able and willing to help him. What more natural, for example, than for the Jewish people to praise the heroic Judith, who slew the leader of their enemies at a critical period in their history, and to exclaim (Judith, xv. 10) in salutations suitable for a litany: "Thou art the glory of Jerusalem; thou art the joy of Israel; thou art the honor of our people!" If such praise was due to Judith for her successful efforts in promoting the temporal welfare of her people, much more must it be due to Mary and the saints, whose conquests were not only in the temporal order—for they were real benefactors of mankind—but also in the spiritual order, for the example, direction, and assistance of men, and the honor and glory of God. Again, Isaias (ix. 6), in the names which he gives the coming Messias, furnishes appellations suited for a litany; as, "His name shall be called Wonderful, Counsellor, God the Mighty, the Father of the world to come, the Prince of Peace."

But the most perfect example of a litany in the Old Law, and the one which is by excellence called the Litany of the Old Testament, is found in Psalm cxxxv. This psalm, which the Jews were accustomed to recite both in the public services of the temple and in their private devotions, recounts the divine attributes in twenty-seven verses, each concluding with the words—answered by the people: "For His mercy endureth forever."[1] There are several other less perfect forms of litanies to be found in different parts of the Old Testament.

In the Old Law religious writings were given with the divine sanction, and it was impossible for anything to be introduced into the services of religion except in proper form; but it is not precisely so in the New Law, although here also there is a proper restraint placed upon those who will submit themselves to its direction.

[1] Ferraris, "Verbum Litanjæ."

But the invention of printing has often aided the mistaken and imprudent zeal of not a few, who have multiplied litanies without end, and gained for many of them a place in the endless number and variety of prayer-books which flood the market. To restrain this pious weakness for manufacturing litanies — some of which were not even free from heresy — the Sacred Congregation of Rites issued a decree, March 31, 1821, strictly forbidding any additions to be made to the litanies approved by the Holy See, or the recitation of others in public that are not approved by the ordinary; and at the same time it enjoined on the bishops to devote particular attention to the enforcement of this decree. Other decrees of a similar tenor had been issued a century and a half before. The litanies approved by the Sacred Congregation for the public functions of the Church are the Litany of the Saints and that of the Blessed Virgin. Upon each of these, as well as upon that of the Holy Name of Jesus, remarks will be made.

THE LITANY OF THE SAINTS.

It is superfluous to observe that this litany derives its name from the fact that it is a form of prayer in which petitions are addressed to various members of all the orders of the blessed, asking their intercession with God for us. It is of great antiquity, but authors do not agree in fixing the date of its origin. Many authorities attribute it to Pope St. Gregory the Great, who ruled the Church at the end of the sixth century. But this is disputed, because a number of councils held before the time of that Pontiff make mention of both the Greater and the Lesser Litany (Ferraris). It is also maintained that it was in use in the East in the time of St. Basil the Great, and even in the days of St. Gregory Thaumaturgus, the latter of whom flourished about the middle of the third century. St. John Chrysostom also makes mention of it in one of his sermons. But this opinion is called in question, and apparently with good reason, on account of the well-known fact that the Orientals call any form of supplication a litany, as may be learned from their liturgies.

It is not strange, however, that this litany should have been attributed to St. Gregory, inasmuch as he had a great devotion to the saints, and had their litany chanted with special solemnity in the processions which he caused to be made through the streets of Rome on the occasion of the plague that raged there during his pontificate. After weighing the evidence, as far as we can secure it, on both sides, the only safe conclusion we can arrive at is that of Baronius, who admits, in his notes on the Roman Martyrology, that he is unable to determine by whom the litany was composed, but that it is of very great antiquity. It cannot, however, have been earlier than the fourth century, because no saints but martyrs were honored by the Church prior to that time; and it is a fact that no saints but martyrs are mentioned in the Canon of the Mass, which was brought to its present form by the labors of St. Gregory more than by those of any other person.

The Litany of the Saints is known in liturgical language as the Greater and the Lesser Litany. The former is chanted in the solemn procession on the feast of St. Mark, April 25; the latter on the Rogation Days. It is maintained by some writers that the Greater Litany derives its name from the fact that it was instituted by a Pope, while the other is called the Lesser from its being instituted by a bishop. But Ferraris holds that the former derives its name from the fact that the procession during which it is sung directs its course toward the Church of St. Mary Major; while the procession during the singing on the Rogation Days is directed toward other churches. Ferraris' opinion is more probably the correct one.

The Rogation Days derive their name from the Latin word *rogatio*, a petition—from the verb *rogo*, I ask, *rogare*, to ask, or petition. And their origin is this: Toward the close of the fifth century the diocese of Vienne, in France, was sorely afflicted with conflagrations, earthquakes, and ravages of wild beasts, and the terrified people were driven almost to despair. The bishop, Mamertus, had recourse to prayer, and instituted three days of penance immediately preceding the feast of the Ascension of Our Lord into heaven, in order to propitiate the divine goodness. And the better to insure the success of his petitions, he begged the intercession of all the blessed by means of their litany. Heaven deigned to hear his prayer; and soon other dioceses, first of his native land, and then of other countries, followed his example, till finally the Sovereign Pontiff, St. Leo III., established the Rogation Days in Rome, in the year 816.

The object of these days' devotions is to ask of God, from whom every good and perfect gift proceeds, that He would be pleased to give and preserve the fruits of the earth, and bestow upon His creatures all those temporal blessings that are necessary for them in the course of their mortal pilgrimage. Besides the actual graces received by the devotions of the Rogation Days, the fact itself of being reminded to have recourse to Almighty God for temporal blessings is of great advantage in this material age, when the all-sufficiency of man has become one of the leading dogmas of misguided persons.

Those who are bound to the recitation of the Divine Office are also bound to recite the Litany of the Saints, with the versicles, responses, and prayers, both on the feast of St. Mark and on the three Rogation Days. Formerly there was a similar obligation to recite the litany on all Fridays during the holy season of Lent; but that was removed by a bull of Pope St. Pius V., *Quod a Nobis*, so far as those are concerned who are not bound to the recitation of the Office in choir.

There is a short form of the litany given in the Roman Missal for the blessing of the baptismal font on Holy Saturday and the eve of Pentecost; but it is strictly forbidden to use this form on any other occasion.

There is no indulgence attached to the recitation of the Litany of the Saints.

THE LITANY OF THE BLESSED VIRGIN.

The sublime prophecy of the Blessed Virgin—one of the most beautiful in the Sacred Scriptures—"Behold, from henceforth all generations shall call me blessed," early began to find its fulfilment in the Church. It could not have been otherwise, considered even from a natural point of view; for the faithful who found in the Son the object of their supreme worship and deepest gratitude could not fail to honor the Mother through whose instrumentality that Son had been given to them. To these claims were added the many others, so to say, of her own which Mary had on them. These devout sentiments found their expression in numerous ejaculations, in seeing in Mary the fulfilment of many of the prophecies of the Old Testament, and discovering in the same sacred volume figures of her whom they loved so much. Mindful of their necessities, especially during

The Litanies.

the persecutions by which the early Church was so severely tried, they soon learned to weave these pious sentiments and expressions into a litany, with a petition for assistance after each, and the litany, substantially as we have it, was formed.

This litany is of the greatest antiquity, and antedates all others, even that of the Saints ; for, as we have said, it was not customary to honor any of the saints but martyrs before the fourth century. Quarti is of opinion that it was composed by the Apostles after the Assumption of the Blessed Virgin into heaven, the better to impress the people with a correct idea of her transcendent greatness, and to induce them to have more frequent recourse to her in their spiritual and temporal necessities. And he arrives at this conclusion from the fact that it is so ancient that no one can be named with certainty as its author. It has doubtless undergone slight changes ; and additional petitions have been placed in it, from time to time, in gratitude to Mary for having granted more than ordinary favors to her suppliants. A few of these will be mentioned, with the circumstances under which they were formed.

The title "Help of Christians" owes its origin to the victory which the Christians gained over the Turks, who were threatening to overrun Europe in the sixteenth century, but who met with a crushing defeat in the year 1572, through the intercession of the Blessed Virgin, in whose honor the Christian world recited the Rosary for the success of the Christian arms. That of "Queen of all saints" is due to the return of Pope Pius VII. to Rome after his long imprisonment in France, in May, 1814, in fulfilment of a vow he had made of placing a golden crown on the statue of Our Lady in the holy chapel of Loretto on the event of his release and return to his own dominions. He fulfilled this vow with great solemnity on the 13th of May of that year, and then saluted his holy protectress as Queen of all saints. The privilege of addressing Mary as " Queen conceived without original sin " was first granted to the Archdiocese of Mechlin, July 10, 1846, and to the United States, September 15th of the same year. It is now common throughout the Christian world, but there is no general decree on the matter.[1] It may not be generally known that the last title of the litany, " Queen of the most holy Rosary," was used two centuries ago. A decree of the Sacred Congregation of Rites dated July 13, 1675, permitted the members of the Confraternity of the Holy Rosary to address the Blessed Virgin by this title.[2] The recent act of the Holy See adding it to the Litany is dated December 10, 1883.

This litany is commonly called the Litany of Loretto because it is sung with great solemnity in the Holy House of Loretto every Saturday—the house in which the great mystery of the Incarnation actually took place, and in which the Blessed Virgin spent the greater part of her holy life.

The various ways of reciting the litany make it pertinent to inquire : What, precisely, is essential in order to secure the indulgences granted by the Holy See ? Some persons are accustomed to begin it with the prayer, " We fly to thy patronage," etc., and end it with a versicle, response, and prayer. This form is found in many prayer-books. Is it necessary ? The most reliable source of information to be had on the point is the *Raccolta*. In the last edition of that work the litany begins with " Lord, have mercy on us," and concludes

---

[1] Schneider's "Maurel," pp. 189, 190.
[2] Ibid.

The Litanies. 201

with the third *Agnus Dei*. Hence this is all that is required to gain the indulgences. But if pious persons want to add a prayer, what prayer should it be? The most common, perhaps, is "Pour forth," etc. This, however, is not the proper one, as we learn by consulting the Typical Edition of the Roman Ritual—a work which is specially approved as the liturgical standard, in its line, by the Sacred Congregation of Rites. There, instead of the above prayer, we find the versicle and response: "Pray for us, O holy Mother of God. That we may be worthy of the promises of Christ. Let us pray. Grant, we beseech Thee, O Lord, that we, Thy servants, may rejoice in continual health of mind and body; and, through the glorious intercession of Blessed Mary ever virgin, be freed from present sorrow, and enjoy eternal gladness, through Christ Our Lord. Amen."

The following are the indulgences granted for the recitation of the litany, as taken from the *Raccolta:* Two hundred days, once a day, granted by Sixtus V. and Benedict XIII.; three hundred days every time, granted by Pius VII.; and to all those who recite it once a day, a plenary indulgence on the five feasts of obligation[1] of the Blessed Virgin—that is, the Immaculate Conception, the Nativity, the Annunciation, the Purification, and the Assumption—on the condition of confession, Communion, visiting a church, and praying according to the intention of the Holy Father.

THE LITANY OF THE HOLY NAME OF JESUS.

This litany is so called because it contains expressions in praise of the various attributes of our holy Redeemer, after each of which His divine Name is invoked. I have

---

[1] Some of these feasts are not of obligation everywhere.

not been able to ascertain anything positive regarding the authorship of this litany, but it is certainly not of so great antiquity as either of the others we have been considering. A more interesting question, however, is that of its approbation by the Holy See. This was long a point upon which there existed great diversity of opinion among authorities; and although it is now settled, a review of the discussion may not be uninteresting.

The Constitution *Sanctissimus*, issued by Pope Clement VIII., September 6, 1601, forbids the recitation in churches, oratories, and processions of any other litanies than those of the Saints and the Blessed Virgin, without the approbation of the Sacred Congregation of Rites. Ferraris, however, maintains that this litany is exempt from that regulation, because it was enriched by Sixtus V. with an indulgence of three hundred days, at the instance of the Discalced Carmelites. But this argument is not conclusive, because the decree of Clement VIII. is of later date than the alleged grant of Sixtus V., and it makes no mention of the Litany of the Holy Name. In the seventeenth century a number of German princes and bishops petitioned the Holy See for the approval of this litany, on the ground that it was constantly recited, both in public and in private, by the faithful under their jurisdiction. The reply of the Sacred Congregation of Rites, April 14, 1646, was: "The aforesaid litany is to be approved, if His Holiness deem proper." It would appear, however, that the Sovereign Pontiff did not accede to their wishes; for when the same Sacred Congregation was asked, two centuries later, whether the litany was approved and enriched with indulgences, the reply, dated September 7, 1850, was "No" to both questions.[1] (By a decree of

[1] Schneider's "Maurel" pp. 159, 160.

Sixtus V., dated January 22, 1585, the jurisdiction of the Sacred Congregation of Rites is restricted to public functions and ceremonies.) But in some other places as well as in Germany the decree regarding this litany was not always complied with, and it was recited both in public and in private.

On the occasion of the canonization of the Japanese martyrs in 1862, a large number of the bishops present petitioned the Holy See for the approval of the Litany of the Holy Name of Jesus and its enrichment with indulgences; and the Sovereign Pontiff so far acceded to their request as to grant an indulgence of three hundred days to the faithful of all those dioceses whose bishops should make that request of him. Finally, his present Holiness, by a decree of the Sacred Congregation of Indulgences dated January 16, 1886, granted an indulgence of three hundred days, to be gained once a day by all the faithful of the Christian world, on the usual conditions of a partial indulgence.[1] But it does not appear that any decree has been issued permitting its recitation in any of the public functions of religion.

We have next to inquire: What, precisely, constitutes the Litany of the Holy Name of Jesus and is necessary to be said in order to gain the indulgences? This litany differs from that of the Blessed Virgin in requiring the recitation of a versicle and response, with two prayers, after it. Beginning with "Lord, have mercy on us," it closes with the versicle and response, "Jesus, hear us. Jesus, graciously hear us. Let us pray. O Lord Jesus Christ, who hast said: Ask, and you shall receive; seek, and you shall find; knock, and it shall be opened unto you: grant, we beseech Thee, unto us who ask, the gift of Thy most divine love; that we may ever love Thee

---

[1] Beringer, "Die Ablässe," pp. 141-143.

with our whole hearts, and in all our words and actions, and never cease from showing forth Thy praise.

"Make us, O Lord, to have a perpetual fear and love of Thy holy Name; for Thou never failest to govern those whom Thou dost establish in Thy love. Who livest," etc.[1]

Although this essay may appear dry to some readers, the frequency with which the litanies here treated of are recited, and the importance which the Church, especially at present, attaches to indulgences, make it not only a matter of instruction, but also one of spiritual interest to Christians, to be acquainted with what is essentially necessary for them to do in order that they may secure those spiritual favors; while the history of the origin and development of the litanies can hardly be regarded as a matter of indifference.

[1] "Rituale Romanum," Editio Typica: Beringer.

XVII.—THE PASCHAL CANDLE.

THE origin of the custom of making and blessing the Paschal Candle has not been ascertained with certainty either as to time or place. It has been attributed by some writers to Pope St. Zosimus, who ascended the throne of Peter in the year 417.; but it seems more probable that the rite had been introduced before his time, at least in the greater basilicas. It is not mentioned of this Pope that he *instituted* the ceremony, but only that he permitted the Paschal Candle to be blessed in the parish churches. What still more pleads, says Cardinal Wiseman, for the antiquity of this rite is the existence of it in distinct churches, and some of these in the East; for St. Gregory Nazianzen, who was a contemporary of St. Zosimus, mentions it, as do other Fathers also. I think it may then be said to have been in general use early in the fifth century.

Some of the Paschal Candles were very large, weighing thirty, fifty, and even a hundred pounds. A favorite weight in many churches was thirty-three pounds, in honor of the thirty-three years of the life of our divine Lord upon earth, whose pure body the virginal whiteness of the wax aptly typifies. In early times the offices of the entire year, which began with Easter, were inscribed on the Paschal Candle. Later, as their number increased, they were written on a parchment, and attached to it, sometimes by means of one of the grains of incense, to be noticed later on. This custom continued in certain dioceses of France as late as the middle of the last century. But with the multiplication of feasts the practice became impossible, and with the invention of printing, unnecessary. The candle was also frequently decorated with flowers, or, as is still done, with designs in wax or other material ; and it had openings for the five grains of incense.

Before the beginning of the fifth century Mass was not celebrated during the day on Holy Saturday ; the offices did not begin before the hour of *none*, or three o'clock in the afternoon ; and the people kept vigil in the churches till midnight, when Mass was celebrated. This custom continued till the latter part of the Middle Ages ; and it accounts for the frequent reference to night both in the blessing of the Paschal Candle and in the Preface and Canon of the Mass of Holy Saturday. It served also to impart a more striking significance to the candle, which shed its light in the natural darkness, and symbolized more perfectly than at present the risen Saviour as the light of the world. It served better to explain, too, the joyous character of the Mass of Holy Saturday, which was then, in point of time as well as in tenor, a more perfect anticipation of the glories of Easter than now ; since the Mass came nearer to the joys of Easter morn than to the dolorous scenes of Good Friday afternoon.

The custom of celebrating Mass on Holy Saturday night is found to have existed as early as the time of Tertullian, that is, at the close of the second century ; and it is, besides, spoken of by that writer as something common and well known, and not as a ceremony but lately introduced. St. Jerome attributes the keeping of the vigil of Easter to apostolic tradition. But about the middle of the twelfth century, as we are informed by Hugh of St. Victor, a custom began to be introduced of anticipating the offices, although it did not become general for some three centuries at least, and vestiges of the old custom were found still later.

No little diversity of opinion exists with regard to the authorship of the *Exultet*, chanted for the blessing of the Paschal Candle. Says Father O'Brien, in his "History of the Mass": "It is almost universally admitted that the composition of this is the work of St. Augustine, but that the chant itself is Ambrosian." Cardinal Wiseman is more probably correct when he states that "the beautiful prayer in which the consecration or blessing of the Paschal Candle takes place has been attributed to several ancient Fathers: by Martene, with some degree of probability, to the great St. Augustine, who very likely only expressed better what the prayers before his time declared." And he continues: "It very beautifully joins the twofold object of the institution. For while it prays that this candle may continue burning through the night to dispel the darkness, it speaks of it as a symbol of the fiery pillar which led the Israelites from Egypt, and of Christ, the ever true and never failing light." The chant is said to be the only specimen of the pure Ambrosian found at present in the liturgy of the Church.

I shall not pause to speak of the ceremony of the blessing of the new fire, the five grains of incense, or the lighting of the candle, and from it the lamps. We are familiar with these, and they are sufficiently explained in the missal and the ceremonial. But it is worthy of remark that it is the deacon and not the priest —or, in smaller churches, the celebrant as deacon and not as priest—who blesses the Paschal Candle, to signify that not to the apostles but to others was entrusted the privilege of preparing the dead body of Our Saviour— which the candle not as yet lighted typifies—for the holy sepulchre. The five grains of incense, which are blessed to be inserted in the candle, represent by their number and arrangement the five wounds of our blessed Lord, which were inflicted before His death, but the cicatrices of which were retained by Him after His resurrection; and the material of these grains represents the spices with which His sacred body was prepared for the holy sepulchre. Hence they are put into the candle before it is lighted, and remain there afterward.

The manner in which the Church attaches mystic significations to many of her sacred rites and ceremonies naturally leads us to inquire still further into the symbolical meaning of the Paschal Candle; and we have the more reason to expect a mystic signification both from the time and the circumstances attending the blessing of the candle itself, and from the days on which it burns. In the first place, it represents our divine Redeemer Himself, dead, and then risen to a new life, to die no more, as the Apostle declares; for the candle is not at first lighted, but only after the performing of a part of the blessing. The grains of incense, too, are inserted in it before it is lighted, to represent the wounds which caused the death of the Saviour of the world. The virginal wax of the candle typifies His sacred body, while the flame and light show Him to be the Word of the Father, enlightening everyone that cometh into the world. Hence it burns on Sundays from Easter to the Ascension, Sunday being the day on which especially the Word is preached for the enlightenment of the people; but it is extinguished when Our Saviour leaves the earth and entrusts the diffusion of His light to the apostles. It also typifies, as we have seen, the cloud and the pillar by which the chosen people were guided in their wanderings, during forty years in the desert, on their way to the Promised Land.

During the blessing of the baptismal font the Paschal Candle, as representing Our Saviour, is thrice lowered into it, the celebrant praying meanwhile that the virtue of the Holy Ghost may descend into the sacred font and sanctify it, as He descended upon Our Lord when He was baptized in the Jordan, thereby imparting to water the power of cleansing from sin those to whom it is applied according to the institution of Christ.

Considerable diversity of opinion exists with regard to the times during which the Paschal Candle should be lighted. The following from De Herdt is perhaps as fair a summary of these opinions as can be had, and will serve all practical purposes. According to a decree of the Sacred Congregation of Rites, of May 19, 1607, it is to be lighted at the solemn Mass and Vespers of Easter Sunday and on the two following days; on Easter Saturday, and on all the Sundays to the Ascension, on which day it burns only to the end of the gospel, when it is finally extinguished. It is not to be lighted on other days or feasts celebrated within the Easter time, unless in churches where such a custom exists, which custom may be continued. According to the *Memoriale Rituum* of Benedict XIII., it is to be lighted also on the feasts of Our Lord, and on the feasts of precept of the saints occurring during the same season. Gavantus holds it to be a pious custom to light it during the entire octave of Easter. In the opinion of Merati it would be proper to have it burn on the feasts of the apostles, of the patron, titular, and of the dedication of the church occurring during Easter time; also on other feasts celebrated with solemnity; during the Masses, though not solemn, on Sundays; and during the celebration of solemn votives.

provided the color of the vestments is not violet. It is not to be lighted on the Rogation Days, according to the same authority. It is to be lighted for the blessing of the baptismal font on the eve of Pentecost. The custom most generally followed in this country, though by no means universal, is to have the Paschal Candle burn on Sundays during Easter time at all the Masses and at Vespers.

Another important question regarding the Paschal Candle is deserving of a few remarks. It is seldom or never entirely consumed; can it be blessed a second time? This is sometimes done after it has been scraped and cleansed from drippings so as to appear in some sort new. Is this in harmony with the rubrics and with their interpretation by the best authorities? De Herdt, who has summarized the authorities on this point, shall again answer. He says: "The candle must be new, or not blessed; or, if not new, must be entirely remoulded —*refectus;* and if not remoulded, other wax must be added, and this in greater quantity than the old wax, otherwise the axiom will hold: *Major pars trahit ad se minorem.*" It may be remarked, parenthetically, that sometimes the lower part of the Paschal Candle is a separate and heavily ornamented piece of wax, which serves as a sort of pedestal or candlestick. This may be used each year, provided it has not been blessed with the Paschal Candle proper during the ceremony of Holy Saturday. Discussing the opinions of those who hold that the same candle may be blessed more than once, De Herdt draws a distinction that is worthy of attention. He says the repetition of a blessing is permitted when the blessing is what is called *invocative*, by which blessing the divine protection merely is besought, as in the case of food, etc. But with regard to that form of blessing which is known as *constitutive*, by which the things blessed become holy in such a manner that they cannot afterward be devoted to profane uses, such as the blessing of a church, of sacerdotal vestments, *and beyond doubt, of the Paschal Candle,* so long as the articles retain their proper form—*quamdiu ipsæ res integræ existunt*—it cannot be repeated.

There is a relation between the Paschal Candle and the *Agnus Dei* which is deserving of notice. As has been said, it is seldom that the Paschal Candle is entirely consumed before the feast of the Ascension. It was not the custom in early times to remould the remnant of the candle left when it was finally extinguished, but the faithful were accustomed to procure small portions of it, and keep them in their homes as a sacred amulet to protect them against evils, especially against tempests. All authors agree that it was from this pious custom that the *Agnus Dei*, which is now almost universally worn by devout Christians, derives its origin.[1]

[1] See the following essay on the *Agnus Dei*.

XVIII.—THE AGNUS DEI.

There is in every rational creature an intuition of the supernatural. Different individuals or peoples manifest it in different ways, but all manifest it in some way. The polished Greek embodied it in an exquisite sculpture; the Egyptian, in a labyrinthian temple; the Druid discovered it in the forest; the Central African places it in a stick or a stone; and the American Indian who wants to shoot the rapids of the St. Lawrence in his frail bark canoe propitiates the manitou of the waters with a few leaves of the tobacco so dear to him. No man can entirely emancipate himself from the influence of this universal belief. The infidel and the scoffer at both pagan and Christian beliefs are not without their superstitions, their lucky and unlucky days, their propitious and unpropitious omens. Deny it as they may, they cannot even conceal the fact. The Christian is the only logical person among them; for he believes in a personal God, creating, preserving, and ruling the universe in its entirety and in all its minute details with a fatherly providence for the benefit of His rational creatures—alive to the wants of the least among them, and ever ready to turn a willing ear to their every petition.

Among the consequences of this intuition of the supernatural, in the different ages of the world, is the desire to propitiate the unseen power, whether good or evil, by the use of amulets or charms worn suspended from the neck or carried about the person, as a means of warding off danger, disease, and all influence of the evil principle, and invoking the aid of the good principle. Among pagans these amulets were fashioned into different forms. Sometimes they were little images of the pagan deities; sometimes they consisted of certain drugs or herbs; again they were certain letters of the alphabet arranged in an abracadabra; and not infrequently they were of a very objectionable character. The Romans, as every classic scholar is aware, hung about the neck of infants amulets of this kind with certain mythological significations, showing to which of the pagan deities the child was consecrated. On attaining the age of fifteen years he assumed the *toga virilis*, or garb of manhood, and consecrated his amulet to the *lares*, or household gods of the family. In no part of the world does this superstition appear to have had so deep a hold as among the Romans, and great difficulty was experienced by the early preachers of the gospel in withdrawing them from the use of these relics of paganism. It was not until the lapse of centuries that it was entirely eradicated, especially in the rural districts.

Christians, too, have their amulets—the crucifix, the scapular, blessed medals, the *Agnus Dei*, etc.—and these are with greater propriety called amulets, for they fulfil the meaning of the term, which, being derived from the Latin word *amolior*, means "I remove." According to this etymology, "an amulet is something worn to remove or ward off danger; and when the thing so worn has not of its own nature power to produce this effect, to use it, confiding in it alone, would be the sin of superstition. Thus, when the old pagans hung around their necks certain stones, metals, or bits of parchment, with mysterious signs and figures inscribed on them, and trusted in them for protection against disease and witchcraft, they only proved the stupid folly into which human nature left to itself is sure to run. . . . But the Christian does not, like the pagan, put his trust in them on account of any inherent virtue which he imagines them to have, nor does he look to the enemy of his soul for assistance. His hope is in the Living God, who, listening to the prayers of His beloved Spouse, the Catholic Church, blesses these material things, and bids His children keep them as memorials of Him—as tokens that His divine providence will ever shelter them beneath its protecting wing."[1]

The *Agnus Dei* is, then, no superstitious object, as some would fain have us believe, but one of those sacramentals by which the blessing of God is invoked upon those who wear it with proper dispositions, and one of those objects which the Church has successfully employed to abolish a real superstition. It is a remarkable fact that those claiming the name of Christians, who discard the pious articles blessed by the Catholic Church, not infrequently themselves fall into real, culpable, and foolish superstitions. A striking instance of this is furnished by Queen Elizabeth of England. In the thirteenth year of her reign it was enacted by Parliament that "if any person shall bring into the realm of England any token or tokens, thing or things, called or named by the name of *Agnus Dei* (which said *Agnus Dei* is used to be specially hallowed and consecrated, as it is termed, by the Bishop of Rome in his own person), and shall deliver the same to any subject, he shall incur the penalty of *Præmunire*."[2] After this it was hardly

---

[1] Barry, pp. 136, 137.

[2] This was a very severe punishment, entailing on the offender, in the words of Lord Coke, that he "shall be out of the king's protection, and his lands and tenements, goods and chattels, forfeited to

to be expected that the very sovereign who enacted such severe laws against "vain and superstitious things" should herself become guilty of gross superstition. But Parson says: "One of her privy councillors presented her with a piece of gold of the bigness of an angel,[1] dimly marked with some small characters, which he said an old woman in Wales bequeathed to her on her death-bed, telling her that the said old woman, by virtue of the same, lived to the age of one hundred and odd years, and could not die as long as she wore it upon her body; but being withered, and wanting nature to nourish her body, it was taken off, and she died. The queen, upon the confidence she had thereof, took the said gold, and wore it on her ruff."[2]

What, it may be asked, is the *Agnus Dei*, and why called by that name? It is scarcely necessary to say that *Agnus Dei* are Latin words signifying "Lamb of God." The *Agnus Dei* has a twofold signification, the first being that it represents the Lamb of God. All the ceremonies of the blessing of it point to this primary signification, as will appear later on. The reader of both the Old and the New Testament need not be told that the lamb was, in the ceremonial law and in the writings of the prophets, the symbol of Christ. Nor need he be referred to the numerous passages in which the long-expected Messias is compared in His meekness to the lamb. In the New Testament He is frequently referred to in the same manner, and is called by John the Baptist "the Lamb of God, who taketh away the sins of the world."[3] But why are these blessed objects

the king; and that his body shall remain in prison at the king's pleasure."

[1] An ancient gold coin of England, worth about ten shillings, and so named from the figure of an angel stamped upon it.

[2] "Discussions," pp. 217, 218. [3] St. John, i. 29.

named the lamb, and not rather the lion, for Christ is called the "Lion of the tribe of Juda"[1] And since they are to be a defence against our spiritual enemies, is it not strength, as typified by the lion, rather than gentleness, as symbolized by the lamb. that we should be endowed with? The reason for this name is found in the second signification of the *Agnus Dei*—its reference to the newly baptized. These, in the words of St. Paul, put on Jesus Christ, are incorporated into His mystical body, and become new lambs of His flock, and as such are bound to imitate His virtues. Now, it is a remarkable fact that, though Our Saviour illustrated every virtue in an infinitely perfect degree during His sojourn upon earth, there are but two which He bids us learn especially from Him. "Learn from Me that I am meek and humble of heart"—the characteristics of the lamb and not of the lion. In His triumph over the powers of darkness He is indeed the Lion of the tribe of Juda; but among His children, as their model, He is the meek Lamb; and, as lambs, they are to walk even as He walked. Hence the name *Agnus Dei*. The purity of their lives is typified by the immaculate whiteness of the wax; the meekness of their conduct by the figure of the lamb impressed upon it. Mystical writers deduce many other symbolical meanings from the part which the lamb played in the religious ceremonies of the Old Law; but they shall be passed over as not being intimately connected with our subject.

Great variety of opinion exists with regard to the origin of the *Agnus Dei* and the date of its introduction. Writers of the time of Charlemagne—that is, near the close of the eighth century—inform us that on the morning of Holy Saturday the archdeacon was accustomed

[1] Apocalypse. v. 5.

to pour melted wax into a vessel prepared for the purpose and mix it with oil. From this admixture he formed figures in the shape of lambs, which, after being blessed, were kept in a suitable place to await the concluding ceremony, which took place on Low Sunday. On that day the lambs, which must have been quite small, were given to the people to be used in fumigating their houses, or to be placed in the fields and vineyards as a protection against the machinations of the spirit of evil, and against danger from lightning and thunder. John Albert Widmanstadius, Jurisconsult and Chancellor of Eastern Austria under Frederic I., writes that when baptism was solemnly administered—which ceremony was performed by the bishop only—if any received this sacrament at Rome, it was the custom to give them, as a holy amulet, a wax seal stamped with the figure of a lamb bearing a banner, which had been immersed in water mingled with consecrated chrism, as a symbol of baptism. Although authors are not wanting who call this statement in question, it is accepted and defended by no less a scholar than Pope Benedict XIV., in his work on the canonization of saints. He proves, further, that the use of wax is of very great antiquity, and furnishes as an evidence the fact that in the year 1544 the tomb of Maria Augusta, wife of the Emperor Honorius, who died before the middle of the fourth century, was opened, and in it was found, besides a great variety of gems, etc., a wax *Agnus Dei*. That the latter was in use among Christians at that early day, the learned Pontiff asserts, is in harmony with the opinion of Cardinal Augustine Valerius, who refers the origin of blessing wax *Agnus Deis* to the beginning of the fifth century. Molanus quotes, without, however, approving, the opinion of those who are in favor of a still more remote antiquity, placing the origin of the *Agnus Dei* as early as the time of the Emperor Constantine, and, therefore, near the beginning of the fourth century. The discovery of the *Agnus Dei* in the tomb of the pious Empress Maria Augusta is the strongest evidence of the antiquity of its introduction among Christians. The annotator of Molanus, quoting from the *Cosmographie Universelle*, gives the following account of it: " Among other things was a *bulla*—one of those which at present are called *Agnus Deis*—around whose circumference was the inscription, ' *Maria Florentissima.*' " Two difficulties here present themselves, which have not escaped the attention of those who deny to the *Agnus Dei* so great an antiquity: namely, whether wax could be preserved for a thousand years; and whether this object was identical with the *Agnus Dei* now in use. Both sides of the question are, naturally, warmly disputed; and I shall not attempt to decide what others have found it impossible to settle.

Mabillon, while disputing the conclusions of those who argue from Prudentius that the custom of blessing the Paschal Candle existed in the fourth century, yet proves from Eunodius, a bishop who flourished before the year 520, that it certainly did exist at the beginning of the sixth century. The "Catholic Dictionary" places the beginning of the custom as early at least as the time of Pope Zosimus, who ascended the throne of Peter in the year 417. When the Paschal Candle was finally extinguished on Ascension Day, the people were accustomed, as we have seen, to procure small portions of what was left of it, and carry them home as a protection agains tempests. All authors are agreed that it was from this custom of the people that the *Agnus Dei* derived its origin. But Molanus still maintains that the custom of blessing the *Agnus Dei* cannot be proved to have existed prior to the eighth or ninth century. In a number of dioceses which he names, as well as in certain others, a custom existed, especially among the inhabitants of the rural districts, of taking portions of the candles blessed on the feast of the Purification of the Mother of God, forming them into crosses, and placing them in their homes, or at the tops of their chimneys (*externæ caminorum oræ*), as it were in the most conspicuous place of their houses. But, evidently, this could not have been prior to the time at which the blessing of candles on the feast of the Purification was introduced into the Church, a point which will be discussed in the next essay. Baronius, no mean authority, would give the *Agnus Dei* a still greater antiquity than any of the writers already quoted.

In such a diversity of opinion among the learned who have made this question a matter of careful study, it is impossible to arrive at any definite conclusion, except that the *Agnus Dei* is of very great antiquity; but of how great no one will ever be able to determine with any degree of certainty. Perhaps the conclusion arrived at by Maurel (p. 267) is as near the truth as we can hope at this distant day to come—that "it is spoken of in the Roman Ordo, which in the opinion of the learned is anterior to the eighth century." But setting these questions aside, it will be more instructive for us to turn to the manner in which the *Agnus Dei* is blessed and comes to us.

At the present day, and for some time past, the *Agnus Dei* is blessed only by the Pope. The ceremony takes place, according to Molanus, during Easter time, in the first year of the reign of the Sovereign Pontiff, and once every seven years thereafter. The "Catholic Dictionary" says the blessing is performed on the

Thursday of Easter week, while Barry will have it on Low Sunday. This last opinion is evidently erroneous, as will be seen from the ceremony of the distribution, which takes place on the Saturday before Low Sunday. The ceremony of the blessing is as follows: The Pope first blesses water, after which he pours balsam and oil into it, in the form of a cross. He then recites a number of prayers and blessings over the masses of wax fashioned into the form of lambs. This done, the wax images are carried on silver trays with great solemnity by the attendants to the Holy Father, who immerses them in the blessed water. The prelates who are in attendance on the occasion lift them out of the water, and, having dried them, put them in a place prepared for their reception, where they remain till the following Saturday. It may be remarked in passing that at first water only was used in the blessing of the *Agnus Dei*, but that afterward oil and balsam were added. It may also be noted that although the masses of wax are formed into lambs, these are not all of the same size; and, further, that certain inscriptions and the images of saints, as well as the figure of a lamb, are sometimes stamped on them.

On the Saturday of Easter week during the Mass of the Holy Father a subdeacon carries the *Agnus Deis* to the altar on a large silver tray, before the Pope's Communion, singing at the same time: "Holy Father, these are the young lambs which have announced to you Alleluia. Behold, they have just come from the fountains: They are filled with light, Alleluia"—words which evidently apply rather to the newly baptized than to the wax images. The Pope then distributes the *Agnus Deis*, with appropriate ceremony, during the singing of the *Agnus Dei* of the Mass—first to the cardinals, who on receiving them kiss his hand; next to the bishops, wearing their mitres, who kiss his right knee; and, finally, to the prothonotaries, who prostrate themselves and kiss the cross on his sandal. From the hands of these several persons the *Agnus Deis* find their way by subdivision and distribution to all parts of the world, where, with the care of pious persons, religious women for the most part, they are divided into small portions and encased in appropriate covers—generally in the form of a heart—for the use of the faithful.

After having learned something of the manner in which the *Agnus Dei* is blessed and reaches us, a very practical question is, What spiritual benefit may we expect to derive from the devout use of this holy amulet? But first it may be remarked, as to the manner of wearing it, that it differs from the scapular; for, while the latter must be worn so that one part hangs upon the breast and the other on the back, with one string passing over each shoulder, the latter may be worn attached to the scapular, or it may be carried in any other way about the person. The manner of wearing it is not prescribed as a condition for securing the benefits attached to it. This premised, it may be said that the benefits which the devout wearer of the *Agnus Dei* may expect to reap from it are well expressed in the prayers recited in the blessing which it receives at the hands of the Holy Father.

By these several benedictions the Church, the divinely appointed dispenser of the mysteries of God, causes inanimate objects to become vehicles for conveying graces and the divine protection to such of the faithful as use them with lively faith, ardent charity, and firm confidence in God; and not only so, but the divine mercy sometimes goes, if we may be allowed the expression, to extraordinary lengths, and by means of them bestows graces upon some persons who, to all human discernment, are manifestly unworthy of them, to convince us that the Spirit breathes where He will, and to encourage sinners to repentance. Few priests but have witnessed a greater or less number of these extraordinary manifestations of the divine mercy. And if this be true, as it certainly is, of a scapular or medal blessed by the simplest priest,—though he has received in his ordination the power that whatsoever he blesses shall be blessed, and whatsoever he sanctifies shall be sanctified,—much more should it be true of the *Agnus Dei*, which is blessed by him who is head of the Church, who sits on the throne of the Prince of the apostles, and has received from Jesus Christ, as His vicar upon earth, the plenitude of power for binding and loosing, for enacting laws and granting privileges.

In the *Agnus Dei*, as an object blessed by the Church, two things are to be considered: first, the power conferred on it as a sacramental, of being an instrument of grace; and secondly, the power it possesses of awakening in the persons who use it with the proper dispositions sentiments of faith, devotion, and confidence, so efficacious in calling down the blessings of heaven.

It is unnecessary to pause to dwell upon the numerous well-authenticated miracles that have been wrought by means of the *Agnus Dei;* for the devout Catholic is always prepared to expect and believe in such manifestations of the divine mercy, when they are for the honor and glory of God and the good of His creatures. It may be remarked, however, that there is no indulgence attached to the wearing of the *Agnus Dei;* and further, that the prayer to be said by those who wear it, found in some prayer-books, is not of obligation. The following is a brief and clear enumeration of the benefits to be derived from the use of this sacramental · "The Supreme Pontiff implores of God to bless, sanctify, and consecrate them in such a way that the faithful who, with a sincere and lively faith, piously use them may obtain the following graces : (1) That the sight or touch of the lamb impressed on these figures, exciting the hearts of the faithful to contemplate the mysteries of our redemption, may induce them to thank and bless and adore the divine goodness, and thus obtain for them pardon of their faults. (2) That the sign of the cross represented on these figures may remove evil spirits, hail, thunder-storms, and tempests. (3) That, through the efficacy of the divine blessing, they may escape the wiles and temptations of the dragon. (4) That women bearing children may be preserved from all harm, and favored with a happy delivery. (5) That pestilence, falling-sickness, water, or fire may have no power over them. (6) That both in prosperity and adversity these pious Christians may be fortified with the divine protection ; and that through the mysteries of the life and passion of Our Lord they may be preserved from a sudden and unprovided death, from every other danger, and from every evil. . . . When we are deprived of these blessings, we are to attribute the privation to our own want of faith and piety, or to some other latent cause, which prevents Our Saviour from enriching us with such extraordinary benefits."[1]

Barry (pp. 140-142) has the following very appropriate remarks on the pious sentiments with which the *Agnus Dei* should be worn : "The *Agnus Dei* represents Our Lord, and he who would wear it devoutly

[1] Maurel, pp. 268, 269.

must imitate Him in His lamblike virtues—meekness, innocence, and indifference to the world. . . . The meek Christian, and only he, has caught the devotion of the *Agnus Dei.* . . . Innocence—spotless purity of soul and body—is another virtue of the wearer of the *Agnus Dei.* Wax and the lamb have ever been the chosen emblems of the angelic virtue. When we touch or look at our holy amulet, let us remember that the breast on which it reposes must be sinless. And if the angel of Satan is hovering around us, striving to inflict the death-blow on our souls, let us press the *Agnus Dei* closer to our hearts, that it may be a sign to him that he has no power over us, as the blood of the paschal lamb on the doors of the Hebrews was a sign to the angel of the Lord. The third virtue which springs from a reverent use of the *Agnus Dei* is indifference to the world. The lamb is dumb before his shearer, teaching us silence when shorn of our fair name; it is shy of a stranger, that we may learn from it to be distrustful of the world and its vanities—that we journey on as strangers and pilgrims, till called to the marriage-feast of the Lamb in heaven. The *Agnus Dei* serves to call to our minds the promises of baptism. It represents the whiteness of our souls after being washed in the saving waters of regeneration." In allusion to this symbolism, the subdeacon who brings the *Agnus Deis* to the Pope for distribution calls them, as we have seen, young lambs just come from the fountains.

There are no decrees of the Roman Congregations with regard to the *Agnus Dei;* but there is one of Pope Gregory XIII. which prohibits all persons whatever, whether lay or cleric, secular or regular, under pain of excommunication, to be incurred by the very act, from painting, gilding, or in any way coloring the *Agnus Dei;*

because, as the Pontiff remarks, it represents the pure and immaculate Lamb, who shed His most precious blood for our redemption. Barry says (p. 143) that the same Sovereign Pontiff also forbade the exposing of the *Agnus Dei* for sale ; but, though this sale is well known to be forbidden, Molanus does not mention it in his extract from the decree of the Pope. The prohibition to paint or otherwise color the *Agnus Dei* refers only to the wax of which it is composed, and not to the covering in which it is encased, which may be, and generally is, very properly ornamented with various pious devices. But the notion of some persons is deserving of censure, to esteem the pretty covering more than the pious object itself. Alas for the vanity of some Christians ! Others are found to value an *Agnus Dei* because they have received it from some particular priest or prelate. While this need not be condemned, being no more than a natural feeling, harmless in itself, it must not be forgotten that the *Agnus Dei* derives all its efficacy from the blessing imparted to it by the Father of the faithful, and from no one else. Other persons not well informed will inquire, on receiving an *Agnus Dei*, whether it is blessed or not. Such persons must be told that all *Agnus Deis* are blessed, and would not be *Agnus Deis* at all if it were not for the blessing they have received at the hands of the Sovereign Pontiff. There are two other classes of persons for whom a word may not be out of place. They are, first, those who make light of *Agnus Deis*, scapulars, medals, etc., and make fun of those who wear them. No true child of the Church will ever be guilty of this fault of making light of anything which the Church approves or blesses for the pious use of the faithful. We are not bound to make use of these objects, but we are strictly forbidden to jest about them.

It may be, and frequently is, true that some people would seem to carry the use of these things to an extreme by wearing all the medals and other pious objects they can find, loading themselves down, it might almost be said, with them. But what matter? It can do them no harm; and their wearing of them can burden no one else. Let them alone; it is their business. The other class is composed of those who do not think themselves good enough to carry such pious objects about them. While they are mistaken, they have this at least in their favor: they are conscious of the fact that these objects are to be treated with a degree of reverence; and they do treat them so, but in an erroneous manner. Here is a point which many persons do not, and it may, in some cases at least, be said will not, understand—these things are not a reward of virtue, but a means of acquiring it.

Much more might be said of the *Agnus Dei*—of the esteem in which it was and is held by popes, prelates, priests, civil rulers of the highest position, and eminent lay Catholics; but it is not necessary to enlarge further on this subject. The solemnity with which this sacramental is blessed and distributed, the graces that are besought of God in the consecration it receives, the benefits derived from its pious use, the true Lamb which it represents, and the innocence of baptism which it typifies, with other considerations which will readily present themselves to the pious Catholic, will hardly fail to impress him with a correct idea of his duty in regard to the *Agnus Dei*. Let everyone take it and wear it devoutly, and God Himself will show what great benefits it bestows.[1]

[1] The authorities referred to in the preparation of this essay are Joannes Molani, in "Cursus Completus," vol. xxvii. coll. 425, *et seq*.; Barry; Maurel; the "Catholic Dictionary;" the London *Tablet*, April 17 and June 26, 1886; and the other authorities named.

XIX.—BLESSED CANDLES.

WITH the Purification of the Blessed Virgin Mary is closed the series of feasts that circle around the cradle of Bethlehem. On Christmas are presented the birth of the long-expected Redeemer of the world, the Desired of nations, and His manifestation to the Jews, in the persons of the poor shepherds, as the One for whom their fathers and the prophets had yearned. Epiphany completes that manifestation by presenting Him to the Gentiles, represented by the Wise Men, as Him in whom the Gentiles should hope. Now Mary crowns the great work by offering Him in the temple to the Eternal Father as the Victim by whose atonement a permanent reconciliation is to be effected between God and man, the gates of heaven are to be opened, and the thrones made vacant by the fall of the angels re-occupied. Did it fall within the scope of this essay much might be written on these points; but we are concerned in this place with the blessing of the candles only and the institution of the feast upon which that ceremony takes place.

Dr. Wapelhorst[1] very properly draws attention to a point which it is well to bear in mind, especially in our day when the mystic is lost sight of to so great an extent, and when everything is sought to be judged, even by many Catholics of the lax and imperfectly informed class, by the criterion of the senses without any relation to the supernatural. He says: "The service of the

---

[1] The opinions of Dr. Wapelhorst given in this essay are taken for the most part from an article, "Liturgical Lights," found in the *American Ecclesiastical Review*, vol. ii. pp. 98 *et seq.*

Church in each detail is eminently what the Apostle of the Gentiles directed the Romans to offer, 'your reasonable service,' which, if rightly understood, renders its strict observance as agreeable as it is beneficial. . . . The two cardinal principles which determine the ecclesiastical legislation regarding liturgical lights are: first, the symbolical meaning of lights, and, second, tradition, or what might be called historical consistency."

The use of lights in the Jewish temple is well known; and, though there is difference of opinion as to whether they burned during the day or not, it is more probable they did, as Josephus expressly states. Inasmuch as the first Christians were converts from Judaism, it would appear but natural for them to continue the use of lights in the New Dispensation; for if they were appropriate in the ceremonies of the worship which was but the shadow of the better things to come, much more appropriate are they in that form of worship which is the reality. Besides, they would aid in reconciling the converts to the change of religion.

The best authorities on the liturgy maintain that the use of lights during the celebration of the divine mysteries is of apostolic origin; an opinion which gains weight from certain passages in the New Testament, especially from St. John's vision in the Apocalypse (i. 12, 13), as well as from the custom of the Jews just referred to. The first mention of the use of lights in the New Law is found in the Acts of the Apostles (xx. 8); but these, it would seem, were used rather from necessity, to dispel the darkness, than as an adjunct to divine worship. The use of lights is mentioned in all the Oriental liturgies. But perhaps the first direct testimony to the use of lights in that portion of the Church is furnished by St. Jerome, in the fourth century, in his reply to the heretic Vigilantius, who attacked their presence as superfluous. The celebrated Father and Doctor replied—and his rejoinder implies that the use of lights was a custom of long standing:—"Throughout the churches of the East, whenever the gospel is read, they bring forth lights ; not certainly to drive away darkness, but to manifest some sign of joy, that under the type of corporeal light may be symbolized that light of which we read in the psalms (cxviii. 105) : 'Thy word is a lamp to my feet and a light to my paths.'"

St. Paulinus, the scholarly Bishop of Nola, who flourished in the first half of the fifth century, bears testimony to the use of lights in the celebration of the divine mysteries in the Western Church. Dr. Rock gives us in his *Hierurgia* the following translation of a part of one of his numerous hymns:

"With crowded lamps are those bright altars crowned,
And waxen tapers, shedding perfume round
From fragrant wicks, beam calm a scented ray
To gladden night and joy e'en radiant day.
Meridian splendors thus light up the night,
And day itself, illumed with Sacred Light,
Wears a new glory, borrowed from those rays
That stream from countless lamps in never-ending blaze."

Although candles were used in all probability from apostolic times in the celebration of the Holy Sacrifice, Wapelhorst concludes, after carefully weighing the authorities, that "during the first ten centuries of the Church's life no candles were placed directly upon the altar, or at least upon the table of the altar ; but there were always quite a number of lights kept round about the altar. Burning lamps were suspended partly in front, partly above the altar, and betwixt the columns of the ciborium, or canopy above the altar." Large chandeliers are also mentioned by early writers, which either in the sanctuary or immediately before it shed light from hundreds of lamps or candles. As an example it may be mentioned that Pope Adrian I. (772-795) had a chandelier made for St. Peter's which held thirteen hundred and seventy candles.

The use of lights in the administration of the sacraments and other sacred functions may be traced to the respect we should have for these sacred rites, and also to the symbolical meaning of wax and light already referred to. But only in baptism is direct reference made to the candle. This is done when, toward the end of the ceremony, a lighted candle is placed in the hand of the newly baptized, or his sponsors, with the solemn admonition: "Receive this burning light, and preserve your baptism blamelessly; keep the commandments of God, in order that when the Lord shall come to the marriage-feast you may run to meet Him with all the saints in His celestial palace, and may have life everlasting and live forever and ever. Amen." Early writers mention the use of lights at funeral obsequies, especially of persons of note; and the number of lamps found in the catacombs and in other early sepulchres of the Christians confirm their statements.

"Light," says Wapelhorst, "is the fittest and most appropriate symbol of God, an absolutely pure spirit Light is itself pure; it penetrates long distances; it moves with incredible velocity; it awakens and propagates life in the organic kingdom; it illumines with its brilliancy all that comes under its influence. Therefore the Holy Scriptures make frequent use of this symbolic meaning. . . . 'God is light, and in Him there is no darkness.'[1] The wisdom of the Son is called 'the brightness of eternal light,' and 'the brightness of glory.'[2] The psalmist exclaims (ciii. 2): 'Thou art clothed with light as with a garment.'"

Light also represents the mission of our divine Lord upon earth. The prophet Isaias (ix. 2) calls Him a great light, and foretells that "to them that dwelt in the region of the shadow of death light is risen;" and holy Simeon declares that He is "a light to the revelation of the Gentiles, and the glory of Thy people Israel." To these St. John adds that He was "the true light, which enlighteneth every man that cometh into this world." And Christ says of Himself, "I am the light of the world."[3] The Sacred Scripture abounds in similar passages, but these are sufficient.

Lights are also significant of respect, and hence they are used on occasions when it is desired to show more than ordinary deference to distinguished personages or to holy things. Both the Greeks and the Romans employed them in the celebration of many of their pagan rites. Josephus informs us that, out of the great reverence which the chosen people entertained for the vestments of the high-priest, a light was kept constantly burning before them. The Grand Lama, or supreme pontiff, of Tartary is never seen in his palace without having a profusion of lamps and torches burning around him. The same custom is found in many abbeys, where at meals two candles, with the crucifix between them, burn on the table before the abbot. And it is a universal, or almost universal, rule of royal etiquette to burn two or more candles before kings and princes on important occasions, such as state dinners, etc.

[1] I. St. John, i. 15.   [2] Heb., i. 3.
[3] St Luke, ii. 32; St. John, viii. 12 and i. 9.

It is a remarkable fact that no work on the liturgy makes mention of any other than beeswax candles in any of the sacred functions of religion, except to condemn them unqualifiedly; and the very name—*cereus*—most frequently made use of is the Latin word for this wax. The law requiring candles for the altar to be made of beeswax is very strict, and it is rarely indeed, as we shall see, that a dispensation is granted for the use of any other material; and *it is never granted on account of poverty, no matter how great that poverty may be.* The only ground recognized by the Church is the impossibility of procuring beeswax; and as soon as it can be had the dispensation ceases by that very fact. The reason the Church has selected the candle as the type of Our Lord is thus explained by St. Anselm: "The wax produced by the virginal bee represents Christ's most spotless body; the wick enclosed in the wax and forming one with it images His soul, while the ruddy flame crowning and completing the union of wax and wick typifies the divine nature subsisting in the human in one divine Person."

The spread of the Church in missionary countries, especially during the present century, and the great difficulty encountered in many instances in procuring the requisites for the celebration of the Holy Sacrifice, rendered it necessary for the perplexed missionaries and their bishops to address numerous questions to the Sacred Congregation of Rites regarding what might be permitted in the peculiar circumstances in which they were placed, so as to comply at once with the requirements of liturgical law and at the same time afford their people, as far as possible, the consolations of religion. It is doubtful whether any question perplexed them more than that of the material which it would be lawful to use for lights at the altar. But while the authorities at Rome attached due importance to the difficulties by which the missionaries were surrounded, they still adhered to the laws, the traditions, and the symbolic meanings of the liturgy, and no general relaxation was permitted, though special indults were granted in a few cases until the existing abnormal condition of affairs could be changed for the better. Again, poverty, added to these difficulties, often led to the making of candles of other material than wax, such as vegetable or artificial wax, sperm, stearine, paraffine, tallow, and sometimes of a mixture of beeswax with one or another of these baser materials. Prelates from various parts of the world appealed to the Holy See for permission to use such candles, partly on the ground of poverty, partly on that of the impossibility of procuring beeswax, and partly because in countries where the proper material could be had there were not wanting some who continued the use of other than wax candles, with the tacit permission of their bishops. The case was put in its strongest light; but of all the multitudinous petitions presented the only one granted was that of the Vicar Apostolic of Corea, who was permitted to use the wax exuding from a tree of that country, because it was impossible to procure beeswax, and because that wax resembled the proper material. The Sacred Congregation, however, it is well to remember, did not reply that it was *lawful* to use this wax, but that they would apply to the Holy Father for special permission to use it till such time as beeswax could be had. It is a point worthy of careful attention that the use of any other material than beeswax is never permitted except provisionally.

A remarkable instance, which shows the unchangeable mind of the Church on this point, is furnished by Dr.

Wapelhorst in the following words: "The superiors of the missions of Oceanica, finding it impossible to obtain beeswax for candles, had requested the Sacred Congregation to allow the use of sperm and stearine candles. The Sacred Congregation of Rites answered that, it being impossible to obtain wax, the missionaries of that country might, by a special privilege which the Holy See granted in their behalf, make use of olive oil instead; and, if this failed, they might celebrate Mass without lights. The superiors had recourse again, stating that it was not in their power to obtain olive oil any more than wax, and that the missionaries were unwilling to celebrate without lights. Upon this the Sacred Congregation of Rites answered, September 7, 1850, that they might make use of sperm or stearine candles till it would become possible to obtain wax or oil." Whatever the opinion of others may be, I cannot, in view of these decisions, see how anyone can use other than wax candles on the altar in this country at the present time. It is beyond all possible question entirely alien from the spirit of the Church. But it will be said that many of the so-called wax candles offered for sale are not pure wax—perhaps are not half beeswax. This question has not escaped the attention of the Sacred Congregation of Rites; for a priest consulted that body on the matter, and the answer, under date of March 8, 1879, was that he should abide by the decision of his bishop.

Before treating of the blessing of candles it will be proper for us to inquire into the origin of the feast of the Purification, upon which that ceremony takes place, and why it is fixed on that day and no other. While the purification was one of the ordinances of the Mosaic law (Exodus, xiii. 2), the date of its institution as a Christian feast, with its procession and the blessing of candles, is not so easily ascertained. Our divine Redeemer came, as He declares, not to destroy the law, but to fulfil it; and, though neither He nor His blessed Mother was subject to the law of purification, they both complied with it to leave to mankind an example of humility and obedience. With them, however, it was not merely a ceremony, in acknowledgment of the supreme dominion of God over His rational creatures, but an act full of the deepest signification. But the purpose at present is to treat of the feast only in its relation to the blessing and use of candles.

There are several reasons why the Church instituted this feast, and fixed on it the blessing of candles. In the first place, it comes forty days after the date usually assigned as that of Our Saviour's birth, and hence corresponds to the purification required by the law of Moses. Again, it is well known that the Church, instead of trying to obliterate entirely the remembrance of a pagan feast in her converts,—and much more of a Jewish one, —sometimes changes it into a Christian solemnity, the better to win the erring to her fold, and avert the danger of a return to their pagan superstitions.

Some writers maintain that it was Pope Gelasius, who ruled the Church at the close of the fifth century, that instituted the feast of the Purification, to take the place of the Lupercalia, which is said to have been established by Evander, and which was celebrated annually on the 15th of February. It was intended as a purification of the people, although its ceremonies were among the most revolting of ancient pagan rites. Other authorities, however, hold that the institution of the feast is of much earlier date, and that the candles which are carried in procession in honor of the Mother of God were intended to withdraw the people from the pagan custom of carrying lights through the streets of Rome in honor of a pagan goddess. To reconcile these conflicting opinions, it is said that Pope Gelasius did away with the Lupercalia, but that the feast of the Purification was established at an earlier date. Benedict XIV., after passing the various opinions in review, concludes that the feast was instituted to take the place of the Amburbalia, a pagan sacrifice which was offered in February every five years, after receiving tribute from the provinces; a feast at which those who participated in it went through Rome carrying torches and performing certain ceremonies for the purification of the city. He concludes that Gelasius did away with the Lupercalia, but did not establish the feast of the Purification, and that Pope Sergius I., at the close of the seventh century, substituted the procession of the feast for that of the Amburbalia. But the discussion does not rest here; for other writers insist that the feast of the Purification was celebrated in Jerusalem in the fifth century, and was not then of recent institution. The Bollandists refer the establishment of it to apostolic times, at least in the Eastern Church. This opinion may, I think, be regarded as the most probable, both on account of the weight of the authority on which it rests, and the fact that it was in the East that Mary came to the temple for the performance of the ceremony of the purification. What more natural than that this event should be first commemorated on the spot where it actually took place, though the ceremony may since have undergone modifications?

The suffix *mas*, connected with the name of certain feasts, as Christmas, Candlemas, etc., was formerly more common than it is at present, especially in England in Catholic times; and it would appear to owe its origin to the obligation of the members of the gilds and trades-unions to assist at Mass on the feasts of their respective patron saints and on certain other great feasts of the ecclesiastical year, which were designated by the name of the saint or the feast with the suffix *mas*, as Michaelmas, etc.[1]

Turning to the blessing of the candles, the mind of the Church is well shown forth in the prayers—five in number—which are recited by the priest during the ceremony, as well as in the antiphons sung during the procession. In the first of these prayers we beg of God, —who created all things, who by the labor of the bees brought this liquid to the perfection of wax, and who, on this day, fulfilled His promise to holy Simeon,—by the invocation of His holy Name and the intercession of the Blessed Virgin Mary, and of all the saints, to bless and sanctify the candles presented for blessing; that they may be for the service of His people and for the health of their bodies and souls wherever they may chance to be, whether on land or water, and that He would at all times hear the prayers of His people who desire to carry these candles in their hands. In the second prayer our divine Saviour, who was received in the arms of holy Simeon, is entreated to bless and sanctify with the light of His heavenly benediction the candles which His servants desire to receive and carry lighted in honor of His holy Name, to the end that they may be made worthy to be inflamed with His sweetest charity, and may deserve to be presented in the temple of His eternal glory. The third prayer entreats Our Saviour to pour forth His blessing upon the candles, and sanctify them with the light of His grace; and mercifully to grant that as these lights, enkindled with visible

[1] Wilford's "Gilds," *passim*.

fire, dispel the darkness of night, so our hearts, illuminated by invisible fire, that is, the Holy Ghost, may be free from the blindness of every vice; that the eye of our minds being purified, we may discern those things which are pleasing to God and profitable to salvation; so that after the darkness and perils of this world we may be found worthy to be admitted to that light which never fails. In the fourth prayer the Almighty God, who commanded Moses to have the purest oil prepared for the lamps to burn before Him continually, is besought graciously to pour forth the grace of His blessing upon the candles, that as they afford external light, so through the divine mercy the interior light of the Holy Spirit may never be wanting to our minds. In the last prayer our divine Redeemer—who in the substance of our flesh was presented in the temple and recognized by the aged Simeon, enlightened by the Holy Spirit—is mercifully besought that we, enlightened by the same Holy Spirit, may truly acknowledge and faithfully love the same divine Redeemer.

It is not forbidden to sell candles that have been blessed, provided no more is asked for them than the ordinary selling price; in other words, provided no charge is made for the blessing itself.

The faithful in general have caught the spirit of the Church with regard to her blessed candles, and have come to look upon them as one of the most efficacious of the sacramentals. This is amply shown by their lighting them in times of danger — especially from the elements — and by their desire to have the dying expire while holding a blessed candle in the hand — the material light being thus made a symbol of the invisible light that is to guide them after death to the realms of everlasting happiness.

XX.—BLESSED ASHES.

The use of ashes, especially the sprinkling of ashes on the head as a sign of humiliation and sorrow, dates back to the cradle of the human race. Numerous references are made to it in the Old Testament. David, the model of penitents, says: "I did eat ashes like bread, and mingled my drink with weeping." The Ninivites, at the preaching of Jonas, "proclaimed a fast, and put on sackcloth from the greatest to the least, and sat in ashes." Judith put ashes on her head when she prayed for strength to overcome Holofernes, the leader of the enemies of her people. And the prophet Jeremias cries out: "Howl, ye shepherds, and cry; and sprinkle yourselves with ashes, ye leaders of the people."

While the pagans retained some vestiges of primitive revelation and religious observance, — corrupted by the lapse of time, the debasing influence of unbridled passions, and their distant separation from the Fountain of Truth, — humility and self-denial, practised from supernatural motives, find no place among their virtues. In their pride and self-indulgence they gradually fell away from the practice of virtue; and the deification of the basest passions was the natural result. Even those whom we regard as having been the most upright among them looked upon taking part in the most abominable orgies as a religious duty. Not so the child of God, whose mind has been illumined by the light of revelation. He early learns that he must chastise his body and keep it in subjection; that if he neglects or refuses to do penance he is in danger of perishing; and that in all things he must remember his last end and his return to the dust from which he was taken, if he is to avoid sin and attain everlasting life. Conscious that he is by nature a child of wrath, he studies to appease an offended God by the practice of penance and mortification; and remembering that he is formed from the dust of the earth, and doomed to return to it again, he humbly sprinkles the noblest of his members, the head, with dust. In the light of revelation this is perfectly natural to him.

The ceremony of blessing and distributing the ashes, as we have it at present, like many of the other ceremonies of the Church, comes down to us from the earliest ages. It is probable that it was introduced by the converts from Judaism, or at least in imitation of a somewhat similar practice in vogue among the chosen people. Like some of the other ceremonies, too, it has undergone certain minor changes before assuming its present form. The principal of these will be noticed as we proceed.

Ash-Wednesday, the day upon which the faithful are signed with the ashes, was called by early writers *caput jejunii*, or, the beginning of the fast, although up to the time of Pope St. Gregory the Great, at the close of the sixth century, the fast did not commence till the Monday following the first Sunday of Lent. With the Sundays deducted, this left but thirty-six fast-days, which constitute about one-tenth part of the year — a circumstance which led some of the Fathers to remark that it was giving a tithe of the year to God, after the example of the Jews, from whom He required a tenth part of their produce. But the forty days' fast of Moses and Elias, and more especially of our divine Redeemer, showed the propriety of increasing the number of fast-days to forty; and accordingly the four days before the first Sunday of Lent were added. This took place about the beginning of the eighth century, first, it would appear, by a capitulary of the Church of Toulon, in 714. Amaury (about 820) describes the Lenten usages of his time as identical with ours. But this manner of celebrating the fast did not become general for centuries; and it was not until the time of St. Charles Borromeo, who flourished in the sixteenth century, that the Church of Milan introduced the custom of beginning Lent on Ash-Wednesday.

At first no persons were signed with the ashes but the public penitents, who were required to appear, clad in the garb of penance, at the door of the church on Ash-Wednesday morning. Says Barry (pp. 67, 68): "The course of penance for those who were to be reconciled on Holy Thursday began on Ash-Wednesday. The penitents, having confessed their sins, came to the church on that day with bare feet and in the habit of mourning, and humbly begged from the bishop canonical punishment. The pontiff then clothed them in sackcloth, scattered ashes on their heads, sprinkled them with holy water, and recited the Seven Penitential Psalms over them, whilst the attending clergy lay prostrate on the ground. The bishop and his ministers then imposed hands on them, to ratify, as it were, their solemn consecration to the course of penance. This ceremony was followed by a pathetic exhortation, in which the bishop announced to the weeping sinners before him that, as God had driven Adam from Paradise, so was he obliged to exclude them for a time from the spiritual paradise of the Church. With sorrowing hearts and countenances, the penitents marched in slow procession to the door of the church. The bishop thrust them out with his pastoral staff, and they passed not again the threshold of the house of God until Holy Thursday. During this touching ceremony the clergy chanted the words which God addressed to fallen man when driving him from the earthly Paradise : ' Remember, man, that thou art dust, and unto dust thou shalt return.' Do penance, that you may have eternal life."

Soon others of the faithful joined the penitents in receiving the ashes, partly out of humility, and partly as a more effectual means of doing penance for their sins ; and the number of these continued to increase as time went on. Local Church authorities next devoted their attention to the matter. The Council of Beneventum, held in the year 1091, decreed that all, clergy and laity, men and women, should present themselves to be signed with the ashes. Other churches followed, and by the thirteenth century the custom became universal, and so it has continued.

The ashes used for this ceremony are procured by the burning of the blessed palm of the previous Palm Sunday ; a circumstance which reminds us that we cannot bear the palm of victory over Satan, sin, and death unless by the practice of humility and mortification during life, and by paying the debt of sin in giving our bodies to the dust at the close of our earthly existence.

The form of blessing the ashes, like all the other ceremonies of our holy religion, is very beautiful and expressive ; but it is difficult to tell at what time this form was adopted, or whether the ashes with which the public penitents were signed in the early ages were blessed or not. It is most probable, however, that they were, on the general principle that whatever the Church makes use of in her sacred ceremonies first receives a blessing. But whether this blessing was less solemn at first than later, when it became general, it would be difficult, if not impossible, to determine. We shall examine it as it is at present, remarking that, according to several decrees of the Sacred Congregation of Rites, the ashes are to be blessed by the priest who is to celebrate the Mass that follows.[1]

In the performing of the blessing the priest is vested in amice, alb, and violet stole and cope. Proceeding to the altar, on which the ashes are placed, at the Epistle side, in a suitable vessel, he reads an antiphon and four prayers. In the first of these Almighty God is besought to spare the penitent sinners who invoke Him, and to send His holy angel from heaven to bless and sanctify these ashes, that they may become a salutary remedy for all who invoke His holy name, and who, conscious of their transgressions, call upon His loving kindness; and to grant to all upon whom they are sprinkled health of body and salvation of soul. The second prayer begs of God, who desires not the death of the sinner, and who knows the frailty of man, to bless these ashes, which are to be used in token of humility and for the purpose of obtaining forgiveness; that we, who know ourselves to be but dust and ashes, may obtain the divine mercy, the pardon of our sins, and the rewards promised to the penitent. The third prayer asks the mercy of God and the spirit of compunction for all those who are signed with the ashes, and that they may be firmly established in the friendship of God. In the last prayer God, who pardoned the Ninevites who did penance in sackcloth and ashes, is besought to grant us the grace to imitate their penance, that we may receive a like pardon. The ashes are then sprinkled with holy water and incensed, after which they are distributed to the faithful, as we

[1] De Herdt, vol. iii. p. 25.

are accustomed to witness; the priest reciting, as he signs each one, "Remember, man, that thou art dust, and unto dust thou shalt return."

During the distribution of the ashes certain antiphons from the Scripture and other sources, which are calculated to awaken a spirit of penance, are sung—at least in such churches as have a choir capable of singing them; and it is greatly to be regretted that, owing to circumstances, many churches have not such trained singers. This part of the ceremony over, the priest returns to the altar and recites the following concluding prayer: "Grant us, O Lord, to begin our Christian warfare with holy fasts; that as we are about to fight against the spirits of wickedness, we may be defended by the aid of self-denial. Through Christ Our Lord. Amen." The celebration of the Mass then follows.

At one time it was customary, at least in many places, to dampen the ashes before using them; but the Holy See has forbidden this, and they are to be applied in a perfectly dry state. It is also a common custom of our time for people to ask the priest to give them some ashes to take home to the sick, or to others who have not been able to be present at the distribution. This is also forbidden by a decree of the Sacred Congregation of Rites; and what remains is to be put into the *sacrarium*, or place where things that are blessed and can no longer be used are thrown, as the water used in baptism, that used at Mass, etc.

XXI.—BLESSED PALMS.

It would be superfluous to begin by stating that the blessing and carrying of palms in procession derives its origin from the action of the people of Jerusalem in going out to meet Our Saviour on the Sunday before He died, and conducting Him in triumph into the city, spreading their garments and strewing branches of trees on the way for the humble animal on which He rode to tread upon. But this very action prompts the reflection that this must have been a customary way of showing respect to a person of distinction, else why did the people resort to it on this occasion? Turning to the Sacred Scriptures, we find the bearing of palm branches to have been one of the principal ways of manifesting joy; and one not only approved but commanded by God at the time of the foundation of the Jewish religion. When the people assembled in the fall of the year, after the gathering in of the harvest, to celebrate the feast of Tabernacles, God said to them, as we read in Leviticus (xxiii. 40): "You shall take to you on the first day the fruits of the fairest tree, and branches of palm trees, and boughs of thick trees, and willows of the brook; and you shall rejoice before the Lord, your God." This custom was observed among the Jews as long as they existed as a nation. In the Second Book of Machabees (x. 7) it is related that, after the temple was purified from the defilements to which it had been subjected by the enemies of God's people, the Jews rejoiced as they had formerly been accustomed to do on the feast of Tabernacles; and "therefore they now carried boughs and green branches and palms for Him that had given them good success in cleansing His place." The martyrs, too, those who have secured the only real triumph, are represented among the blessed carrying palms in their hands (Apoc. vii. 9).

Nor was the bearing of palms confined to religious triumph. The palm is the recognized symbol of victory throughout the world, as the olive branch is of peace. Philo relates that Agrippa carried palms and flowers on his entry into Jerusalem; and Josephus tells the same of Alexander the Great.

The palm is admirably adapted to symbolize. It is one of the most useful of Oriental trees. Its foliage forms a delightful shade in those hot countries; it supplies dates, a delicious and useful fruit, and a species of wine exudes from its bark. It is thus emblematic of the overshadowing protection of Divine Providence, the strength of supernatural grace, and the nourishment which Our Saviour gives us in the Holy Eucharist.

Great variety of opinion exists with regard to the date of the introduction of the blessing of palms into the ceremonial of the Church, and it is impossible to fix it with precision. The custom is admitted, however, to be of ancient origin. Among the works of St. John Chrysostom there is a sermon on Palm Sunday; but it is held by some writers that this is not genuine, and has been interpolated. Martene, a reliable authority on such matters, asserts that no vestige of the ceremony of blessing palms can be found before the eighth or ninth century; and a Roman Ordo of the eighth century, edited by Frotone, would appear to confirm this opinion; for, treating of the ceremony of Palm Sunday, it makes no mention of the blessing of palms. But this is only negative testimony, while there is much that is positive on the other side. Meratus, a consultor of the Sacred Congregation of Rites, produces a number of solid arguments which go to prove the antiquity of this rite. Among these is a calendar of the close of the fourth or the beginning of the fifth century, edited by Martene himself, in which occur the words "Palm Sunday at St. John Lateran"—"*Dominica ad Palmas ad S. Joannem in Lateranis.*" Reference is also made to Palm Sunday in the "Sacramentary" of Pope St. Gelasius, who ruled the Church at the close of the fifth century, where occur these words: "Palm Sunday of the Passion of Our Lord"—"*Dominica in Palmis de Passione Domini.*" Also in the "Sacramentary" of St. Gregory the Great, who occupied the chair of Peter at the close of the sixth century, mention is made of the faithful who were present at Mass with leaves and palm branches in their hands. Other authorities of the same early date are not wanting, but these are deemed sufficient. Venerable Bede (born 672) is the first writer of the West who speaks of palms; but he is immediately followed by St. Aldhelm, Bishop of West Saxony (d. 709), who also makes mention of them.

The custom of blessing and carrying palms in procession appears to have had its origin in the East. And this is but natural; for in the Old Law it was in the East, as we have seen, that God commanded them to be carried; it was in the same region that they were borne before Our Lord; and it was to be expected that those with whom these traditions were local should be the first to imitate them. Most probably the idea of the procession preceded that of the blessing; and the latter was introduced on the general principle that whatever is used by the people of God in His service should first be sanctified by the blessing of the Church. The importance of the event which the procession commemorated would naturally lead to a solemn form for the blessing of the palms to be carried in it.

It may be remarked in passing that Palm Sunday corresponds to the tenth day of the moon, on which the Jews were commanded to select and set apart the lamb without blemish, that was to be eaten on the feast of the Passover. It was also customary in the early ages of the Church to baptize the catechumens either on Holy Saturday or on the eve of Pentecost; and those who were to receive that sacrament on the former occasion were examined some days before, and on Palm Sunday were declared competent to receive the sacrament of regeneration. Hence it is sometimes called the "Sunday of the Competent."

According to the rubrics of the Missal, the palms presented to be blessed must be the branches of the palm or olive, or other trees. And, although it is not expressly stated, it seems proper that the "other trees" taken in place of the palm or olive, where it cannot be had, should be some sort of evergreens; at least this is the interpretation put upon the words by the universal practice of the faithful. The spruce, or hemlock, being the most common species of evergreen tree found in many parts of this country, is frequently used; but it is hardly to be recommended, as its leaves soon drop off, and leave nothing but the bare twigs.

A decree of the Sacred Congregation of Rites, of June 9, 1668, requires the blessing of the palms to be performed by the priest who is to celebrate the Mass that follows the procession.

Commenting on the prayers recited in the blessing of palms, Cardinal Wiseman remarks: "Of the prayers employed in this benediction I shall say nothing but what may be said of all that occur in the Church offices—that they possess an elevation of sentiment, a beauty of allusion, a force of expression, and a depth of feeling which no modern form of supplication ever exhibits." It is believed that no one who attentively studies these prayers will regard the words of the learned Cardinal as an exaggeration.

In the act of blessing the palms the celebrant—vested in violet cope, and standing at the Epistle corner of the altar—after the recitation of a short prayer, continues with the reading of a lesson from the Book of Exodus, in which mention is made of the children of Israel coming to Elim, near Mount Sinai, on their journey to the Promised Land, where there were a fountain and seventy palm trees. Here they began that long series of murmurings against Moses, for leading them out, as they said, to starve in the desert, far from the fleshpots of Egypt; and here it was that God in His mercy promised to rain down the manna for their subsistence. After a few verses from the New Testament, that portion of St. Matthew's Gospel is read which narrates the coming of Christ into Jerusalem the Sunday before His death, on which occasion the people were aroused to a degree of enthusiasm regarding Him which they had never before manifested. Cutting down boughs from the trees and strewing them, together with their garments, on the way, they made the air resound with their joyous hosannas. Next in the blessing follows a prayer begging of God that we may in the end go forth to meet Christ, bearing the palm of victory and laden with good works, and so may enter with Him into eternal happiness. Then follow a beautiful preface and five prayers, all invoking a blessing on the palms, and beseeching God that they may be sanctified, and may become a means of grace and divine protection, both for soul and body, to those who carry them to their homes and keep them there in a spirit of faith and devotion. Reference is also made to the olive branch that was brought by the dove to Noe, after the waters of the deluge had subsided, as a symbol of the peace established between heaven and earth, and to the palm as the emblem of victory. Another prayer follows, and the palms are ready for distribution among the people.

According to the directions of the ceremonial, the palms should be distributed at the communion rail, those receiving them kissing first the palm and then the hand of the celebrant; but this ceremony is not carried out in most of our churches. The palms are more commonly carried through the aisles by the altar-boys or others, and given to the people in their pews. There is some excuse for this departure from the ceremonial, but what its precise value is I shall not attempt to say. The Church in many places in this country is yet in process of organization, and in most others it is but just organized; and this, like many other ceremonies, it was impossible to carry out in the beginning. A departure from the rubrics took place from sheer necessity; and it has since, it may be said, been generally tolerated. After the distribution of the palms, certain verses of Scripture are read, which, with another prayer, closes the blessing, and preparations are made for the procession.

The procession is frequently dispensed with for the same reason as the strict rubrical form of distributing the palms, and can hardly be said to take place except in the larger churches and cathedrals. Speaking of the hymn "Gloria, laus et honor," etc., which is sung during the procession, Cardinal Wiseman remarks: "It is said to have been composed by Abbot Theodulf, when in prison at Angiers for a conspiracy against Louis the Pious, and sung by him in a moving strain as the Emperor in procession, on that Sunday, passed under the prison wall. The words and music touched the offended monarch's heart, and procured the prisoner's liberation. This is said to have taken place in the year 818; and even if the legend be inaccurate, as some have thought, it proves the character and power which the public voice attributed to the composition."

The palms are to be held in the hand during the singing or reading of the Passion and the Gospel.

Reference might here be made to certain local customs connected with the blessing and procession of the palms, and more especially to those which belong to the Eastern Church. The writer just mentioned informs us that " in the East they have from the earliest ages practised the ceremony of carrying palm and olive branches to the church on Lazarus Saturday, as the eve of Palm Sunday used to be called, and have them blessed the next day. At Constantinople it was customary for the Emperor to distribute the palms with great solemnity to all his courtiers."

The Maronites were accustomed to bless an olive tree and give it to the person who contributed the largest alms. This favored one passed it to his son or to some other youth, whom he, with the assistance of his friends, carried in procession amid the acclamations of the people. At the conclusion of the procession the tree was distributed among the people, or, perhaps more correctly, they distributed it among themselves, each striving to secure a branch or twig of it, and deeming himself fortunate if he succeeded. Other local customs existed in different places, and perhaps still exist, to which we need not refer.

A concluding remark is, however, to be made. The palm is the symbol of victory ; but our divine Redeemer, who gained the greatest of all victories, did so by humbling Himself to death, even the death of the cross, to teach us that all true victories are those won by triumphing over ourselves, with our unruly passions and evil inclinations. The palm is made to teach us this salutary lesson among others ; for whatever remains after the distribution is laid aside to be burned for the ashes used on the next Ash-Wednesday. These ashes, after having been blessed with solemn prayers, as we have seen, are used to mark the sign of the cross on our foreheads, the seat of that pride infused into our nature by the arch-enemy of mankind at the time of the fall of our first parents. This solemn ceremony is accompanied with the words : " Remember, man, that thou art dust, and unto dust thou shalt return." It is only by returning to dust, the doom of all the children of Adam, that we can hope to rise to a new life like our divine Model, to die no more, but to bear to His eternal home and ours the palm of our final victory.

The authorities consulted in the preparation of this essay were, among others, Benedict XIV., "De Festis ;" Cardinal Wiseman, "The Ceremonies of Holy Week ;" "Kirchen-Lexicon ;" Barry, "The Sacramentals ;" De Herdt, etc.

XXII.—THE NUPTIAL MASS AND BLESSING.

THE end which I propose to myself in the present essay is an explanation of the marriage ceremony and the Nuptial Mass, that the reader may better understand them; may learn more clearly their beauty and appropriateness; appreciate more highly the graces which they convey to the souls of those who worthily participate in them, and by that means conceive a greater love and reverence for them. The mystic ceremonies of religion are not so attractive to the minds of many Christians in this material age as they should be, and are not sufficiently studied; and hence it is not to be wondered at that many persons make little account of neglecting or dispensing with these sacred rites and fountains of grace which holy Church has prepared for those who are about to enter the married state. Yet, considered merely from a natural point of view, and altogether apart from the importance which faith teaches man to attach to it, the question of marriage is one demanding the most serious reflection. The very intimate and life-long association of one person with another, which the bond of marriage supposes and obliges to; the attendant temptations and dangers; the training of a family, with all the privations, trials, and sufferings inseparable from it, under the most favorable circumstances; and the countless accidents which checker the life of everyone, are points which common prudence forbids us to pass over lightly. But when in addition to these are included the obligations which religion imposes on the couple in relation to each other and to the children with which Almighty God may and most probably will bless them, matter is presented for still more serious consideration. It is true, indeed, that the sacrament of matrimony is an abundant and never-failing source of grace; but it is so to those only who receive it worthily, and live according to the laws which it imposes. How few there are who perfectly observe those sacred laws!

He who seriously reflects on these points will not be surprised that God in His infinite wisdom should have made matrimony the subject of special legislation in the world's infancy, in the very groves of Paradise; nor that the Church should from the earliest times have devoted her special attention to seeing that her children entered into that union with the proper dispositions and according to the ceremonies which she, guided by the Holy Spirit, had prescribed. Few matters have received so large a share of her attention. Read ecclesiastical history, the writings of the saints, fathers, and theologians, the decrees of councils and the utterances of Sovereign Pontiffs—all manifest her zeal for the purity and sanctity of marriage, and at the same time show the waywardness of the human will when excited and blinded by the basest and most unruly passion of the heart of man. But so far from victory having declared for the Church, the struggle is waging more furiously in the present than it did perhaps at any previous period. Scarcely had the illustrious Leo XIII. ascended the throne of Peter than he found it necessary to raise his voice in solemn admonition to Christians to conform themselves to the wise regulations which the Church has established. And if attention is directed to the instructions which the Holy See sends to the bishops of missionary countries like ours, it will be seen that by far the greater number have to do with the sacrament of matrimony. Happy is it for society that there is still one authority respected on earth, although it be only by the few. What is marriage outside the pale of the Church? A contract, or the semblance of a contract, subject to the caprice of the basest passion that tyrannizes over the heart of fallen man—this and nothing more. It may truly be said that there is no longer any respect for the bond of marriage except in the Church. It goes for the saying that a divorce can anywhere be had for the most flimsy pretext, and the laws are so framed in some States as to put a premium on crime. Nor need it be wondered at that some Catholics, breathing this pestilential atmosphere, should long for freedom from a restraint so galling to rebellious nature.

But the circumstances of the Church, not only in herself but also in her surroundings, must be taken into consideration when we attempt to account for the distaste which many persons have for the Nuptial Mass and the blessing which accompanies it. The Church among us is still in many respects in its infancy; until recently it was impossible to surround the reception of the sacraments with that external pomp which delights the Christian heart; and in not a few places this is true even at the present day. Hence it is that many persons have grown up ignorant or but indifferently instructed in regard to some of the most touching and beautiful ceremonies of religion. But without further preface let us approach the subject that is to engage our attention, and for which I beg the young reader's careful consideration.

When a person enters the religious life he or she has half a year's time as a postulant, and two years as a novice, all of which are spent in the learning and practising of the rules and usages that are afterward to become obligatory; but when one is married, as St. Francis of Sales remarks, there is no novitiate. Two persons unite themselves together for life, and, of course, they expect to live long lives, say at least fifty years, together; and this in the most intimate relationship known on earth, and one that can never be dissolved, for "what God hath joined together let no man put asunder."[1] And how little do the two often know of each other before marriage? Their main object then is to show off all their good qualities to the best advantage and conceal their weak points. When they are united, however, the realities of life begin to present themselves; but it is then too late to retrace their steps. Hence the necessity of the most mature deliberation, and of calling down all the blessings of Heaven.

Let it be supposed that after a sufficient acquaintance a young man and woman have mutually agreed to marry; that their parents have been informed, and proper regard paid to their authority; and that the pastor of the church has been notified in due time, the banns proclaimed, and no impediments discovered, and the hour for the solemn ceremony approaches. Being Christians, they are resolved to comply not only with the essential laws, but also with the wishes of holy Church, and enter into their union with the Nuptial Mass and Blessing.

Before proceeding to speak of the Nuptial Mass and the benediction which accompanies and forms a part of it, the reader must be reminded that the latter is entirely distinct from the ceremony of marriage and the sacrament of matrimony, each of which is perfect without it.

The Nuptial Mass takes its name from the object for

[1] St. Matthew, xix. 6.

which it is celebrated, and consists, as has just been said, of the Mass with the special blessing for the married couple. Certain questions here present themselves for solution before we can proceed to consider the Mass in itself. And first, For whom can the Nuptial Mass be celebrated, and to whom can the Nuptial Blessing be imparted? In answer we must first say that it cannot be celebrated in the case of a mixed marriage; for such a marriage cannot even take place in the church. "The Nuptial Benediction is not to be given when either of the parties received it in a previous marriage; but where it is usual to give it in all cases in which the female was not previously married, the custom, according to the rubric, may still be retained. The benediction, from its form, seems directed chiefly to the female, and hence probably the custom, as well as the sanction given to it. . . . It is to be observed that the benediction is not to be withheld at the second marriage unless it was given at the first, and therefore may be given to a widow who did not receive it at her previous marriage, whatever may have been the cause of the omission."[1] We are to conclude from this that, although the husband may receive the blessing more than once, where custom permits it, the wife cannot receive it the second time. The reason of this appears to be that the Church expects it always to be received at the first marriage, and this marriage represents more perfectly than any subsequent one the union of Christ with His spouse, the Church.

It may be further asked, Where is the Nuptial Blessing to be received? O'Kane replies (No. 1092): "The Nuptial Benediction can be given only in the church, according to a decree of the Sacred Congregation; but

[1] O'Kane, Supplement to the "Notes on the Rubrics," Nos. 1089, 1090.

this is because, according to another decree, it can be given only at Mass. Such, at least, is the opinion of Cavalieri, who further maintains that if there be an oratory annexed to the house where the marriage takes place the Nuptial Benediction may be given at the Mass celebrated there. Suppose, then, that a marriage is for some sufficient reason celebrated in a private house, and that there is at the same time permission to say Mass there, it would appear to us that the Nuptial Benediction may, and should, be given." Permission to receive the Nuptial Blessing in a private house, it is clear from the above, is ruled by the permission to say Mass there. Where the latter is permitted the former is also allowed.

When can the Nuptial Blessing be received? This question admits of a threefold reply: as regards the occasion, the season of the year, and the dignity of certain solemn feasts. As regards the occasion, whatever customs or privileges may have obtained in other times or countries, a decree of the Sacred Congregation of Rites, dated June 23, 1853, and another of August 14, 1858, forbid the Nuptial Blessing to be given except in the Mass. There is a benediction, distinct from that found in the Nuptial Mass, given in the ritual of certain European countries, which may be imparted at any other time.[1] But with this we are not concerned, there being no such blessing given in the ritual prescribed for the use of the clergy in this country. In the second place, as regards the season of the year during which the Nuptial Blessing may be given, it can be imparted at any time except during what is called "the closed time," which extends from the first Sunday of Advent to Epiphany, and from Ash-Wednesday to Low Sunday,

[1] De Herdt, vol. iii. N. 278.

inclusive.[1] I use the expression "Nuptial Blessing" instead of "Nuptial Mass," for, though the blessing can be given only at Mass, it may be imparted, as we shall see, at another than the Nuptial Mass, on feasts when that Mass is not permitted to be celebrated. Marriage being an occasion of joy, it is the wish of the Church that her children should not, without grave reasons, contract it during penitential seasons ; and, although its solemnization is also forbidden on the great festivals that immediately follow these times of penance, it would appear to be because the Church would wish that the Christian heart should be so occupied with the thought of God as to forget even the lawful pleasures which this miserable world affords. The sacrament of matrimony can indeed be received at any time of the day or year ; but it cannot be solemnized, that is, received with the Nuptial Mass and Blessing, during the "closed time," nor is it in the power of the bishop to dispense from that law.[2] The Council of Trent and the Roman Ritual earnestly exhort those who, for any reason, have been married without the Nuptial Blessing not to live together until they shall have received it, the intention of the Church being that they should not consummate their marriage without this salutary blessing ; and, according to a decree of August 14, 1858, they could not receive it if they had lived together in the same house even for one day. But a decree of the Congregation of the Holy Office, dated August 31, 1881, has made a radical change on this point, declaring that it is to be granted "to such as did not receive it at the time of marriage, from whatever cause this may have arisen—even if they petitioned

---

[1] Council of Trent, sess. xxiv., chapter x., De Reformatione Matrimonii.
[2] Decree S. C. R., February 6, 1858.

for it after living a long time in the married state, provided that the woman, if a widow, had not received it at a previous marriage. Moreover, Catholics who did not receive this blessing on their marriage should be exhorted to ask for it as soon as possible." Although the reception of this blessing is only a matter of counsel, not binding, most probably, under pain of sin, as O'Kane remarks, still it shows the mind of the Church, and the importance she attaches to the Nuptial Blessing; and it is, at the same time, a rebuke to those—and they are not a few—who make light of this source of divine grace.

With regard to the third question, it may be said that, apart from the "closed time," the Nuptial Mass may be celebrated on any day, with a few exceptions, and on these exceptional days the Nuptial Blessing with the commemoration of the Nuptial Mass may be inserted, with the sole exception of the vigil and feast of Pentecost, with the two following days; and the same would appear to apply to the feast of the Ascension and Corpus Christi.[1] And although on the commemoration of All Souls the celebration of a Mass for the living is not permitted, yet the Nuptial Mass may be celebrated, according to a decree of the Sacred Congregation of Rites, dated September 7, 1850; and, though this decree is not promulgated, it is yet authentic.[2]

The many privileges which the Church grants to the Nuptial Mass are an evidence of the earnest desire she has that her children should avail themselves of it. No one doubts her devotion to the souls in purgatory; but she grants, as we see, far greater privileges to the Nuptial Mass than she does to that for the dead, even in cases

[1] De Herdt, vol. iii. N. 285.
[2] S. Alphonsi, "Ceremoniæ Missæ," Schober, p. 238.

where the body is present. The antiquity of the Nuptial Mass is no less an evidence of the importance the Church attaches to it, being anxious, as she is, that those from whom her ranks are to be recruited should be enriched with special blessings for the discharge of their onerous duties. Pope St. Evaristus, who ruled the Church at the beginning of the second century, ordained, in accordance with apostolic tradition, that marriage should be celebrated publicly, and with the blessing of the priest;[1] and, although this is not conclusive evidence that the blessing meant was that found in the Nuptial Mass, it is probable that it was one similar to it, both on account of the importance the Church has always attached to the sacrament of matrimony, and also because Tertullian, who flourished but a century later, speaks of marriage with the Mass as a custom common among Christians.

Inasmuch as we are not here treating of the sacrament of matrimony, but only of the Nuptial Blessing, as one of the sacramentals, much is omitted that would otherwise be both interesting and instructive.

The marriage should take place immediately before the Mass. This Mass, it is to be noted, the priest is not bound to offer for the intention of the contracting parties, unless he has been requested to do so. Formerly the rituals of different countries were not uniform with regard to the vestments in which the priest should appear for the performance of the ceremony; but according to a decree of the Sacred Congregation of Rites, dated August 31, 1867, the priest is to be vested as for Mass, except that he does not put on the maniple, which is to be placed on the altar till the ceremony is over.

We have now to examine the Nuptial Mass, with the blessing that forms a part of it, omitting, however, those

[1] Roman Breviary, October 26th.

portions that are common to every Mass. The *Introit* is taken from the 7th and 8th chapters of the Book of Tobias, and from the 127th Psalm; and reads thus: "May the God of Israel join you together: and may He be with you who was merciful to two only children: and now, O Lord, make them bless Thee more fully. V. Blessed are all they that fear the Lord: that walk in His ways. Glory be to the Father, etc. May the God of Israel," etc., repeated. The following is the *Collect* or prayer: "Graciously hear us, almighty and merciful God, that what is performed by our ministry may be abundantly filled with Thy blessing. Through," etc.

The *Epistle* is taken from that of St. Paul to the Ephesians (v. 22-33); and however much its ideas may differ from those of the present day, they give the only correct basis upon which human society can be firmly established in any age. "Let women be subject to their husbands, as to the Lord: because the husband is the head of the wife, as Christ is the head of the Church. He is the saviour of his body. Therefore, as the Church is subject to Christ, so also let the wives be to their husbands in all things. Husbands, love your wives, as Christ also loved the Church, and delivered Himself up for it: that He might sanctify it, cleansing it by the laver of water in the word of life, that He might present it to Himself a glorious Church, not having spot or wrinkle, or any such thing, but that it should be holy and without blemish. So also ought men to love their wives as their own bodies. He that loveth his wife loveth himself. For no man ever hated his own flesh, but nourisheth and cherisheth it, as also Christ doth the Church: because we are members of His body, of His flesh, and of His bones. For this cause shall a man leave his father and mother, and shall cleave to his wife, and they shall be two in one flesh. This is a great sacrament: but I speak in Christ and in the Church. Nevertheless, let every one of you in particular love his wife as himself: and let the wife fear the husband."

The *Gradual*, recited during the greater part of the year, is composed of the following verses of Scripture: "Thy wife shall be as a fruitful vine on the walls of thy house. Thy children as olive branches round about thy table. Alleluia, alleluia. May the Lord send you help from the sanctuary, and defend you out of Sion. Alleluia."

The *Gospel* is taken from that of St. Matthew (xix. 3–6): "And there came to Jesus the Pharisees tempting Him, and saying: Is it lawful for a man to put away his wife for every cause? Who answering said to them: Have ye not read that He who made man from the beginning made them male and female? And He said: For this cause shall a man leave father and mother, and shall cleave to his wife, and they two shall be in one flesh. Therefore now they are not two, but one flesh. What therefore God hath joined together let no man put asunder." The *Offertory* is also from the Sacred Scriptures: "In Thee, O Lord, have I put my trust: I said, Thou art my God: my lot is in Thy hands." The *Secret* prayer is couched in these terms: "Receive, we beseech Thee, O Lord, the gift which we here offer up in behalf of Thy holy law of marriage: And as Thou art the Giver of the work, be Thou also the Disposer thereof. Through Our Lord," etc.

Immediately after the *Pater Noster*, the first part of the Nuptial Blessing is recited over the married couple, who come forward and kneel at the foot of the altar. The priest, turning round to them, prays: "Be propitious, O Lord, unto our supplications, and graciously assist Thine own institution, which Thou hast ordained for the propagation of mankind : that the union made by Thy appointment may be preserved by Thy aid. Through Our Lord Jesus Christ, Thy Son, etc.

"O God, who by the might of Thy power didst create all things out of nothing; who when the beginnings of the universe were set in order, and man was made to the image of God, didst ordain the inseparable assistance of woman, in such wise that Thou gavest beginning to her body out of the flesh of man, teaching thereby that what it had pleased Thee should be formed of one it should never be lawful to put asunder ; O God, who didst create the bond of matrimony by such an excellent mystery, that in the covenant of marriage Thou wouldst signify the sacrament of Christ and His Church ; O God, by whom woman is joined to man, and society, as ordained from the beginning, is furnished with a blessing, which alone was not removed, either in punishment of original sin or by the sentence of the deluge ; look mercifully on this Thy handmaid, who, being now to be joined in wedlock, earnestly desires to be fortified with Thy protection. May it be to her a yoke of love and peace ; may she marry in Christ, faithful and chaste, and be an imitator of holy women. May she be amiable to her husband, like Rachel ; wise, like Rebecca ; long-lived and faithful, like Sara. May the author of sin have no share in any of her actions. May she remain constant to the faith and commandments : united to one spouse, may she fly all unlawful approaches ; may she protect her weakness by the strength of discipline; may she be grave in bashfulness, venerable in modesty, learned in heavenly doctrine. May she be fruitful in offspring, approved and innocent ; and may she arrive at the repose of the blessed in the heavenly kingdom ; and may they both see their children's children, even to the third and fourth generation, and arrive at their desired old age.

Through the same Jesus Christ, Thy Son," etc. At the conclusion of these prayers the Mass continues as usual.[1] The *Communion* prayer is: "Behold, thus shall every man be blessed that feareth the Lord: and mayest thou see thy children's children: peace upon Israel." The *Post-Communion* is: "We beseech Thee, O Almighty God, to accompany with Thy gracious favor what Thy providence hath ordained, and preserve in continual peace those whom Thou hast joined in lawful union. Through Our Lord," etc. Immediately before the ordinary blessing given in Mass is the concluding one of the Nuptial Benediction. Like all the special prayers of this Mass, it includes three petitions: fecundity, peace, and everlasting happiness. It is addressed to Heaven in these words: "May the God of Abraham, the God of Isaac, and the God of Jacob be with you, and may He fulfil His blessing upon you, that you may see your children's children unto the third and fourth generation, and may afterward have everlasting life, without end, by the help of Our Lord Jesus Christ, who, with the Father and the Holy Ghost, liveth and reigneth God, world without end. Amen."

Such is the Nuptial Mass and Blessing, ordained in her maternal solicitude by holy Church for her children who are about to enter into married life—a life enriched, indeed, with many graces for those who enter it with the proper dispositions, but strewn for all with more than ordinary trials and temptations. Happy are they whose early training and spirit of piety prompt them, on realizing the existence of these trials and temptations, to fortify themselves with the graces of the Nuptial Mass and Blessing, and to call down upon the new path they have entered the plentiful dews of heavenly benediction!

[1] The couple are earnestly exhorted to communicate, by a decree. S. C. R., March 21, 1874.

XXIII.—THE CHURCHING OF WOMEN.

WHEN our first parents were so unfortunate as to transgress the divine command by eating the forbidden fruit, Almighty God called them to Him, and in punishment of their disobedience the woman, who was the first to transgress, was told: "I will multiply thy sorrows and thy conceptions: in sorrow thou shalt bring forth children." And though it was promised at the same time that the seed of the woman should crush the head of the serpent which had seduced her, this was to take place only after the lapse of centuries, during which the woman was to hold an inferior position, and her noblest function of motherhood be regarded as necessarily associated with defilement. The memory of this, which was traditional among all the peoples of the world, assumed in the true religion of the Jewish Dispensation the sanction of a liturgical law. It was left for Mary, the highest type of true womanhood, to change this decree, and to elevate woman to the sublimest heights to which it is possible for her to aspire. What can ennoble her more than to have the greatest creature that ever came or ever can come from the hand of Omnipotence given her as a model? If sin came by woman, redemption from sin came also by woman, as the Church sings of Mary: "Through whom we have received the Author of life, Christ Our Lord."

As our divine Redeemer by eating the Paschal Lamb on the eve of His sacred Passion gave that Mosaic rite an honorable termination, as certain of the Fathers have remarked, so did Mary, by conforming to the law of purification, give to it an honorable ending.

The rite of Churching differs essentially from the ceremony of legal purification among the Jews, as we shall see in the sequel. The Jewish rite was founded on the idea of legal defilement ; Mary removed this, and by becoming the mother of our divine Redeemer made maternity truly honorable. The Jewish rite was necessary to fit the mother for assisting at religious ceremonies ; the Christian rite is an act of thanksgiving. The Jewish rite was of obligation, commanded by the voice of God Himself ; the Christian ceremony does not bind even under pain of venial sin. Hence through Mary the whole current not only of public opinion but also of religious observance on this point is changed, and results in the true elevation and ennobling of woman. Happy would it be for woman if the refined paganism of our day did not seek to degrade her once more, while eloquently prating about her rights. But by no other means than by the example of Mary can she be truly elevated, and the sooner the world learns this the better.

A spirit of humility, so natural to the true Christian heart, as well as a desire of imitating the Blessed Virgin, equally natural to Christian mothers, induced the early Christian women to abstain from entering the church for a certain time after they had received the blessing of motherhood, although no legal defilement attached to them under the New Dispensation. They then asked the blessing of the priest at the door of the church, before entering, and made their first visit as an act of thanksgiving for their safe delivery.[1] Hence the origin of churching, which was a natural outgrowth of the Mosaic rite. The date of the origin of this pious custom is not certain ; but that it is very ancient there can be

[1] O'Kane, pp. 244 *et seq.*; " Kirchen-Lexicon."

no question. Perhaps the first authentic mention we have of it is in an Arabic canon of the Council of Nice.

Turning to the persons to whom this blessing is to be imparted, it is to be remarked that it is not to be given to all women indiscriminately. And as there is no obligation binding even under pain of venial sin, women are only to be exhorted to receive it, but it is not to be imposed as an obligation. Nor is it of obligation that the mother should bring her infant with her, as there is no law to that effect, nor is there anything in the ceremony that necessarily supposes the presence of the child. When a provincial council of Mechlin decreed to make churching obligatory, the Sacred Congregation at Rome changed the decree. The blessing is not to be denied those whose infants have died without baptism. Says O'Kane: "The pastor may refuse it in any case in which the birth is notoriously illegitimate, even when there is no diocesan or provincial statute requiring him to do so." And the Sacred Congregation of Rites, on being consulted on the subject, decided that none but those whose children were born in lawful wedlock could claim a right to this blessing.[2] Also, according to the Second Plenary Council of Baltimore (N. 242), the blessing is not to be given promiscuously, but regard is to be had to the honorable condition of the person asking it. In short, it is a blessing for honorable, not for dishonorable, motherhood.

There is no special legislation with regard to the priest by whom the blessing should be imparted, nor is there any need of it; the pastor of the church to which the mother belongs, or his representative, is the person who, according to the most ordinary rules of propriety, should give it.

[1] "Kirchen-Lexicon."
[2] Felise, Decree, June 18, 1859; O'Kane; De Herdt.

The blessing is not to take place outside the church, even in the case of a mother who is in danger of death ; because as there is no obligation to receive it there can be no sin in omitting it; but in missionary countries where Mass has frequently to be said in a hall, a schoolhouse, or a private dwelling, the blessing can also be imparted there. The rule, then, is that wherever Mass can be celebrated the blessing can be given, but not elsewhere.

With regard to the manner of giving the blessing, the circumstances of this and perhaps other missionary countries have made certain inroads on the strict requirements of the ritual. It directs that if a woman desires this blessing she shall kneel at the door of the church, holding a lighted candle in her hand ; and the priest, vested in surplice and white stole, and accompanied by an acolyte, shall proceed to the door of the church, where he shall sprinkle her with holy water, and recite the twenty-third psalm, with an antiphon. Then he presents her the end of the stole which hangs from his left shoulder, which she takes with her right hand, while holding the candle in her left ; and they come up to the foot of the altar, the priest saying the while : "Enter into the temple of God, adore the Son of the Blessed Virgin Mary, who has given thee fruitfulness of offspring." After certain versicles and responses, with the "Our Father," the priest recites the prayer : "Almighty, everlasting God, who through the delivery of the Blessed Virgin Mary hast changed the pains of the faithful in childbirth into joy, look mercifully on this Thy handmaid, who comes in gladness to Thy temple to offer thanksgiving ; and grant that, after this life, through the merits and intercession of the same Blessed Mary, she may be found worthy to attain.

together with her offspring, to the joys of everlasting happiness. Through Christ Our Lord. Amen." The priest then sprinkles her with holy water, gives her a blessing, and the ceremony is ended.

But it has just been said that the full ceremonial of the ritual is not always carried out in many places. Among us in this country it is not the general custom to meet the woman at the church door; she more commonly comes to the altar rail, where the priest, standing at the inner side of the railing, performs the ceremony How far this departure from the strict requirements of the ritual is justified it is not the intention to inquire in this place; but where it does exist it is known and at least tolerated by local ecclesiastical authorities.

It may further be noted that while in many of the blessings, and in the administration of the sacrament of baptism, there are rubrics directing the plural number to be used when there is more than one person, there is no such rubric with regard to churching. But this is not always regarded, and there are frequently several women churched at the same time. Nothing is said in the ritual as to when the candle should be extinguished, or what is afterward to be done with it; but it is commonly extinguished at the conclusion of the ceremony, and left to the church to be burned on the altar.

This blessing is asked in imitation of the Blessed Virgin presenting herself in the temple, and submitting to the ceremonial law of purification; and, inasmuch as she made an offering on that occasion, it is customary with many Christian mothers to make an offering on the event of their being churched. It should not be regarded as strange that offerings are made to the priest or church on the occasion of baptisms, marriages, churchings, and the like. There are at least two very good reasons for this. In the first place, there is a propriety in the faithful making voluntary offerings for the spiritual benefits they receive through the ministry of the priests, as those cannot be estimated at a price, as labor or merchandise can be ; and as they are the free gifts of God to His people, there is a fitness in making some return for them in the same manner. And in the second place, there is no professional man of the same education, and holding a position at all as responsible as that of the priest, who receives so small a salary ; and while professional men have only certain hours in which they are engaged, and seldom more than six or seven in the day, the priest is liable to be called at any moment, night or day, and when called he is strictly bound in conscience to render prompt service. The new-born infant can call him to the furthest end of his parish, were he ever so fatigued. And these offerings are commanded by God Himself, both in the Old and in the New Law.[1] The statutes of every, or almost every, diocese have made his salary comparatively small, knowing that he will receive certain voluntary offerings, thus making these offerings a part of his necessary income ; and this gives him a sort of claim on the people for them. It is well for the faithful to have a correct idea of this matter ; for while some of them imagine the priest is fond of money, the fact is he is the poorest paid man of education in the community. In large congregations, however, these perquisites do not, as a rule, go to the officiating priest, but are thrown into a general fund from which the salary of the pastor and his curates is taken in whole or in part, according to the amount.

[1] Deut. xvi. 16 ; I. Cor. ix. 43.

XXIV.—THE BLESSING AND THANKSGIVING AT MEALS.

It is not the intention to treat in this brief essay of the various forms of blessing and thanksgiving which are authorized by the Church and practised by different religious communities and some other persons, but rather to speak of the act itself—its propriety, its antiquity, the favor with which it has ever been regarded by the faithful, and the approval it has received from many holy personages of the Old Law, and from our divine Saviour and His apostles and saints in the New. It is proper to remark in the beginning that while the priests of the Church, by the power they receive in ordination—having their hands anointed, that whatever they bless shall be blessed, and whatever they sanctify shall be sanctified—are the proper persons to bless articles officially as the ministers of God, and in His name; still any person, even a child, is permitted to make the sign of the cross over any proper object, with the intention and desire that the blessing of Heaven may descend upon it, and upon those who use it in the spirit of faith and in conformity to the divine will. For this reason it is not only permitted, but recommended, that lay persons should ask the blessing of God upon such things as they have occasion to use, and for which there is no special blessing. But as nothing in the natural order is more common or necessary than the food we eat, it is very fitting that it should be sanctified by the word of God and prayer. Under the head of the blessing of food thanksgiving is also commonly included, whether it is made before or after the meal.

Turning to the authorities on the subject, we learn that the blessing of food was enjoined on the Jews by God Himself. Moses, laying down the law for the chosen people, says: "When thou hast eaten, and art full, bless the Lord."[1] According to the Talmud, the form of prayer recited by the Jews after each meal was this: "Blessed be Thou, O Lord, our God, the King of the world, who hast produced this food (or drink) from the earth (or the vine)."[2]

Monsig. Gaume, however, gives a more particular account of this ceremony, which will doubtless be interesting to the reader. He informs us that at meal-time "the father of the family, surrounded by his children, said: 'Blessed be the Lord our God, whose goodness gives food to all flesh.' Then taking a cup of wine in his right hand, he blessed it, saying, 'Blessed be the Lord our God, who has created the fruit of the vine.' He first tasted it, and then passed it to his guests, who also tasted it. Then followed the blessing of the bread. Taking it between his hands, the father of the family said: 'Praised and blessed be the Lord our God, who has drawn bread from the earth.' He then broke the bread, ate a piece, and gave some to his guests. It was only then that the meal began. When they changed the wine or brought in new dishes, a particular blessing was made over each, so that every kind of nourishment was purified and consecrated. The meal being ended they sang a hymn of thanksgiving."[3]

Turning to the New Dispensation, we have the highest

---

[1] Deuteronomy, viii. 10.
[2] "The Life of Jesus Christ," Maas, p. 220.
[3] "The Sign of the Cross in the Nineteenth Century," pp. 244, 245.

sanction for this universal custom in the example of our divine Redeemer, who on several occasions is said to have blessed the simple fare prepared for Himself and His apostles or the multitudes, as in the institution of the Blessed Eucharist and in the multiplying of the loaves and fishes, as well as at other times. St. Paul, too, frequently admonishes the early Christians to receive the gifts of God with thanksgiving.

It is impossible that a custom so perfectly in harmony with the promptings of a generous nature, as well as with the practice of holy men of earlier times, should not have been adopted and practised by Christians from the beginning; and that such was the case we have abundant evidence. The extracts from the Fathers which I shall proceed to give are taken for the most part from Monsig. Gaume, above quoted.

Says Tertullian: "Prayer begins and ends the meal." St. Athanasius bears witness, in the following words, to the custom of his early day: "When we sit down to table, and take the bread to break it, we make the sign of the cross over it three times, and return thanks. After the repast we renew our thanksgiving by saying thrice: 'The good and merciful Lord has given food to them that fear Him. Glory be to the Father,'" etc. The austere St. Jerome follows with the admonition: "Let no one ever sit at table without having prayed, and let him never leave it without having given thanks to the Creator." Carried away by his ardent zeal, St. John Chrysostom rebukes some of the Christians of his time in such forcible terms as these: "We must pray before and after meals. Hear this, ye swine who nourish yourselves with the gifts of God without raising your eyes to the Hand that gives them."

Not only in families was the blessing of food practised, but even in camp among the soldiers, where, if in any place, we should expect to see it omitted. St. Gregory Nazianzen, among others, bears witness to this fact, and that, too, in the time of Julian the Apostate—a circumstance which is worthy of note.

It is needless to add further evidence on this point. The custom is so well known that no one at all familiar with the daily life of the early Christians will presume to call it in question. But the reader will be interested in having placed before him some of the forms of prayer made use of on such occasions at that early day. The two following are taken from Origen, one of the earliest writers of the Church. The blessing before meals is in these words: "O Thou who givest food to all that breathe, deign to bless the food we are about to take. Thou hast said that if we should ever drink any poisonous thing, we should receive no injury thereby, provided we would invoke Thy name, for Thou art all-powerful. Take away, then, from this food all that is dangerous and hurtful in it." And the thanksgiving was couched in these terms: "Blessed be Thou, O Lord our God, who hast nourished us since our infancy, and with us all that breathe. Fill our hearts with joy, that we may abound in all kinds of good works. Through Jesus Christ Our Lord, to whom, with Thee and the Holy Ghost, be glory, honor, and power. Amen." How profound the philosophy, how simply beautiful the language, of these invocations!

Whenever a priest was present, the honor of asking the blessing was very properly conferred on him. And indeed the practice of asking the blessing at table was regarded as so holy that when, in the ninth century, the Bulgarians were converted to the faith, they asked Pope

Nicholas I. whether a layman might take the place of a priest in performing this function. "Without doubt," answered the Pontiff; "for it has been given to each one to preserve by the sign of the cross all that belongs to him from the snares of the demon, and in the name of Our Lord Jesus Christ to triumph over his attacks."[1]

Different nations have different customs in this as in almost everything else; but among some, especially among the Germans, in this country at least, it is usual to have one of the children pronounce the blessing at meals. I have been at table in their houses, when, though a priest, I was passed by, and one of the children asked the blessing. I approve of this custom, because it familiarizes children with such pious exercises; and the great, the crying want of our day is more prayer, and prayer on ordinary occasions.

So natural to man is the blessing before meals, and so deeply grounded in his nature, that even the pagans saw the propriety and felt the necessity of it, as may be learned from their writings. And here again I shall beg leave to quote from Monsig. Gaume: "Never," says Athenæus, "did the ancients take their meals without having first implored the gods." And speaking of the Egyptians, the earliest of all the pagan nations of whom we have an authentic history, he continues: "Having taken their places on the banquet-couches, they arose, knelt down, and the chief of the banquet or the priest began the traditional prayers, which they recited after him; after that they resumed their places."

The pouring out of libations to the gods, not only at the beginning of the feast, but at the bringing in of the several courses, is so well known as to require the merest reference. The Romans had a proverb which the learned

[1] "The Sign of the Cross," etc., p. 240.

Erasmus translates as meaning: "Do not throw yourselves on the food like beasts, but eat only after having offered the first-fruits to the gods." Even among the pagans, according to their best writers, the daily repast was regarded as something sacred. The reason why these blessings were pronounced and libations poured out, according to Porphyrius, a high authority in such matters, is given in these words: "It must be known that the dwellings are full of demons. This is why we purify them by expelling those malevolent hosts every time we pray to the gods. Moreover, all creatures are full of them, for they particularly relish certain kinds of food. So when we sit at table, they not only place themselves beside us, but also attach themselves to our bodies. Thence comes the use of lustrations, the principal end of which is not so much to invoke the gods as to expel the demons."

There is no indulgence attached to the mere asking of a blessing before meals, or the returning of thanks after it; but prayers are sometimes said at meals which have been indulgenced by the Holy See without reference to the occasion on which they are recited.

All fair-minded persons then, whether Christian or not, must, by the weight of the most irrefragable proofs, conclude with the learned Monsig. Gaume that "prayer over food is as ancient as the world, as widespread as mankind." The virtue of prudence will teach that it is not advisable to make the sign of the cross over food on some occasions and in some company, but it will not teach that it is ever advisable to omit at least a secret blessing of the gifts of God.

It is much to be regretted that contact with an unbelieving world has exercised a baneful influence over many Christians, causing them to forget or neglect the pious custom of blessing before and thanksgiving after meals, so reasonable in itself, so consonant with the spirit of our holy faith, and so highly sanctioned and consecrated not only by the practice of the noblest portion of the human race—the saints—but commanded by the voice of God, and practised by His Incarnate Son during His sojourn upon earth. Can a custom so recommended carry with it anything but a blessing? Can a faithful child of the Church regard it lightly, or blush to practise it? It were to brand himself as more negligent or forgetful than even the pagans, much less the favored children of a kind and merciful God. Far be it from any Christians in our day so to dishonor their fathers in the faith.

XXV.—SACRED VESTMENTS.

In treating of the holy sacrifice of the Mass the Council of Trent uses the following words: "Whereas such is the nature of man that, without external helps, he cannot easily be raised to the meditation of divine things, therefore has holy mother Church instituted certain rites, to wit, that certain things be pronounced in the Mass in a low and others in a louder tone. She has likewise employed ceremonies, such as mystic benedictions, lights, incense, vestments, and many other things of this kind, derived from an apostolical tradition, whereby both the majesty of so great a sacrifice might be recommended and the minds of the faithful be excited by those visible signs of religion and piety to the contemplation of those most sublime things which are hidden in this sacrifice."[1]

This passage reveals a very important truth of which we are all conscious, but to which perhaps we too seldom advert; yet it exercises an influence on our civil, religious, and military life. The simple dais on which the school-teacher sits gives him an influence which he would not have without it. So, too, the elevation of the royal throne, the pulpit, etc. The effect with regard to a uniform or a religious habit is still more marked, because its influence is both objective and subjective: it not only impresses others with the position of the person who wears it, but it also reminds him that he should " walk worthy of the vocation whereunto he is called." For this reason it is that soldiers, policemen, firemen,

[1] Session xxii., chapter v., Waterworth's translation.

and others are uniformed, that they may respect themselves and may the better command the respect of those around them. Much more is this true of religious; for, though there is a saying that the habit does not make the monk, it is nevertheless true that it has a great deal to do with making him. All this is in perfect harmony with right reason; and whatever is in harmony with reason is pleasing to God, the Author of reason.

While the sacred vestments are sacramentals, answering all the requirements of the definition, they are something besides, which the other sacramentals are not. They are an appropriate dress, fitting the minister of God to perform his sacred functions in a more dignified and becoming manner. And here it may not be out of place to correct an erroneous impression on the minds of not a few Catholics: that, namely, that the vestments give the priest power. They do not. He receives all his powers directly from God, through the ministry of the bishop, in his ordination. But it is for the bishop of the diocese in which he is to labor to define the limits and the circumstances in which he shall exercise some of these powers, such, for example, as hearing confessions.

We have but meagre information regarding what may be called the priesthood of the Patriarchal Church; all that we know is that the patriarch, or some one designated by him, officiated at the sacrifices; but whether he wore a distinctive dress or insignia during the sacrifice, or whether his venerable appearance was sufficiently characteristic of his office, we have no means of knowing at the present time. But I am of opinion that even then there must have been some peculiarity in his dress, from the fact that among all nations, no matter how civilized or how barbarous, the priest —who among the latter was generally the medicine-man—was and still is dressed differently from the rest of the people when performing his religious rites. And, as I have frequently insisted in these pages, paganism is a corruption of true revelation, and even in its greatest deformity it bears evidence to that fact.

When it pleased Almighty God to give a fuller revelation of His holy will, in the establishment of the Mosaic law, He prescribed in the minutest manner the material and form of the sacerdotal vestments, and enjoined them under the severest penalties; and so deeply did the people venerate the vestments of the high-priest that Josephus tells us they had a light constantly burning before them in the place in which they were kept. The kind and form of the vestments of the New Law were not prescribed by a divine command, and this for two reasons: in the first place, because by a miracle of omnipotence our divine Redeemer gave to the head of His Church the plenitude of power, promising the sanction of Heaven to his enactments; and, in the second, because the Christian Church, unlike the Jewish, was not intended for one nation only, but for the world, and for all time; and must vary somewhat in external matters, according to times and peoples, in the lapse of time in which it is to exist, and the countless variety of nations to which it is to be preached.

The word *vestment*, like most of the terms used in the liturgy, is of Latin origin, and has, derivatively, the same meaning as the English word *clothing;* but usage has long since restricted it to garments worn by the ministers of religion during the performance of their sacred functions.

In the first four or five centuries the vestments worn by the clergy were the common dress of men in the

Roman Empire; and it was not till the repeated incursions of the barbarians had wholly changed the customs of southern Europe, and introduced new fashions in dress, that sacerdotal vestments became peculiar to one class and to religious functions. This change was effected gradually, of course, and rather by the force of circumstances than by the decrees of ecclesiastical authority. But though this is true, two points are to be noticed: in the first place, that the uses to which vestments were devoted would cause them, though conforming in pattern to the every-day dress of men, to be made of more costly material than other garments and to be more richly ornamented; and, in the second place, that the use for which they were intended would suggest the propriety of reserving them for sacred functions only. History confirms what propriety suggests; for about the middle of the third century Pope Stephen ordained that the Levites should not wear the consecrated vestments in common life, but only in the church.

There are five colors of vestments: white, red, green, violet, and black. There is also gold-cloth; but this, in the sense of the rubrics, is no color, but only a substitute for certain other colors. Different writers on liturgy held different opinions as to what colors gold-cloth is permitted to represent, but by a decree of the Sacred Congregation of Rites of April 28, 1866, it is permitted to be used for white, red, and green, according to the custom of the place. But the decree supposes that it is real gold-cloth, and not an imitation. In some places rose-colored vestments are worn on the third Sunday of Advent, the fourth of Lent, and the feast of the Holy Innocents, when it does not fall on a Sunday. Formerly this color was also worn in some places on the feasts of martyrs. The various colors came gradually into use.

At first, and up to the sixth century, only white was used. About that time other colors were added, but violet does not appear to have been worn till about the beginning of the thirteenth century. Pope Innocent III. is the first writer to mention four colors. The necessity the early missionaries of this and other countries were under of making the parcel which they were required to carry from one missionary station to another as small as possible, led to the use of vestments which combined two colors, as red and white, the cross on the back and the bar in the middle in front being of one color, and the rest of the vestment of another. This has been forbidden by the Holy See, and is seldom or never seen at present. Beyond these remarks it is not the intention to refer to any of the numerous local customs of churches, dioceses, or countries. While the existence of these customs tends to show the tolerant spirit of the Church in matters not essential, they also show the unity in variety of the Church's liturgy; for if order is heaven's first law, variety is the second. There can be no success without the one, and there can be no pleasure without the other.

Examining the vestments worn by the priest in the light of ecclesiastical tradition, we find them to have a practical use and a mystic signification, both of which will appear as we proceed. The mystic holds so important a place in the liturgy of the Church that an inquiry into the signification of the several colors will be instructive. Says O'Brien: "*White*, being symbolic of purity, innocence, and glory, is, as a general rule, employed on the special feasts of Our Lord and the Blessed Virgin, and on those of the angels, virgins, and confessors. *Red*, the symbol of fortitude, is the color proper to Pentecost, in memory of the tongues of fire; it is also used on the feasts of the apostles and martyrs, and on those of Our Lord's Passion. *Green*, symbolic of hope, is used as the color of the time from the octave of the Epiphany to Septuagesima, and from the octave of Pentecost to Advent. *Violet*, the penitential color, is used on all occasions of public affliction and sorrow, in time of fasting and penance, and in all those processions which do not immediately concern the Blessed Sacrament. This color is also used on the feast of the Holy Innocents, on account of the lamentations and weepings heard through Jerusalem when they were massacred by order of Herod. But should this feast fall on Sunday, the color of the occasion is red, as also the color of the octave, from the fact that the lamentations taken up are supposed to have ceased by this time, and the eighth day is always significant of beatitude and glory. *Black*, from its gloomy appearance, and because it is the negation of all color, is used in Masses and Offices of the Dead, and on Good Friday in memory of the profound darkness that covered the land when Our Lord was crucified." [1]

It is the intention to speak of those vestments only which the people are accustomed to see the priest wear ; for it is thought more interesting and instructive for them to understand these than to be told, for example, of the archbishop's pallium, or something which they seldom or never see. The cassock, being the ordinary dress of the priest, does not come under the name of a vestment. The vestments proper are the amice, the alb, the cincture, the maniple, the stole, and the chasuble ; to which will here be added the cope, the shoulder-veil, and the surplice, as being in common use in religious functions.

Propriety would dictate that the vestments used in the

[1] " History of the Mass," p. 63.

service of religion should first receive an appropriate blessing. This is confirmed both by the custom of the Church to bless all things which she makes use of, and also by the fact that God Himself directed that the vestments employed in the service of religion in the Mosaic law should be consecrated with a solemn ceremony. It is not known with certainty when the custom of blessing them was first introduced, but it must be very ancient. The first mention of it is found in the Gregorian "Sacramentary"; and the Council of Poitiers, held in the year 1100, forbids anyone but bishops to give this blessing, and Pope Innocent III. confirmed this decree. Bishops, however, very often impart this faculty to their priests in missionary countries.

Worn-out vestments are not to be turned to profane uses, but are to be devoted to some other purpose in the church, or else be burnt, and the ashes thrown into the *sacrarium*, on the general principle that whatever has been consecrated to God cannot be turned to the use of man.

Turning to the several vestments, we have first to treat of the *amice*, which is an oblong piece of white linen with strings at two of its corners by which it is to be adjusted. The name is derived from the Latin word *amictus*, which means to wrap around or about; and the amice is intended, with the alb, to conceal the everyday dress of the priest, so that, on approaching the altar, he may lay aside all that savors of the world, and may in very truth appear what St. Paul calls him—"a man of God." At first the amice was not worn, but it appears to have come into general use about the commencement of the eighth century. Formerly it covered the head, and it is so worn at present by several religious Orders till the beginning of the Mass. Nor was it first invariably made of linen as now, but occasionally of silk or other material, and it was sometimes richly ornamented.

Inquiring into the symbolical meaning of the amice, we need not be surprised that writers have assigned various significations, as they have also done with regard to the other sacred vestments. But the best means of arriving at a correct idea of the mind of the Church is to examine the prayer recited by the priest while clothing himself with the amice. He says: "Place, O Lord, on my head the helmet of salvation, for repelling the attacks of the Evil One." From this it appears that the amice is symbolical of the helmet worn by soldiers to protect them from the blows of their adversaries.

The alb derives its name from the Latin word *alba*, white, because it is always of that color. It is simply the undergarment formerly worn by both the Greeks and Romans. The name was not incorporated into ecclesiastical terminology before the end of the third century, although the garment itself was in use from the beginning. Nor was it always made of linen, as at present, but was sometimes of other material, and more or less richly ornamented. The use of lace for the lower part of the alb is of still more recent introduction. The prayer recited by the priest while putting on the alb affords the most correct idea of the mystic signification of the garment. It is couched in the following terms: "Purify me, O Lord, and make me clean of heart, that, washed in the blood of the Lamb, I may possess eternal joys." In vesting himself, then, with the alb the priest is reminded of those "who washed their robes and made them white in the blood of the Lamb," and of the purity of soul and body with which he should approach the altar to offer the same immaculate Lamb to the Eternal Father for his sins and those of the whole world.

The *girdle* or *cincture*, with which the priest or other sacred minister secures the alb about his person, was in use among both the Greeks and Romans, and was introduced as a matter of necessity into the list of sacred vestments. In the Middle Ages cinctures were richly ornamented, and were made of various materials. The shape, too, was more or less arbitrary; and they were sometimes found in the form of lampreys, eels, etc. According to the present discipline of the Church it should be of linen rather than of other material, but it may also be of wool, and may vary in color with the vestments.[1] It is the symbol of continence and self-restraint, as is expressed in the prayer which the priest says while girding himself: "Gird me, O Lord, with the cincture of purity, and extinguish within me the humors of concupiscence, that the virtues of continence and chastity may abide in me."

The next vestment which the priest puts on, and which is also worn by the deacon and subdeacon, is the *maniple*, which is of the same material and color as the stole and chasuble. It is worn, as is well known, on the left arm, and is fastened just below the elbow by a tape or pin. It is not until the eighth or ninth century that any trace of the maniple is found. As its name— *manipulus*—indicates, it was originally simply a handkerchief for wiping away perspiration or the tears of devotion shed by the pious celebrant; but it has undergone various changes in the course of time, such as being enriched with ornaments, so that its original use has altogether been lost sight of, and it is now nothing

---

[1] Decrees, January 22, 1701; January 8, 1709; and December 23, 1862.

more than an ornament. But the original use of the maniple is still referred to in the prayer recited by the priest while putting it on: "May I merit, O Lord, to bear the maniple of weeping and sorrow, that I may receive with joy the reward of labor."

After the maniple comes the *stole*, a vestment which has undergone many changes, and has been the subject of no little controversy among liturgists. The word is derived from the Greek, and means a robe of any kind, while the Latin term designated the outer garment worn by women of rank. In the earlier ages it was frequently, and indeed generally, called the *orarium*, which means a handkerchief; and it is mentioned by this name as early as the middle of the fourth century in the decrees of the Council of Leodicea. From that time forward frequent mention is made of it in the canons of councils. But the first mention of it by the now familiar name of *stole* does not occur before the ninth century. Its use was gradually restricted both as to the functions in which it should be worn and the persons who were permitted to make use of it, till the present discipline was finally adopted. This was about the time of Charlemagne, that is, near the close of the eighth century. It is the most frequently worn of all the sacred vestments; and it is the privilege of the Pope to wear it all the time. With the adoption of the name *stole* that of *orarium* fell into disuse; but just why the one was substituted for the other it is at present impossible to determine.

Among the vestments the stole is the symbol of immortality, and also of the obedience of our divine Redeemer. The prayer recited while the priest vests himself with it refers both to the original signification of the Greek term and to the mystic meaning of the word.

It reads: "Restore unto me, O Lord, the stole of immortality, which I lost by the fall of our first parents, that, although I am unworthy to approach Thy holy mysteries, I may, notwithstanding, merit an eternal reward."

Lastly comes the *chasuble*, about which more has been written, wisely and unwisely, than about any other vestment. Its material, its shape, its size, its uses, etc., have been subjected to an endless torture. But, inasmuch as this essay is written for the general reader rather than for the learned antiquarian, such points only will be dwelt upon as are believed to be of general interest and instruction. The more learned will readily know where to look for fuller information. The word *chasuble* is of Latin origin, although it is not found in the writings of the classic authors of that vigorous and polished tongue. In its stead they use the word *pœnula*, which means a mantle or cloak, and was the outer garment worn by the Romans when on journeys or in military service. The Latin word *casula*, which is translated chasuble, is the diminutive of *casa*, and literally means a little house, because, in its original form, the garment covered the entire body, like a little house. The term is first met with in the will of Cæsarius of Arles, near the middle of the sixth century, and in the biography of his contemporary Fulgentius of Ruspe; but in both cases it means a garment used in every-day life. It is also called *planeta*, from a Greek word which signifies to wander, because, as St. Isidore of Seville remarks, its ample folds seem to wander over the body rather than to fit it closely. It was only in the early half of the sixth century that it became exclusively a sacerdotal vestment. It was then a very ample garment, having a hole in the centre for passing the head through. It retained this shape till about the eleventh century, when it began to undergo changes, the first of which was introduced for the sake of convenience, the sides being cut away to give the arms of the celebrant freer action. It is needless to enlarge on the numerous changes that have taken place in the form of the chasuble till at present it scarcely retains a vestige of its original appearance; of the attempts that have been made by well-meaning persons to bring it back to its primitive form; of the manner in which it came to be made of stiff material and ornamented; or of the many other points that might prove interesting and instructive to the learned, but which are of little practical use to the general reader. It remains to remark briefly on its mystic signification.

Early writers have attributed several mystic significations to the chasuble, based for the most part on the fact that it originally covered the entire body. The first and most generally adopted was charity; but it is also regarded as the emblem of justice, humility, and peace, which should, as it were, cover the priest as the minister of Him in whom all these virtues shone with a lustre infinitely perfect. But the prayer recited by the priest while vesting himself with it regards it rather as symbolical of the yoke of Christ. He says: "O Lord, who hast said, My yoke is sweet and My burden light, grant that I may so bear it as to obtain Thy grace. Amen."

The cope, which is called *pluviale* in the Latin liturgical language, as a protection against rain, from the Latin word *pluvia*—rain—does not appear to have had its equivalent among the garments of the ancient Romans. But strictly speaking it is only another form of the chasuble, better adopted to processions and outdoor religious functions, and the cape on it is a remnant of the hood which those who wore it were formerly accustomed to draw over their heads in inclement weather. It is so well known to the faithful that nothing need be said of its form or material. It is not, however, an exclusively sacerdotal vestment, as it is worn by the chanters at Vespers, where Vespers are celebrated according to the strict requirements of the ceremonial. It would be difficult to determine the time when it became a vestment distinct in form and use from the chasuble ; but it is mentioned in one of the Roman Ordos. No special blessing is given for the cope, and whether it is to be blessed or not is disputed by liturgical writers. Nor is any prayer to be recited by the priest while putting it on.[1]

The *humeral*, or *shoulder-veil*, is made of the same material as the cope, and is used by the subdeacon in solemn Masses to hold the paten, from the Offertory to the *Pater Noster*, in imitation of the Levites of the Old Law, who were not permitted to carry the sacred vessels till they had been wrapped up in the coverings by the priests. It is also worn by the priest while giving benediction with the Most Blessed Sacrament, and when carrying the same Holy Sacrament in procession. It is impossible to fix the date of its introduction ; but from the use to which it is put by the subdeacon it or a substitute for it must have been early brought into requisition. No blessing is required for it, and nothing is said while putting it on.

Much more, however, is to be said of the *surplice*. This term, derived from the Latin word *superpelicium*, literally means a garment worn over another made of skins. It is related of many of the anchorites of the

[1] London *Tablet*, 1891, p. 941.

early ages that they had outer garments made of the skins of animals, as well as of other materials; and, indeed, it is but natural for the pioneers of any country, who have often to subsist to a great extent on the flesh of animals killed in the chase, to clothe themselves with the skins of the same animals. Persons familiar with the history of our country need not be told of this. Obeying this law of necessity, as well as carrying out a cherished spirit of poverty, it was but natural that the anchorites and monks of early times, who are well known to have been the pioneers of civilization as well as of religion in many parts of Europe, should, in the absence of a better outfit, have clothed themselves with the skins of the animals they were obliged to kill in order to prevent them from destroying their fields or flocks. These rustic garments were admirably suited to protect the monks in the north of Europe, or in other cold climates, from the severity of the winters, when they entered their chapels in the dead of night to recite the Divine Office. But their sense of what was becoming the house of God, however humble it may have been, and much more their ideas of propriety in approaching the sacraments, would suggest some sort of covering for this humble garb on such occasions. Hence the introduction and the name of surplice—something worn over this ruder garment of skins. The important Synod of Aix-la-Chapelle, held in 817, decreed that each monk should have two garments of fur. Over this the linen garment, or *surplice*, was worn; but it is uncertain when this latter custom was introduced, although it is mentioned by the Council of Coyaca, in 1050. Durandus, who flourished near the close of the thirteenth century, and who had a most extraordinary talent for discovering mystic significations, speaks of it as already ancient, though not universal. At first it was longer than at present, resembling rather an alb than a surplice ; and it was made of linen instead of lace, as it is generally made in our day. In other words, the useful feature predominated over the ornamental, which is not the case in our time. The use of lace for the mere purpose of adding effect does not date further back, perhaps, than two centuries. At first it was the exception, now it is the rule.

In the conferring of Orders, the giving of the surplice with the right to wear it in religious functions is found in the conferring of tonsure, the step by which a person ceases to be a layman and becomes an ecclesiastic, and which is neither one of the Minor nor of the Holy Orders. The bishop recites the following words, adapted from St. Paul's Epistle to the Ephesians (iv. 24) : "May the Lord clothe thee with the new man, who according to God is created in justice and in the holiness of truth."

No blessing is required for the surplice ; and it is needless to remark that the altar-boys of our churches, who wear it in serving at Mass or Vespers, do so by a privilege which custom has sanctioned and of which the Church tacitly approves.

XXVI.—CHURCH BELLS.

THE history of bells is full of romantic interest. In civilized times they have been intimately associated, not only with all kinds of religious and social rites, but with almost every important historical event. Their influence upon architecture is not less remarkable, for to them indirectly we probably owe all the most famous towers in the world. Gross, in his "Antiquities," observes: "Towers at first scarcely rose above the roof, being as lanterns for the admission of light, an addition to the height was in all likelihood suggested on the more common use of bells."[1]

It does not enter into the purpose of this essay to discuss the question of bells in general further than is necessary for an understanding of them in their connection with the services of religion, much less to speak of their form, the material of which they are made, or the manufacture of them.

The word *bell* is of Anglo-Saxon origin, being derived from *bellan*, which means to make a hollow sound; from which also we have the words *bellow*, *bawl*, and *peal*. Bells are very ancient, but the date of their coming into use cannot be determined. They are said to have been used in the worship of Osiris in Egypt at a very early day; and it may be due to this fact that Moses, who was learned in all the sciences of the Egyptians, introduced them into the Jewish liturgy, as we read in Exodus (xxviii. 32-35). But there was, doubtless, a development in bells, as there is in almost

---

[1] "Encyclopædia Britannica," vol. iii. p. 538.

everything else, from a ruder to a more perfect form and tone; and it is, besides, difficult to determine whether the words translated *bell* from the ancient languages, whether Egyptian, Hebrew, Chaldean, Greek, or Latin, meant an instrument such as the bells of our day or not. Mr. Layard, a distinguished Orientalist, believes that he has found some small bells among the ruins of Nimroud. If this be true, it would tend to throw light on the subject.

"The Romans used bells for various purposes. Lucian, A.D. 180, mentions an instrument — clepsydra — mechanically constructed with water, which rang a bell as the water flowed to measure time. Bells summoned the Romans to the public baths; they were also used in processions, and so passed naturally into the service of the Western Church. The first recorded application of them to churches is ascribed by Polydore Vergil to Paulinus (about 400 A.D.). He was Bishop of Nola, a city of Campania (hence *nola* and *campana*, the names of certain bells). It has been maintained that Pope Sabinianus, 604, first used church bells; but it seems clear that they were introduced into France as early as 550. In 680 Benedict, abbot of Wearmouth, imported them from Italy; and in the seventh century Bede mentions them in England. . . . In the eleventh century they were not uncommon in Switzerland and Germany. It is incredible that the Greek Christians, as has been asserted, were unacquainted with bells till the ninth century; but it is certain that, for political reasons, after the taking of Constantinople by the Turks in 1453, their use was forbidden, lest they should provide a popular signal for revolt. Several old bells are extant in Scotland, Ireland, and Wales; the oldest are often quadrangular, made of thin iron plates hammered and riveted together."[1]

Small bells were in use long before large ones; and it was customary in very ancient times, as it is at present, to hang them around the necks of animals, the easier to find them if they went astray. It is not the intention to speak of the enormous bells of Russia and China; but it may be remarked that as late as the eleventh century a bell was presented to the church at Orleans, France, which weighed only 2600 pounds, but which was thought very large.

Bells received different names according to the uses to which they were devoted. This was especially true of those used in monasteries; but this is a matter of local, or at least of only minor, importance. Nor is it necessary to refer to the little bells used at Mass and certain other religious functions, as they are not blessed. Names were given to bells as early at least as the time of Pope John XIII., who, on blessing the great bell of the Lateran basilica, named it after his patron saint, John.

The custom of blessing bells was introduced early, and one of the capitularies of Charlemagne, of 787, speaks of it. Later a form of blessing for the metal of which a bell is to be cast was also found in the ritual, but it is seldom used, and will be passed over.

There are two forms of blessing bells given in the ritual; the one for a church bell, the other for a bell not intended to be used for the church, but for some other purpose, as for a school or monastery. This latter blessing will be passed over. The bell that is to be blessed, or christened, as the people sometimes say, should be brought into the church and placed at the

[1] "Encyclopædia Britannica," vol. iii. p. 536.

head of the middle aisle, or at some other convenient place, in such a manner that the officiating ministers may easily pass around it in the performance of the various ceremonies. The blessing must be performed by the bishop, or by a priest having the necessary faculties from him. The bishop, seated near the bell, begins by reciting, alternately with the clergy present, the 50th, 53d, 56th, 66th, 69th, 85th, and 129th psalms. He then rises and blesses the water to be used in the ceremony with the ordinary blessing for holy water, except that an additional prayer is recited calling down the benediction of Heaven on the water, to fit it for the particular use for which it is intended. The bishop then begins to wash the bell with this water, and the assisting ministers continue it till the bell is washed inside and out, the bishop in the meantime reciting with the clergy the psalms from the 145th to the 150th, inclusive, sitting the while. He next rises and recites a prayer, in which reference is made to the command of God to Moses to make trumpets for calling the people together for the sacrifices, and begging that at the sound of this bell the devotion of the people may be enkindled; that all the wiles of the spirit of evil may be frustrated; that all disturbances of the elements may be calmed; that the air may be healthful; and that at the sound of this bell the spirits of evil may depart at the sign of the cross marked upon it. He now intones the 28th psalm, with an antiphon before and after it.

The bishop then takes the oil of the sick, and with it makes seven signs of the cross on the exterior of the bell at different places, reciting at each the words: " May this signal, O Lord, be sanc✠tified and conse✠crated. In the name of the Fa✠ther, and of the Son✠, and of the Holy ✠ Ghost. Amen." He next recites a prayer similar in its petitions to the first one.

Then with the same formula he signs the interior of the bell with four crosses, equidistant from each other, with the holy chrism. He now recites another prayer similar to the first in its petitions. The 76th psalm with an antiphon is then recited, which is followed by a prayer addressed to the Second Person of the Blessed Trinity, calling, as the others did, for spiritual and temporal blessings. and protection. Particular stress is laid in all these prayers on the power of the sound of the bell to expel evil spirits and calm disturbances of the elements.

The deacon then reads or chants a gospel taken from St. Luke (x. 38-42), which narrates the entering of Our Saviour into the house of Martha and Mary, where Martha remonstrated because her sister did not help her in preparing the meal; but Our Lord declared that Mary had chosen the better part. The bishop then makes the sign of the cross over the bell in silence, and the ceremony is concluded.

It is needless to speak of the various uses of the church bell. One of the most important has been referred to in the essay on the *Angelus;* the others are well known to all Christians.

Many beautiful inscriptions, expressive of the piety and generosity of the faithful or the donors, are to be found on church bells, and some expressive of their vanity, or of the quaint groove in which their minds chanced at the time to run.

It is not a matter of surprise that church bells should be consecrated with so solemn a ceremony, considering the important uses to which they are devoted. They are, we may say, the voice of God calling His children to the foot of His altar to receive His blessing ; to rejoice with the joyful, to mourn with the sorrowful, to illustrate by their union the oneness of the Church herself here, and the assembly of the blest before the throne in heaven. Or, again, it is the same consecrated voice reminding us thrice in the day of the great mystery of the Incarnation; the humiliation of the Son of God; the dignity of the Mother of God. The experience of the devout child of God bears witness to the efficacy of the blessing pronounced on the church bell at the time of its consecration; for it speaks to him whether from far or near a language that only faith can understand

XXVII.—THE LAST BLESSING, OR THE BLESSING "IN ARTICULO MORTIS."

"THE Church, anxious about the spiritual welfare of her children at every period of their lives, becomes more and more solicitous about them as death approaches, knowing that their salvation depends upon their dying in the state of grace. Hence she is ready to administer to them over and over again the holy sacrament of Penance, instituted by her divine Founder as the sovereign remedy for sin."[1] But besides the eternal punishment due to mortal sin there is also a temporal punishment, which must be either cancelled in this world by works of penance or indulgences, or atoned for in the next world in the purifying flames of purgatory. The love of the Church for her children is not wanting here. Aware that it is better to satisfy the divine justice in this world than in the next, she has provided a remedy by which it may be done not only in life, but what is more important and more deserving of our gratitude, at the moment of death. Besides the sacraments of Penance, Extreme Unction, and the Holy Eucharist, to the last of which, as all Christians know, a special privilege is granted by which it can be received by those who are not fasting—there is yet another favor which the Church in her maternal solicitude grants at that time, and with which it is to be feared many Catholics are not sufficiently familiar. For that reason it will be made the subject of the present essay.

The devout Christian, who knows not the day nor the

[1] O'Kane, "Notes on the Rubrics of the Roman Ritual," No. 970.

hour when God shall call him to account, and who has been assured by the words of Eternal Truth that death shall come as a thief in the night, and that a man shall not know the time of his coming, cannot afford to be indifferent to any assistance that is within his reach at that decisive moment. What a boon for him, then, that the Church has provided him with a blessing to which a plenary indulgence is attached, which, when gained in its full extent, is capable of remitting, and actually does remit, all the temporal punishment due to him, and thus frees him from the painful obligation of languishing in the fires of purgatory for perhaps a long period of years. It is the blessing *in articulo mortis*,—at the moment of death,—better known as "the last blessing." Maurel, having treated of other indulgences that may be gained at the hour of death, and of which something will be said further on, continues: "Besides these indulgences for the hour of death, there is another much more solemn, and of great antiquity in the Church, which through a special grant of the Roman Pontiffs bishops impart personally, or by delegated priests, to the sick in their agony. At first they acquired the privilege merely for a limited period, but by his Constitution *Pia Mater*, of April 5, 1747, Benedict XIV. extended it to the entire term of their episcopate, or as long as they held their sees, together with the power of sub-delegating their priests, secular and regular, to apply the indulgence to the dying."[1]

Regarding the origin of this indulgence, O'Kane remarks (No. 958): "From the earliest ages of the Church bishops were invited from time to time to give their blessing to the dying, and when given by the popes, or those specially delegated by them, it was, no doubt, very

[1] Maurel, p. 298.

often accompanied by a plenary indulgence. We have, most probably, an instance of this in the indulgence granted to St. Clare by Innocent IV., as we read in her Life given in the Roman Breviary. At all events it is certain that the popes have power to grant such indulgences, and that this power has been frequently used in the Church." It is to be given after the sick person has received the last sacraments, or such of them as the nature of his ailment or the condition of his mental faculties permits him to receive. It may be given not only to those who ask for it in express terms, or to those who, although they do not ask for it, either through negligence or forgetfulness, yet show signs of sorrow for their sins; but "this indulgence should be communicated even to the dying who have lost the use of their senses; for we may always presume, at least in ordinary cases, that it would be their desire to receive this blessing had they the use of their reason. It may also be applied to children who, by reason of their age, have not made their First Communion." [1] This is to be understood, of course, of children who have come to the use of reason; for those who have not attained the years of discretion, and persons who have never had the use of reason, being incapable of sin, have no need of it. Nor can it be imparted to excommunicated persons, nor to such as, to all appearances, are dying impenitent. "It may be doubted, however, whether the benediction is restricted, like Extreme Unction, to such as are in danger of death from bodily sickness, whether it may not be given to one who is in danger of death from any other cause, e.g., to a convict about to be executed. The words of the bull *Pia Mater*, as well as the rubrics, undoubtedly seem to suppose that the person receiving the

[1] Maurel, pp 298, 299.

benediction is sick, infirm, etc. Now, it may be that this is supposed or required *as a condition;* or it may be that the words are used, not to express a condition, but simply to describe the case that usually occurs. It is quite uncertain, and depends altogether on the intention of the Pontiff. But in the absence of authority against it, the benediction may be given at least conditionally." [1]

With regard to the circumstances under which the blessing may be repeated, the same author remarks (No. 962) : "It is certain that the benediction may be repeated in the circumstances in which Extreme Unction may be repeated, that is, when the sick person, having partially recovered, relapses, and is again in danger of death. But in case of protracted illness, where the danger still continues, it cannot be repeated. Both points have been expressly decided by the Sacred Congregation of Indulgences. It has been long before decided by the same Congregation that a plenary indulgence *in articulo mortis* given simply and without any other declaration, should be understood strictly as gained only when death actually occurs." It would seem, however, that a more recent decree permits the repetition of the last blessing. Says Maurel (p. 299) : " In the same danger, or in the same *articulo mortis*, said the ancient decrees, it is not permitted to recite many times the benediction for a dying person, with an application of the plenary indulgence. But Pius IX. has given leave to repeat the form of the indulgence over the same invalid and in the same danger. He furthermore allows priests vested with the power to impart several times— *pluries*—to a dying person the different indulgences *in articulo mortis*, to which he may have a right under

[1] O'Kane, No. 960.

various titles. Notwithstanding this, the indulgence cannot be gained more than once, and is not truly applied to a sick person, except when death actually ensues. Thus the *articulo mortis* is that moment which is actually followed by death, the intention of the Supreme Pontiff in granting the indulgence being, according to Theodore à Spiritu Sancto, 'that the faithful might have nothing to expiate after this mortal pilgrimage.'" The conditions for gaining this indulgence are: first, at least an habitual intention of gaining it; secondly, the eliciting of an act of contrition and of love, if the sick person is able to do so; thirdly, the invocation, at least mentally, of the name of Jesus; and fourthly, the sick person is admonished to bear with resignation the inconveniences and sufferings incident to his sickness, in expiation of the sins of his past life, and to be ready to accept from the hand of God whatsoever it shall please Him to ordain, even death, which he has deserved by his sins.[1]

A necessary condition for receiving the last blessing is that the sick person be in the state of sanctifying grace, for no one can gain a plenary indulgence in the state of sin.

"The most important condition for gaining a plenary indulgence is to have a true hatred of all sins, even venial, and to be wholly free from any attachment to them. This condition is absolutely necessary; for, as St. Alphonsus teaches, 'it is certain that, so long as the guilt of venial sin is not remitted, the punishment due to it cannot be remitted.' So that while the soul bears the guilt of a single little venial sin, or even any attachment to such sin, it is clear that it cannot obtain the total remission of its punishment, or, in other words, a

[1] Wapelhorst, p. 462, No. 3.

plenary indulgence ; for a plenary indulgence is nothing more nor less than the complete remission of the temporal punishment due to sin, of which the guilt has been already remitted." [1]

On this point O'Kane remarks (No. 963): "If the person, however, be not in the state of grace when the benediction is given, it is of no avail, and should be repeated when he recovers the state of grace. But should he, after having received it in the state of grace, again fall into mortal sin, he would receive the fruit of the indulgence at the moment of death, provided he had in the meantime recovered the state of grace ; and therefore in this case the benediction should not be repeated." Recent legislation on the subject of the last blessing has somewhat modified the conditions, and for that reason the above is not now strictly correct. The blessing cannot be repeated in the same sickness, although the sickness continues for a long time, nor can it be imparted by several priests, nor is it to be repeated if the sick person was in the state of mortal sin when he received it, nor in case he relapses into mortal sin after it is given.[2] It should be given while the sick person has the use of his mental faculties, and not be deferred till the last moment. The faculties now granted to priests in general include that of conferring this blessing, and hence sick persons are seldom deprived of the opportunity of gaining this indulgence so profitable and necessary for them.

With regard to certain other indulgences that may be gained at the hour of death, O'Kane remarks (Nos. 978, 979) : "It may be observed that this is not the only plenary indulgence that can be obtained at the hour of

---

[1] *Raccolta*, p. xxiv.
[2] Wapelhorst, p. 463. No. 6.

death. A great many have been granted for this hour to the faithful who are members of certain pious confraternities, who practise certain devotions, or who have rosaries, crosses, medals, etc., to which indulgences are attached, provided they comply with the requisite conditions. The titles on which these indulgences are granted are altogether distinct, and the conditions are not incompatible. It has been decided by the Sacred Congregation of Indulgences that, when Communion is required as a condition of the indulgence the same Communion may suffice for several plenary indulgences. The conditions required for those *in articulo mortis* are very easy. They are for the most part those acts which should in any event be frequently elicited by Christians in danger of death: acts of contrition, acts of the love of God, and of perfect resignation to His holy will, and the invocation of the holy name, with the heart if not with the lips. To gain the indulgences attached to the rosaries, crosses, medals, etc., it is enough to take the blessed object in the hand, or to have it about or near the person, while making the acts prescribed, which are usually those just mentioned. The ministry of a priest is not necessary, though it is, of course, very useful in assisting the sick person to make the acts required. It is probable that even by virtue of a single concession the indulgences may be gained as often as the prescribed acts are repeated, but there is no reason to doubt that several may be gained when the titles are distinct. With respect to the intention, it is sufficient that one have that of gaining all the indulgences he can by the acts he performs. It is not necessary to think of them in particular, nor even to know that they are attached to the acts. It is even probable that an intention of gaining the indulgence is not required at all, provided the work to which it is attached be done. St. Liguori seems to think that at all events it is enough to have an interpretative intention."[1]

Whatever may be said of the necessity, no one can fail to see the advantage of an intention made at the time the indulgence is to be gained, nor the extent to which it will contribute in disposing the sick person to receive it with the most abundant fruit. For this reason it is advisable for Christians to accustom themselves to make sometimes during life, and more especially when sick, although the sickness may not endanger life, an intention of gaining the indulgences of the last blessing, as well as all the other indulgences to which they may be entitled at that hour; and they should frequently pray God to grant them that inestimable favor. Nor should they neglect in time of sickness to beg of those who have care of them to see that this blessing is imparted to them at the proper time. Any request coming from themselves shows their good disposition; and, besides, friends sometimes lose sight of the needs of the soul in their zeal to provide for those of the body. But it is a sacred duty of those who assist at the bedside of the sick to see that they are not deprived of so powerful a means of grace; and in addition to calling in the priest they should endeavor to dispose the sick person in advance for the visit of the minister of God. A fatal delusion sometimes seizes the sick person, and those also who have care of him, by which they imagine that he who receives the last sacraments and sacred rites of religion must necessarily die — that these are a kind of death warrant. No good, but many evils are the result of this delusion. It prevents the sick person from trying earnestly to excite those dispositions so necessary, or at least so expedient, for receiving the last blessings of the

[1] See also Wapelhorst, p. 462, No. 3.

Church; it imposes on the priest the obligation of disposing him at the very moment he is to receive these sacred ministrations; and even then his friends may, unconsciously, place obstacles in his way by continuing to deceive the sick person with delusive hopes. We should not, indeed, fill anyone with despair of recovery; neither should we, on the other hand, conceal from the sick person the danger in which he is, at least in so far as the consciousness of this danger will aid him in disposing himself for a profitable reception of those graces that are to be his ultimate preparation for a judgment upon which an eternity of happiness or misery depends. What kind of love is that which permits, or runs the risk of permitting, the sick person to lose the use of his mental faculties before he is alive to his danger? It is a folly that may and often has cast souls for long years into purgatory, and has endangered the eternal salvation of not a few who were unhappily in the state of mortal sin; for, had they been conscious of the near approach of death, they would have endeavored to elicit an act of perfect contrition if they had not an opportunity of going to confession. That love which prefers the life of the perishable body to that of the immortal soul cannot be called Christian; and, besides, the peace and tranquillity of mind which usually follow perfect reconciliation with God are often very conducive to the restoration of bodily health. A secondary end of Extreme Unction is the restoration of health, whenever such is the will of God; and it not unfrequently happens that recovery dates from the reception of the last sacraments.

One of the plenary indulgences most easily gained is that which is imparted to the prayer to our holy guardian angel. It is granted, says the decree, "at the hour of death to all those who, during life, shall have frequently said this prayer, provided they shall have the required dispositions."[1] With regard to these indulgences O'Kane says (No. 980): "It is true that if he had the happiness of gaining one plenary indulgence he could not gain a second for himself at the same time, for even one includes a complete remission of all the punishment due to his sins; but it is hard to reckon in any instance on the presence of all those conditions, and especially of those perfect dispositions which are necessary to gain a plenary indulgence in its full extent. But although it be not gained in its whole extent, it may be gained partially; and if many be gained in this way, the effect of all united may come very near, and when there is a renunciation of all venial sins, may be equal to, the full effect of a plenary indulgence."

Too much importance cannot be attached to the inestimable grace conferred by this blessing. We should be grateful at all times for the favors of Heaven, and anxious to profit by them; but for this one, which is bestowed upon us in the hour of our greatest need, we should be especially thankful. Another circumstance, also, shows the wisdom and love of the Church for her children; for, while other indulgences may be gained, and the graces of them afterward forfeited by sin, this one is reserved for the moment of death, when there is no fear of it being lost. Thrice happy the soul that merits so great a blessing and receives it in its plenitude, for it will be immediately admitted into the joy of its Lord. "Oh, let us, then, strive at this last moment, before entering on our road to eternity, to gain as many indulgences as possible! for how do we know what debts we have to pay to the divine justice, or

[1] *Raccolta*, p. 308.

whether these plenary indulgences have been applied to us in their full extent, or in what proportion they are applied? It is also of the utmost importance to us to qualify ourselves in life for such an abundant application of the merits of Jesus Christ, the Blessed Virgin, and the saints at the hour of our death. The most effectual means for attaining this end is carefully to keep ourselves in the friendship of God, especially by a frequent worthy reception of the sacraments, as also by being devout to the Blessed Virgin, and to St. Joseph, the patron of a happy death."[1]

[1] Maurel, pp. 299, 300.

XXVIII.—THE BURIAL SERVICE.

IT is much to be regretted that a large number of Catholics do not better understand the many claims which the Church has on her children of being called their mother. And it is equally to be regretted that these same children are the principal sufferers. Let us, then, pause for a few moments and reflect on this point, especially in its bearing on the funeral ceremonies among Christians.

Love of the departed is deeply seated in man's nature; and there is no people, whether barbarous or civilized, whether enlightened by the true faith or groping in the darkness of error, but honors its dead. The imperishable pyramids of Egypt are sepulchral monuments, and the dead of the same nation are found as mummies after a period of more than three thousand years. So, too, sepulchral monuments are met with throughout the entire East, dating back to a time long anterior to the beginning of the Christian era. The cities of the dead in ancient Greece are pointed out even in our day, where the dust of heroes has returned to its parent dust for more than twenty centuries; while the cromlechs of Ireland and other countries of western Europe, once inhabited by the Celts, stood for ages before the glad tidings of the Gospel awakened those peoples to a new life. But it was left to the Christian Church to pay a fitting homage to the departed, and this with regard to both the soul and the body: to the soul, because faith teaches that it is immortal, and can be assisted in its spiritual necessities by those whom it leaves behind ; to the body, because the same faith teaches that it was once the temple of the Holy Ghost, and is destined hereafter to be reunited to the soul after the General Judgment, to share its eternal destiny.

We appreciate everything according to our estimation of its value. What more noble than man! When God formed the various orders of the visible creation, whatever their excellence, He simply said, as we read in the Sacred Scriptures, "Let them be made, and they were made;" but when He was about to form the masterpiece of His infinite wisdom, power, and love, He could find no model worthy of the noble work He proposed, and He said: "Let us make man to our image and likeness."[1] And He endowed him with an immortality like His own in this, that he cannot die; but unlike His in this, that man's immortality is dependent, while God's is absolute. This is true, as has just been said, not only of the soul, but also of the body. And both the mercy and justice of God shine forth admirably in this; for, as the body was the instrument by which the soul was greatly assisted in the service of God, it is but just that it should share in the soul's reward. Without the body the soul could not, according to the designs of God, have attained to its happiness; the body then should share with the soul in that happiness. Such is the divine decree. How noble is the human body! Even a pagan poet was struck with admiration in contemplating it.[2] So also holy Job declares: "I know that my Redeemer liveth, and in the last day I shall rise out of the earth, and I shall be clothed again with my

---

[1] Genesis, i. 26.

[2] Pronaque cum spectent animalia cætera terram;
Os homini sublime dedit: cœlumque tueri
Jussit, et erectos ad sidera tollere vultus.
    Ovid, Metamorphoseon.

skin, and in my flesh I shall see my God, whom I myself shall see, and my eyes shall behold, and not another."[1] The words of St. Paul are also well calculated to impress upon Christians the sanctity of their bodies.[2] He writes: "Know you not that you are the temple of God, and that the Spirit of God dwelleth in you? But if any man violate the temple of God, him shall God destroy: for the temple of God is holy, which you are." Again: "Know you not that your bodies are the members of Christ? Shall I take the members of Christ and make them the members of a harlot? God forbid. . . . Or know you not that your members are the temple of the Holy Ghost, who is in you, whom you have from God, and you are not your own. For you are bought with a great price. Glorify and bear God in your body."

In no ceremony of the Church does the respect which she pays to the bodies of her children shine forth so admirably as in her funeral obsequies. Mindful of the dignity of the human body, she has the infant brought to the church at as early a day as possible after its birth, that it may be born again of water and of the Holy Ghost; its breast is then anointed with the holy oil, as we have seen in the essay on the Holy Oils, that it may ever bear the thought of God in its heart; on the back it is anointed between the shoulders, that it may learn to bear the sweet yoke of Christ; and the top of its head is anointed, after the infusion of water has blotted out original sin, that it may be entirely consecrated to God. No sooner does it begin to live than it begins to live for God, verifying the words of St. Paul, that Christ died for all, that those who live may live only for Him. Again, in confirmation, when the child has grown to youth, and is called upon to battle

[1] Job, xix. 25-27.   [2] I. Corinthians, iii. 16, 17; vi. 15, 19, 20.

more fiercely with the enemies of its salvation, it is once more consecrated, by having the sign of the cross marked on its forehead with the holy oil, that it may bear fearlessly before the world the standard under which it has vowed to do battle. And, finally, when the time comes for it to bid adieu to its earthly habitation, its senses are signed with the holy oil to remove the remains of sin which they may have been instrumental in committing. The body is also nourished with the Most Holy Sacrament, so that Almighty God, not satisfied with forming it in a more noble mould than that of any other creature, visits it frequently during life to consecrate it more fully to Himself. Would that this truth were more frequently remembered; then fewer would sin against their bodies as well as against their souls. Conscious of this innate dignity, the Church does well in honoring the body even after the soul has departed. It is brought into the church in solemn procession, the adorable sacrifice of the Mass is offered in its presence, the fumes of incense ascend around it, and the saving dews of holy water are shed upon it before it is carried to its last resting-place. The ground also in which it is to return to dust is sanctified by the solemn prayers of the Church.

The Church looks upon death as the punishment of sin;[1] and, remembering that nothing defiled can enter heaven, she treats her deceased members as persons upon whose souls at least slight stains of sin may have been found by the all-searching eye of God at the hour of death; or who may not have fully satisfied the debt of temporal punishment due for forgiven offences. For this reason her funeral services are supplicatory. She does not canonize the dead, as it were, on the spot, or

[1] Genesis, ii. 17; Romans, vi. 23.

perform a pagan apotheosis upon them, regardless of the sort of lives they may have led, as is too often done outside the Church. On the contrary, she banishes, or desires to banish—for there are unfortunately found Catholics who would fain cling to irreligious and pagan customs—all signs of paganism from their obsequies, and she covers their remains in the burial casket only with a plain, black pall. No Christian who is possessed of a lively faith can absolutely rejoice in the death of anyone who has attained the use of reason, as if he were already in the fruition of the beatific vision, no matter what may have been the purity of his life. No one knows with absolute certainty whether he is deserving of love or hatred; and St. Paul, who declared that he was not conscious of any fault, did not, for all that, regard himself as justified.[1] Our hope must always be seasoned with a salutary fear.

The Church has a separate ceremony, however, for the interment of those little innocents who die before they have come to the use of reason. In their case the ritual recommends that, besides the white vestments with which the priest is clothed, a crown of flowers or of odoriferous herbs be placed on the coffin, as a symbol of the purity of both the body and the soul of the deceased. And with the chant of psalms of joy, and the recitation of prayers suggestive of the virginal purity of the departed and radiant with Christian hope, the tender remains are consigned to their final resting-place.

Since, then, in the good pleasure of God we are all destined to return to dust before we can rise to immortality, it will be both instructive and encouraging for us to pass briefly in review the services which are to usher us into the unseen world.

[1] Eccles. ix. 1 ; I. Cor. iv. 4.

Let us suppose a person dead, and about to be carried to the church for the funeral obsequies. The entire ceremonial, it is true, is not, as a rule, carried out among us, owing to the fact that we are not living in a Catholic country, and must be influenced by circumstances in this as in many other things not essential. The remains are not usually accompanied from the house where death took place, but are met at the door of the church by the priest. Sometimes, too, they are not met at the door, but are carried to the foot of the altar, where the priest performs the part of the ceremony appropriate to that place. Nor is it a uniform custom to attend the funeral to the cemetery; for, as was remarked in the essay on the *Asperges*, the circumstances in which most of the early missionaries were placed rendered it difficult, and often impossible, to carry out the entire ceremonial of the Church in many of her sacred functions. But without further preface or apology, we shall take up the funeral ceremony as it is found in the ritual, and make such comments on it as will be thought interesting and instructive.

The priest, vested in surplice and black stole—and in a black cope, if the church has one—at the house where the remains are, begins the solemn ceremony by sprinkling the body with holy water; he then recites an antiphon and the psalm *De profundis* (the 129th), at the conclusion of which and of the *Requiem æternam*,—which always in funeral ceremonies takes the place of the *Glory be to the Father*, etc., recited after each psalm on other occasions,—he repeats the antiphon. The remains are then taken up by the pall-bearers, and the procession moves toward the church. The priest, having recited an antiphon, begins the psalm *Miserere* (the 50th), and, if the distance is considerable, at the conclusion of it he continues with what are called the *Gradual Psalms*, which are fifteen in number, and begin with the 127th. If there are other priests present they recite the psalms in alternate verses with the officiating clergyman. On arriving at the door of the church the antiphon is repeated, and the chanters—if there are any—and the officiating priest sing certain versicles and responses ; but in most churches the choir has to take the place of the chanters properly so called. The Mass is then celebrated, unless the Office of the Dead is first to be recited.

At the conclusion of the Mass the celebrant lays aside the chasuble and maniple, and putting on the black cope. proceeds to the foot of the altar, and turns to the remains. While the choir is chanting the *Libera*—which is a most pathetic appeal of the soul, trembling with fear before the judgment-seat for mercy at that awful hour— he reads a prayer beseeching God to deal mercifully with His departed servant, and extend His grace to him who during life was signed with the seal of the Most Holy Trinity. He also recites the *Libera*. The celebrant then puts incense into the censer ; the chanters (or the celebrant, where there are no chanters) sing the *Kyrie eleison*, the choir answering *Christe eleison*. The priest then repeats a second *Kyrie*, and intones the *Pater Noster*, which he continues in silence while he passes twice around the coffin, first sprinkling it with holy water, and then incensing it, two acolytes with candles and one between them with the processional cross standing at the head of the body the while. Then follow a number of versicles and responses appropriate to the ceremony, and the prayer : "O God, whose property is always to have mercy and to spare, we humbly beseech Thee for the soul of Thy servant *N*., which Thou hast this day commanded to depart from this world, that Thou wouldst not deliver it into the hands of the enemy, nor forget it unto the end ; but command it to be received by Thy holy angels, and conducted into its true country ; that as in Thee it has hoped and believed, it may not suffer the pains of hell, but may take possession of eternal joys. Through Christ Our Lord. Amen." The body is then borne to the cemetery, the priest in the meantime singing or reading the antiphon : "May the angels lead thee into Paradise ; at thy coming may the martyrs receive thee, and bring thee into the holy city Jerusalem. May the choir of angels receive thee, and with Lazarus, once a beggar, mayest thou have eternal rest." Here there is a prayer for the blessing of the grave, if the cemetery is not consecrated. But whether the body is immediately taken to the cemetery, or is left in the church for a time, for example, that the relatives and others may take a last view of it, the canticle of holy Zachary, commonly called the *Benedictus*,[1] is sung or read, with the antiphon : "I am the resurrection and the life ; he that believeth in Me, although he be dead, shall live : and everyone that liveth and believeth in Me shall not die forever."[2] This, with the following prayer and the versicles before and after it, must, according to the ritual, never be omitted : "Grant, O Lord, we beseech Thee, this mercy unto Thy servant deceased, that having desired to do Thy will he may not suffer in return for his deeds. And as by the true faith he was joined to the multitude of the faithful here below, so may Thy tender mercy give him a place above among the angelic choirs. Through Christ Our Lord. Amen." The priest retires from the cemetery reciting the *De profundis* in a low tone.

[1] St. Luke, i. 68–79.   [2] St. John, xi. 25, 26.

How radiant with hope is not this important ceremony in which we all occasionally take part during life, and which we sincerely trust will be performed over us in death, as our mortal remains are borne to their last resting-place? It passes admirably between the two extremes of the feeling of total annihilation, which the infidel would fain have us believe he considers awaits him, on the one hand ; and on the other the apotheosis; which is so commonly and indiscriminately pronounced on the dead among too many of the sects. It is a sweet consolation to the living, and at the same time an exhortation to the practice of the noblest acts of Christian charity, those of offering prayers and good works for the repose of the souls of the faithful departed. It teaches the bereft that their separation is only for a time, and that even during this corporeal separation there still exists a union of souls in the communion of saints.

XXIX.—THE SELECTION OF MARY CONCEIVED WITHOUT SIN AS PATRONESS OF THE UNITED STATES.

THE student of ecclesiastical history need not be told through what stages the pious belief of the faithful in and the devotion of religious Orders to the Immaculate Conception of the Blessed Virgin passed, from the beginning of the Christian era to the day when, amid the acclamations of more than two hundred millions of Catholics, the saintly Pius IX. defined it as an article of faith. Nor can the attentive reader of American history fail to see the finger of God manifested in the way in which Mary Immaculate claimed America, and America Mary Immaculate, from the earliest period of the authentic history of the New World. It is not necessary to speak of these : they are too well known to American Catholics. The following, however, may be given as an example. When Alexander O'Reilly came to Louisiana in 1769, as the Spanish governor of that province, he gave the form of oath which was to be taken by all the officials, containing, among other things, the following : "I, ——, appointed ——, swear before God, on the holy Cross and the Evangelists, to maintain and defend the mystery of the Immaculate Conception of our Lady the Virgin Mary."[1] It may be interesting to pass in review the action of the American prelates in authoritatively promoting devotion to the Immaculate Conception, until the time when they obtained their petition from the Holy Father, that our Blessed Lady

[1] Shea, " Life and Times of Archbishop Carroll," p. 548.

under the title of the Immaculate Conception should be the patroness of the United States, and later, that her feast should be a holyday of obligation. It is worthy of note that the Blessed Virgin under this beautiful title was not chosen merely as Patroness of the *Church* in the United States, but as *Patroness of the United States.* Neither in the decree of the Fathers of Baltimore, as will be seen later on, nor in the document from Rome confirming their action, is the phrase "of the Church" found; Mary is everywhere called Patroness "of the United States." It cannot, of course, be doubted that the Mother of God takes a livelier interest in her devoted children than in others; but the mantle of her protection covers all who dwell in the Great Republic.

No sooner had the illustrious John Carroll been consecrated bishop of the Church in the United States—which event took place on the 15th of August, 1790—than the special devotion to Mary which had characterized the Church here received new life and vigor. It was decreed in the fifth session of the first Synod, held in Baltimore in November, 1791, that the Litany of the Blessed Virgin, the principal patron of the vast diocese of Baltimore, should be sung or recited before Mass on Sundays and holydays. The bishop declared in another decree that from the beginning of his episcopate he was most anxious to select the holy Mother of God as the principal patron of the diocese, that, through her intercession, the faith and piety of the people committed to him might flourish and be more and more increased. And he further decreed that the feast of the Assumption should be the principal feast of the diocese, urging upon both clergy and people to celebrate it with the greatest solemnity.[1]

[1] "Concilia Baltimorensia," 1829-1852, pp. 19-21.

But it was not until the Sixth Provincial Council, held in May, 1846, that devotion to the Immaculate Conception was solemnly discussed by the American prelates. In the third congregation, held May 13th,—an auspicious date,—the first decree of the council was promulgated in these memorable words, which show clearly that, although this was the first solemn pronouncement, the devotion had long been flourishing. The decree reads as follows: "The Fathers, with ardent desire, and with unanimous applause and consent, have chosen the Blessed Virgin conceived without original sin as the Patroness of the United States; without, however, imposing the obligation of hearing Mass and resting from servile works on the feast itself of the Conception of the Blessed Mary; and therefore the Sovereign Pontiff shall be humbly petitioned that the solemnization of the feast may be transferred to the following Sunday,—unless the feast falls on a Sunday,—on which day the Masses, both private and solemn, of the feast shall be celebrated, and Vespers of the same feast shall be recited."

The decree was not, however, approved and confirmed by the Holy See until February 7, 1847. In his letter to the Archbishop of Baltimore, July 3d of that year, Cardinal Fransoni, Prefect of the Sacred Congregation for the Propagation of the Faith, announced the decision, and enclosed the decree, remarking that the Holy Father had most willingly confirmed the choice of the council.

In the fourth private congregation of the same Council, held May 15th, it was decreed that the Holy See should be petitioned for the privilege of adding, throughout the United States, the word "Immaculate" before "Conception," in the Office of the Conception of the Blessed Virgin and in the prayers and Preface of the Mass of the same feast, and the invocation "Queen conceived without original sin, pray for us," to the Litany of Our Lady. The Pope granted these petitions in perpetuity, September 13, 1846.[1]

A remarkable circumstance connected with the selection of Mary conceived without sin as our patroness is given by the late celebrated Indian missionary Father De Smet, S.J., in a letter to the editor of the *Precis Historiques*, Brussels, dated New York, May 16, 1857, on the life and labors of the Rev. Theodore de Theux. Says Father De Smet: " In 1844 the Bishop of Cincinnati found himself frequently menaced, as well as the Catholics of his diocese, by tumultuous mobs, composed of the enemies of our holy faith. He asked counsel of Father de Theux. After some moments of reflection the father answered that he should obtain peace and security in those difficult times if he would have recourse to the Sovereign Pontiff, and would encourage the other bishops of the United States to follow his example, so as to obtain the favor of adding, in the Preface of the Mass, to the word 'Conception' the prefix 'Immaculate.' The worthy bishop received the advice with respect, and the request was soon after made at Rome and crowned with success."[2] The acts of the Council do not state by whom the question was introduced; but this being the first provincial council after the Bishop of Cincinnati had spoken of it to Father de Theux, it may safely be presumed that it was brought up at the instance of the ordinary of that see.

While the Holy Father was still in exile at Gaeta, he commenced the preliminaries for the definition of the dogma of the Immaculate Conception. He established a special Congregation to take the matter into considera-

[1] " Concilia Baltimorensia," pp. 240–257.
[2] " Western Missions and Missionaries," p. 480.

tion, and addressed a circular letter to all the bishops of the Christian world asking them to lend their aid and co-operation, to ascertain the devotion of their clergy and people to this mystery, etc. In reply, the Fathers of the Seventh Provincial Council of Baltimore, which was held in May, 1849, declared, in their first decree, that the clergy and faithful of the United States were animated with a most ardent devotion to the Immaculate Conception ; and, in the second decree, expressed, with but one dissenting voice, the joy they would feel at its definition as an article of faith, if the Holy Father should deem such definition opportune.[1]

The Church in this country having been divided, in 1850, into several ecclesiastical provinces, matters relating to discipline among Catholics in general were, thenceforth, to be discussed in Plenary Councils, or assemblies of all the prelates. The first of these was held in May, 1852, when it was decided that a Plenary Council should be held every ten years. No action remained to be taken by the Fathers of the First Plenary Council, from the fact that the Blessed Virgin had already been chosen the Patroness of our country, and the prelates had already expressed their opinion regarding the definition as an article of faith ; all that was left was to await the actual definition by the Vicar of Christ. But with the decree of the Congregation for the Propagation of the Faith approving the decrees of the Council, the members of that body expressed a wish that the bishops of the Church here would labor to have the feast of the Immaculate Conception added to the other days of obligation in the United States.[2]

The civil war, which was unhappily waging in 1862,

---

[1] "Concilia Baltimorensia," pp. 274-278.
[2] "Concilium Plenarium," etc., vol. l. p. 56, nota.

prevented the assembling of the Second Plenary Council at the proper time, and it was not until October, 1866, that it was deemed expedient for the Fathers to meet. In the tenth private congregation of this Council, which was held on October 19th, the question of raising the feast of the Immaculate Conception to the dignity of a holyday of obligation throughout the Union was discussed by the prelates, and decreed, five only voting in the negative. The Congregation for the Propagation of the Faith, whose province it is to examine and pass upon the decrees of Councils held in missionary countries like ours, examined the question in their general assemblies on the 17th, 23d, and 27th days of September, 1867, and issued their decree. Finally, the decree was approved January 24, 1868, by His Holiness, Pius IX., who had labored so strenuously and so successfully during his long pontificate in promoting the honor of the Immaculate Mother of God. The Catholics of our day should deem it a special privilege to have been permitted to live at a time when their Mother in heaven received so precious a jewel in her glorious crown.

www.ingramcontent.com/pod-product-compliance
Lightning Source LLC
Chambersburg PA
CBHW030738230426
43667CB00007B/765